LIVING DHARMA

LIVING DHARMA

Teachings of Twelve Buddhist Masters

JACK KORNFIELD

SHAMBHALA
Boston & London
1996

SHAMBHALA PUBLICATIONS, INC.
Horticultural Hall
300 Massachusetts Avenue
Boston, Massachusetts 02115
http://www.shambhala.com

9 8 7 6 5 4 3

Printed in the United States of America
⊗ This edition is printed on acid-free paper that meets the
American National Standards Institute Z39.48 Standard.
Distributed in the United States by Random House, Inc., and in
Canada by Random House of Canada Ltd

LIBRARY OF CONGRESS CATALOGING-IN-PUBLICATION DATA

Living dharma: teachings of twelve Buddhist masters/[by Jack
    Kornfield].—1st Shambhala ed.
        p. cm.
    ISBN 1-57062-138-1 (alk. paper)
        1. Spiritual life—Buddhism.   2. Vipaśyanā (Buddhism)
    3. Theravāda Buddhism—Doctrines.   I. Kornfield, Jack, 1945–   .
    BQ5612.L58   1996   95-15859
    294.3'443—dc20   CIP

CONTENTS

DEDICATION

This book is dedicated to my father—from whom I learned the power of virtue and good intentions.

Also, this work could not have come about without the compassion and assistance of Stephen Levine, Sumedho Bhikku, Achaan Chaa, Joseph Goldstein, Achaan Asabha, Dan Goleman, Jim Harris, Achaan Jumnien, Eric, Sharon, Ram Dass, Dell, Seth, Chani, Achaan Tawee, Kenny, Kitti Subho, Irv, Tori, Molly, Trungpa Rinpoche, Joyce, Khun Prasom, U Thondera Sayadaw, Josie Stanton, Mahasi Sayadaw, Wicki, Larry and Dayle, Nyanasugato, Winston and Joslyn King, Kalu Rinpoche, Buzz and Janet, Maharaji, Vimalo Bhikku, Mimi, Susan, T. Lobsang Rampa, Soeng Sahn Roshi, Charlie, Richard, Guru Michael, Robert, Jacquie, Achaan Dhammadaro, Dr. Palos, Abbot Yen Boon, Achaan Buddhadasa, Chao Khun Raj, Lao Tzu, Professor Penner, Suzuki Roshi, Pannavado Bhikku, Achaan Maha Boowa, Krishna, David and Mary, Wing Tsit Chan, and all other Dharma friends.

And especially the compassion of Gotama Buddha for us all.

FOREWORD

During its 2,500-year history, Buddhism has manifested itself in a multitude of different schools and styles. Always the dynamic nature of living Dharma has brought about, in different cultural and historical environments, new modes of expression. But at the heart of all of these manifestations lies the practice of meditation, as exemplified and taught by the Buddha himself. Only through personal meditative practice is the student of Dharma enabled to slow down the speed of neurotic mind and to begin seeing the world with clarity and precision. Without this, he will only be able to increase his confusion and perpetuate his aggressive grasping for self-confirmation. Without meditation, there is no approach to genuine sanity, no path to enlightenment, indeed no Dharma.

The practice of meditation presents itself as an especially powerful discipline for the shrinking world of the twentieth century. The age of technology would like also to produce a spiritual gadgetry—a new, improved spirituality guaranteed to bring quick results. Charlatans manufacture their versions of the Dharma, advertising miraculous, easy ways, rather than the steady and demanding personal journey which has always been essential to genuine spiritual practice.

It is this genuine tradition which is embodied by the teachers presented in this book. They are holders of an unbroken lineage of transmission which has succeeded in surviving and communicating itself in its pure form. The teaching of these masters and the example of their lives provide the impetus and inspiration for further practitioners to follow, properly and fully, the path of Dharma.

Vajracharya the Ven. Chögyam Trungpa

FOREWORD

Jack Kornfield, a 'kalyana mita' (the name given to teachers in the
Theravada tradition which is translated 'spiritual friend') has offered us in this volume a compilation of the philosophy and practices of Theravadin Buddhism interspersed with rich anecdotes
and interviews—the situations through which he received his
training.

Jack spent much time traveling and studying in monasteries
throughout Burma, Laos, Thailand, and Cambodia and conveys in
his writing the profound simplicity and sustained effort that
surround the practices of Theravada Buddhist meditation.
Through his anecdotes he shows the way in which a practice is
linked to a lineage. The interviews with these ascetic monastic
bhikkus convey a sense of the 'intense serenity' and assurance
that permeates the teaching vessels of an ancient tradition. Each
teacher emphasizes a specific aspect of the transmission of the
Buddha, yet each is representative of the essence of the lineage.

There are many ways to read a book such as this. Intellectuals
can speed-read their way through, satisfying curiosity. Or you
may 'read' this book with an empty mind, allowing its purifying
waters to penetrate heart and mind and soul. In the course of
allowing these words to pour through you, perhaps a practice here,
a turn of phrase there, a jungle scene or a bit of clearly enunciated
wisdom will attract you, will attach itself to you, will be something to which you will cling. Calm insight will show you why that
particular thought came into your focus. And when you have absorbed what you need, then that bit of stuff will be dislodged to
float on down the stream of your passing thoughts, leaving you,
more than ever, here now.

Blessings, Ram Dass

PREFACE

Today, during the cool morning hours, one can still enter tens of thousands of monasteries across Southeast Asia, in Thailand, Burma, Sri Lanka, Cambodia, and Laos, and hear chanted the timeless teachings of the Dharma, the path of awakening. The practices of this lineage, called the Elders, or Theravada, which have been followed for thousands of years, were offered by the Buddha as "openhanded, universal, inviting all to come to see for themselves."

Even in the 1990s, sincere seekers continue to join in the training of the great Theravada meditation centers or enter the mindful life of simplicity and renunciation in the thick groves of Buddhist forest monasteries.

In the 1960s, when I and other Westerners who were drawn by this living tradition went to Southeast Asia, we found that many of the greatest masters of the twentieth century were still alive. Some of us had the privilege of studying with a whole generation of these masters, such as Ven. Mahasi Sayadaw, Ven. Achaan Chaa, Ven. Buddhadasa, Ven. Taungpulu Sayadaw, Ven. U Ba Khin, and others. We were even able to bring several of them to teach in America.

Since that time thirty years ago, there has been an enormous blossoming of Buddhism in the West. Buddhist America has grown to encompass over a thousand temples and centers of practice, in the Theravada, Zen, Vajrayana, and Pure Land traditions. And while only three of the Theravada masters represented in this book are still alive, their monasteries and others like them are still flourishing. Even more remarkable, a whole generation of Western disciples who studied with these teachers have now established centers to offer their teachings in many parts of the West.

The first edition of this book, *Living Buddhist Masters*, was published shortly after the founding of the Naropa Institute, the first Buddhist university in America. It was Stephen Levine, a keen Dharma student, kind friend, and publisher of Unity Press, who designed the book and brought it to life. Samuel Bercholz of Shambhala Publications and Bhikkhu Bodhi of the Buddhist Publication Society each produced subsequent editions.

At the time of first publication, *Living Buddhist Masters* was unique. It presented the heart of Buddhist practice, insight meditation, in a new way. It offered a systematic and profound series of trainings from a whole lineage virtually unknown to most Westerners. While Zen had been popularized in the 1950s, and interest in Tibetan Buddhism was growing, the ways of practice of Theravada Buddhism were yet to be offered widely in the West. And it is just this, the actual *practices*, offering deep and direct study of the human mind and heart leading to inner freedom, that is presented by these masters.

In this book, masters like Mahasi Sayadaw, U Ba Khin, Mohnyin Sayadaw, and Achaan Maha Boowa offer lengthy and systematic descriptions of the techniques of meditation and maps of consciousness. These teachings lead to the dissolution of our limited sense of self, to an awakening of insight, to compassion, and the realization of Nirvana. In other chapters, masters such as Achaan Chaa, Achaan Buddhadasa, and Sunlun Sayadaw spell out a variety of wise ways of undertaking the many insight practices, clarifying the essential underlying attitudes and spirit that will directly allow each practitioner to discover the truth of the Dharma here and now.

One purpose of this collection is to help dispel any sectarian notion that there is only one right way of practice. What is offered by these masters are dozens of ways to practice, emphasizing the central principles used by the Buddha to awaken "all those with eyes to see." Readers will note that different means of practice are juxtaposed. We hear from masters who emphasize heroic effort and then from those who recommend a relaxed and natural mind. We read of those who urge careful theoretical study and others where only the immediate meditative experience is of value. Yet, taken together, these teachings all embody the virtue and truthfulness, the mindfulness and insight, that are the hallmarks of the Buddha's way. They all foster patience, wisdom, compassion, and clarity, and they all ask for the eyes and heart to open to the truth.

The Buddha taught in a thousand skillful ways—through dialogue and meditation practices, through direct pointing to the truth, by emphasizing wise conduct and clear seeing, through his great compassion and presence—and each way led people to freedom. In the ancient accounts of his teaching, those who heard him and deeply understood would exclaim: "Wonderful! It is as if you have set up what has been knocked down, pointed the way to one who has been lost, brought a lamp into a dark place so that all with eyes can see."

In the same way, it is the intention of the words and teachings of the masters in this book to lead all who follow these practices to confidence, understanding, clarity, compassion, and freedom, like a lamp dispelling the darkness. May it be so.

JACK KORNFIELD
Spirit Rock Center
Woodacre, California
1995

ACKNOWLEDGMENTS

The materials in this book have been collected or translated over a number of years. They represent an intimate record of spoken Dharma, the teachings of many of the greatest living Buddhist masters. They are intended to be shared and used by all in the development of the wisdom and compassion of the Buddha.

In making these teachings available, I have tried to secure blessings and assistance from the masters represented. However, due to difficulties of time and half a world of distance, some of this material has not had the formal acknowledgments and blessings as are traditional in publishing such a volume.

I have endeavored to print in as clear a fashion as I find possible this sample of practical meditation Dharma, for the benefit of all those who wish to put into practice the unexcelled teachings of Buddhism. This Dharma is offered openly, as were the teachings of the Buddha himself, and as is surely the intention of the teachers represented here.

If any errors have been made or important Dharma points confused in the process of translating or editing this material, I must take full responsibility for this. It is simply my hope that in presenting this wide variety of living Theravada Buddhist Dharma that it will be of some practical assistance to those on the path of purification.

LIVING DHARMA

ESSENTIAL BUDDHISM

CHAPTER
ONE

The Buddha, after his enlightenment under the Bodhi tree, was undecided about teaching. Who, he wondered, would be able to understand the Dharma to the depth he had penetrated? Who, in fact, would listen?

His concern was not that the Dharma was too complex to understand, but rather, that the truth of the Dharma was so simple that no one would believe it! With great compassion, he chose to teach, especially for those beings 'with but a little dust covering their eyes'.

The core of this book is a recent transmission of his teachings from twelve of the greatest masters and monasteries in the Theravada tradition. Hundreds of thousands of saffron-robed monks and tens of thousands of temples still exist throughout Southeast Asia and Ceylon. Amidst the prayer flags and ceremonies is found the essence of twenty-five hundred years of teachings, the path of wisdom and compassion outlined by the Buddha for the sake of all sentient beings.

How to write about this teaching, this truth? In a sense, there is nothing to write. The Dharma is everywhere already. East and west, the truth is the same. A Western monk once asked permission of his forest teacher to journey to Burma to try the intensive meditation systems of several other well-known teachers. Permission was readily granted. After several years he returned to his first teacher.

"What did you learn?" the teacher inquired.

"Nothing," answered the monk.

"Nothing?"

"Nothing that is not already around, that was not right here before I left."

"And what have you experienced?"

"Many teachers and many meditation systems," the monk answered. "Yet, the more deeply I penetrated the Dharma, the more I realized there was no need to go anywhere else to practice."

"Ah yes," replied his teacher. "I could have told you that before you left, but you could not have understood."

2   This book is an odyssey. It takes you on a journey through many Buddhist systems and teachers. Outwardly they may appear different, even contradictory. We need not compare and judge better or worse. These words and systems are simply different expressions of a single underlying truth. Dharma does not change. Just as the bending of leaves of grass and the skimming by of clouds indicate the presence of wind, so the words and teachings of these masters all point to the same experience, the same truth.

In our spiritual journey we must be pragmatic. How can the Dharma and paths of practice we encounter be useful to our own understanding? The famous image in the Chinese tradition of the transmission of the lamp is that of a finger pointing to the moon, the truth. Each teacher is pointing . . . be careful not to get caught up in the different fingers and lose sight of the moon!

The masters represented here emphasize the use of meditation as a powerful tool to understand and come into harmony with the Dharma. Meditation must be used as a tool to come to the freedom beyond all tools, all methods. When a Thai teacher was asked if meditation was like self-hypnosis, he replied, "No, it's de-hypnosis."

Meditation techniques are mental disciplines that allow us to calm, focus, and examine the mind. This de-conditioning process is a slowing down and observation of the usual mad-monkey stream of thoughts, perceptions, reactions, feelings. Usually we are dragged along by our desires, prejudices, conditioning, and instincts. Meditation is practicing being clear and alert, freeing ourselves from conditioned reactions to the constant flow of events and mental process.

Buddhist meditation leads to the clear perception of three things: impermanence, suffering, and the lack of an abiding self. As the mind becomes concentrated and observant, the constant change of all physical and mental phenomena is realized. Absolutely all we know, see, hear, feel, think, smell, and taste—even the 'watcher', the knowing of these—is changing from moment to moment. As this constant flow is seen more fully, any involvement or attachment becomes clearly undesirable, a cause of suffering. The meditator sees all events of the mind and body as an empty process that happens by itself. He sees that there is no one, no 'self' behind it. Although this process possesses order, following the Law of Karma or cause and effect, there is nothing in us that can be seen as permanent, an abiding self or soul. Simply the orderly unfolding of mind and matter, arising and perishing moment to moment.

To see this clearly, to experience deeply the true emptiness of self, is enormously freeing. The mind becomes detached, clear, and radiant. It is the illusions of permanence, of happiness, and especially of self-hood that bind us to the world of duality and keep us separate from one another and from the true flow of nature. A deep perception of the void, the emptiness of all conditioned phenomena, undercuts our desire to grasp and hold on to any object or mind-state as a source of lasting happiness. Final happiness comes from this non-attachment, this balance. It is freedom from all suffering. Peace.

It is important to distinguish meditation as a particular form and practice from meditation as a way of life. We may start by practicing meditation much like practicing piano. Eventually, when we become proficient, we will not need to practice anymore. Just as playing becomes practice, everything we do will become meditation. However, we must begin by practicing.

The meditation techniques described in this book are tools. They are not to be used just in isolation. Meditation is not merely a selfish practice or a cultivation of states of bliss; it encompasses all of our experience. It is a tool to develop clarity, an awareness and acceptance of the flow of events whatever they may be. In the end, meditation techniques must transcend even themselves. Then, there will be neither meditation nor non-meditation. Just what is.

WISDOM, POWER, AND KNOWLEDGE

The diversity of techniques and teachings in the spiritual realm is often confusing. This stems in part from the lack of clear distinction between wisdom, power, and knowledge.

Knowledge is infinite. Modern science fills libraries each year with its new discoveries. Spiritual knowledge is equally vast. One can know past lives of individuals and the effects of planets on present lives, the existence of other planes of being or higher levels of consciousness, spiritual healing techniques, and endless other spiritual topics. But knowledge is not wisdom.

One night a Western monk sitting under the stars was talking with several village-born forest monks from Laos. He looked up and noticed a very bright star in the middle of the bowl of the Big Dipper. Astonished he never had seen it before, he looked more closely and saw that it was moving. He recognized it as an Echo satellite moving across the heavens and pointed it out to his fellow monks.

"What's that?" they asked.

"A satellite," he answered.

"What's a satellite?" they queried.

Where to begin? "Well," he said, "did you know that the earth is round?"

No, they didn't. So he dug a small flashlight out of his bag and using a round rock for the earth began an elementary-school-level demonstration of how the earth moves around the sun and rotates on its axis. The usual questions came up, such as "Why don't we feel the earth moving?" and "Why don't the people at the bottom fall off?" In the end, though they listened patiently about planets, satellites, and rockets, he suspected they really didn't believe him.

One of these monks was a very calm, wise old man, an advisor and mentor to many people. He was honest, simple, and, because he was not attached to things being a certain way nor deluded into thinking he had a self to protect, was always happy and at peace. He accepted the changing nature of life and flowed with it. "So you know the earth is round," he shrugged. "Ultimately, what good will all your knowledge do you?" Then the Western monk understood—it is only wisdom, the development of a clear, detached mind that is important for liberation and peace.

It is much as when the Buddha held up a handful of leaves and asked his monks which was more, the leaves in his hand or those on all the trees in the forest. This handful of leaves, he continued, is the knowledge I have given you compared to the infinite knowledge of the Buddha mind. Yet it is all that is necessary to know to attain enlightenment, to come to the end of all suffering.

Power's relation to wisdom is similar to that of knowledge's. Just as the power acquired by science is vast and continually expanding (power over nature, electrical and chemical power, nuclear power), so too the power that can be acquired through spiritual practice is vast and varied. Astral travel, psychokinesis, and telepathy are just some powers that are often described as being developed through spiritual practice. Astral travel, though, will not end your suffering, and even the greatest psychic healer must eventually get sick and die. The Buddha himself lived only to eighty. Quite to our good fortune too, for imagine if the Buddha had not died but lived on for centuries. People would be much more interested in living forever (The deluded mind holds tightly to his old body!) than in finding the wisdom to end all suffering.

Omniscience and even omnipotence are associated with some great saints and yogis and hence many people expect these as necessary results of spiritual development. However, the powers that one can develop are limited by one's past karma. Some powers arise spontaneously with concentration developed in practice. Others can be increased through certain exercises. Not only are these powers different from wisdom, but they often become blocks to insight and understanding. Over and over it is stressed that the thought of gaining anything in meditation is strengthening the illusion that there is anything worth gaining and that there is anyone there to benefit from these powers. More delusion, more suffering.

Wisdom is simple. It is not knowledge, it is not power, it is simply being in harmony with the here and now. Nothing to gain, nothing to lose. Mindful of the flow, the wise person is not deluded; his life is in perfect harmony with the four noble truths. The happiness that comes from wisdom is beyond all knowledge and power. It is the happiness of true inner peace. Happiness that does not waver with the constant change of mental and physical phenomena, peace beyond even birth and death.

THE ORIGIN OF THESE TEACHINGS

These teachings come from the living Theravada Buddhist tradition of Southeast Asia. In the past, much attention in the West has been given to Zen and Tibetan forms of Buddhism, with Theravada usually mentioned in relation to early history or scriptures. In fact, the largest living Buddhist tradition in the world is found among almost half-million Theravada monks and the millions of lay disciples in the countries of Southeast Asia.

Southeast Asia was one of the first areas to which Buddhism

spread from India. There is indication that even during the Buddha's life, and certainly a few centuries later, Buddhism was introduced into Southeast Asia. Over time, as it has mixed with older animist cultures and Brahmin customs, it has risen and declined. Rearising, it has been firmly established as the major religion of the area for the past thousand years.

6 Both the ascetic forest monastery and the intensive meditation center with their respective approaches to practice presented here have long histories in Laos, Thailand, and Burma. There, meditation masters are the current living patriarchs of Theravada Dharma, and the practices taught have developed out of a long tradition based on the Pali scriptures and transmitted by their teachers. With this transmission, each new teacher in the lineage, as a new vessel, lends a special shape and color to the Dharma, the clear wisdom within.

The Dharma in this book was given freely, openhandedly. It seems only natural to share it. Most likely the teachings collected here will not be totally sufficient for you. All the better. Seek out a teacher; find a suitable place to learn and practice. Hopefully the variety of styles and approaches here will help you find one appropriate to you. And this variety will remind you that there are many valid paths to the one freedom. Each must find the one that suits him best. You may take this as a practice manual, but do not hesitate to ask questions, to find a teacher for yourself. These meditations come from only a dozen Theravada Buddhist teachers. There are many more masters, ways, and traditions. I only wish that this may encourage you in your practice, that it may help you find your own true path.

PENETRATING THE ILLUSION EAST AND WEST

Americans have visions of a mysterious Orient, incense-filled temples inhabited by serene, wise Buddhist monks. But just as only a small minority of the Christians in this country really understand and practice their religion, so too do only a small minority of Asian Buddhists understand and practice theirs. Even among Buddhist monks, only a small percentage, perhaps less than ten percent, meditate. What do the rest do? They study, teach, and perform ceremonies, and some just sit around and enjoy not working. The monkhood and the whole of Buddhism is intricately interwoven into the social, political, and economic structure of Southeast Asia.

Politically and economically, the monkhood allows those who wish to leave lay life to be supported by the society. Monks may fill religious roles as religious scholars or as teachers and counselors in social and political undertakings. In the midst of this larger Buddhist setting is a smaller number of sincere practitioners of the Buddha's teachings who concentrate on the development and purification of the mind, supported in their endeavor by both the monastic and lay communities. So although neither the southern Buddhist countries nor the monkhood as a whole is the mythic wise and saintly society of which many Westerners dream, a small but extremely important community of sincere practicing Buddhists does exist. In contrast to the empty ritualism and materialism of the society surrounding them, the great meditation teachers, monasteries, and associated disciples are a living reminder of the human potential for purity of conduct, unselfishness, and wisdom. They are repositories of the practical wisdom for man's awakening, ever available to those who are ready to use it.

7

While elite in terms of numbers, these centers of meditation and spiritual development are not at all elite in their teaching. Dharma is openhanded; meditation and spiritual practice are freely offered to all who come. Nothing is held back. The meditation temples are non-mysterious. Practice is straightforwardly explained, and all who come are welcome to ask questions and participate. Spiritual practice is most simply the development of certain qualities of mind: cultivating non-greed, non-hatred, and non-delusion; or developing concentration, mindfulness, equanimity, and compassion. Meditations, useful tools for this work, are free for the asking.

The Setting Meditation centers and monasteries can be seen simply as special educational environments. In Buddhist countries the purification of mind is valued enough that specially created environments are provided for the needs of those embarked on the path.

First, basic bodily needs are met: Food, clothing, and shelter are provided in moderate but sufficient amounts. Emotional and social needs are met, as one lives in a supportive group with similar values and interests. The psychological need for seeing one's activity in life as meaningful and important is also met, since inherent in the society's support of the monastic community is a great respect for the work of self-purification.

Besides meeting basic needs, the environment of the meditation centers and monasteries provides special conditions for learning mind control and developing concentration and wisdom. There is little talking and little noise. There is quiet for the other senses as well: simple, unadorned food, empty meditation cottages, and few visual distractions. These factors all aid in quieting the turbulent mind.

Social aspects of the community also aid in the process of purification. One is surrounded by good friends, wise people who value honesty and clarity. The community's norms are those of non-greed, non-hatred, and non-delusion. Love, compassion, and concern for others are practiced and valued, supported and modeled. Awareness is the watchword. Inner and outer harmony and patience in the individual are rewarded and built into the social system.

Daily activities are uncomplicated and straightforward. The community structure and outward discipline further simplify life. There is no need to think what to do next or how to behave. This frees the mind to concentrate on the various meditation exercises.

For Westerners, a highly structured, disciplined environment would seem the antithesis of freedom. A Western monk relates this story: "After only two weeks in an ascetic Lao monastery I was going crazy. The conformity of dress and behavior, the sameness, was stifling for me, having grown up in a culture that emphasizes individuality and bold self-expression. I thought of tie-dyeing my saffron robes green or blue, or of painting my begging bowl with flowers. Anything to be different!" Some time later it became clear to him that true freedom is found not in terms of outward form, true freedom is found only in the mind. In such a structured, disciplined, and seemingly unfree environment are found some of the freest beings in the world.

It is important to remember too that these are not closed communities, but rather places of teaching where outsiders are welcome. Visitors are welcome to come, practice, and experience the possibilities of a harmonious human community where unselfishness prevails.

Discipline and Morality Discipline and morality are essential tools in the path of purification. This is an extremely important point. Though Westerners often reject moral rules and discipline as interfering with their supposed freedom, these are indispensable means for achieving real inner freedom.

Meditation is a discipline. Ramana Maharshi, perhaps the most respected Hindu teacher of the last few centuries, said: "No one succeeds without effort. Mind control is not your birthright. Those who succeed owe their liberation to perseverance." Only practice continuously with effort and awareness and you will succeed.

Patience, perseverance. Traditionally a monk stays with his first teacher for a minimum of five years. Keeping to a regular disciplined practice is very important. From the stability of our regular practice we can observe the changes in our life and in the practice itself without reacting and making new difficulties. Regular balanced effort, sustained energy independent of results is needed. Since in fact there is nothing to gain in meditation, no result to be grasped, we are simply uncovering the Dharma.

One full moon evening shortly after a Western monk friend arrived at a Lao ascetic monastery, the monks were reciting the monthly ceremony, the rules of the order. This evening was special for him not only for the ceremony and the inspiring Dharma talk that followed, but also for the hot, sweet coffee that the villagers offered on these monthly holy days. After many days of one simple meal in the morning and nothing but water after noon, this coffee was a special treat. With it he could comfortably sit up all night and meditate.

This particular full moon, one of his teacher's teachers had come to visit. They sat after the ceremony in the temple sanctuary waiting for their Dharma lecture and the offering of the sweet coffee served in the main hall fifty yards away. That night they sat. There was no talk and they were not excused to leave. Silently they continued to sit. Imagining how his coffee was cooling, his agitation grew to extremes. Still they sat. Two hours passed. He was getting very restless and angry. Why couldn't he have his coffee so that he could go and meditate, he grumbled to himself. He was cold and hungry. Didn't the teacher realize how much better it would be if he could have his coffee and go to meditate instead of sitting there wasting his time? More time passed. The teacher looked over and smiled at him. He smiled back politely, angry at the teacher's lack of concern for his welfare and the uselessness of this situation. He could be doing something better, he thought, and thought and thought and raged and fumed, until his thoughts were exhausted after many hours. He was finally empty of anger and expectation. He looked up and smiled broadly at the teacher. The teacher smiled back. It was like coming home. At sunrise he left to collect alms in his bowl with a light heart, meditating with each step.

Meditation needs no special place. Simply work from where you are right now with patience and discipline.

In practice, discipline includes both right morality and right effort. What is right effort? Simply the effort to be mindful, to remember in the present moment what is happening without judging it. In Zen it is called effortless effort. Effortless effort is not an effort to gain or attain anything, but simply the discipline and effort to stay aware in the present. As practice continues, mindfulness as a quality of mind becomes strengthened. Life gets lighter and easier, mindfulness takes over as a way of life. The mind becomes silent and the heart opens. Discipline, effort, patience are very important.

Even more than discipline, morality has a bad name in the West. It is seen as the attempt of fearful Victorian society to control and limit our natural freedom and expression.

In fact, morality or virtue is of great value in practice. Traditionally, in Buddhism certain moral precepts are the foundation upon which concentration and wisdom are built. In the West, the reverse order is often experienced. Many Westerners begin by first understanding the unsatisfactory nature of their current life and society, for some through the daily news, for others perhaps through psychedelics. Often their recognition is accompanied by a complete abandonment of all moral codes. Then comes a search for peace and consciousness through various spiritual and meditation techniques. Finally, the importance of establishing a moral lifestyle as a basis for practice is understood. It helps to free the mind from worry and distraction, from greed and from hatred.

What is morality and where does it come from? Moral rules for self-restraint are simply verbal approximations of inner morality or wisdom and are the basic ways of relating that help reduce selfish action and keep a society harmonious and peaceful. Actions such as killing, lying, and stealing come from a mind that is attached to desires, separateness, selfishness. Formal rules are used to decrease selfishness and sense restraint is used to stop stimulating our desires.

Virtuous action is enormously powerful. The person who is always honest and practices non-harming becomes a beacon of quiet strength in the world. Among Buddhist monasteries, some practice is based almost solely on mindfulness of moral precepts, especially the refined set of 227 rules for monks. Strict, disciplined practice leads to a rapid giving up of one's own desires and selfishness. To a mind grounded in complete honesty and truth, tranquility and wisdom come easily.

We use the form of rules until virtue becomes natural. Then from the wisdom of the silent mind true spontaneous virtue arises. A silent mind which clings to nought, mindful and non-judging, is automatically virtuous and filled with love. This is the natural state of the mind. For when wisdom arises the emptiness of self is known. No self, nothing to protect. Just us, all together, no separateness, no selfishness. We use moral rules to create the conditions by which we can go beyond form and beyond rules to the deepest peace and unity.

11

CONCENTRATION AND INSIGHT MEDITATION

It is useful in understanding the variety of spiritual practices to distinguish between concentration and insight meditation. Basically, concentration meditations are those which develop one-pointedness and tranquility. These are practiced by fixing the mind on any single object and developing the ability to hold it there. Insight meditation, also called process meditation, does not fix the mind on one object. Instead, it develops the quality of concentration on changing objects as a tool for probing the nature of the mind-body process. Insight meditation is practiced by developing bare attention, a seeing-without-reacting to the whole process of our world of experience, to consciousness, and to all the objects of consciousness. Rather than fix the meditation on one object, the ongoing stream of the changing mind-body continuum becomes the meditation object, and through balanced, clear observation comes insight and wisdom into what we really are.

Concentration meditations are numerous. Traditionally, Buddha taught forty kinds; however, any single object of attention can be used for concentration meditation. This includes fixed concentration on a visual object such as a candle or mandala or inner light; concentration on a sound such as music, a mantra, the sound current; concentration on a feeling such as love, compassion, equanimity; or concentration on any part of the body, such as breath at the nose or the heart center or any other object where the mind is fixed and held steady.

Concentration develops high states of bliss and tranquility, and often certain powers. It can lead to experiences of cosmic consciousness and astral realms and the temporary elimination of greed and hatred from the mind. Much has been written in all the great spiritual traditions about the use of various pure concentration practices and the benefits of the mental states that result.

Concentration is also a necessary element in process or insight meditation, but for that it must be applied to changing objects. Process meditation focuses attention on the body, feelings, mind, and mind objects as they are experienced in their moment-to-moment flow. As concentration and attention increase, the mind becomes clear and balanced. More and more sharply we see how all things are changing in each instant, how these are ultimately not a source of lasting happiness, and how the whole mind-body process flows according to certain laws (karma), empty of any permanent self or individual soul. These profound insights become clear simply from increasing mindfulness, penetrating awareness of our own process. With these insights wisdom arises, bringing equanimity, loving-kindness, and compassion, for in experiencing the emptiness of self we see the unity of all beings. When the mind is completely balanced, tranquil, and keenly alert, one may experience the cessation of this whole moving process, the peace of nirvana. With this comes the deepest insight into the emptiness of all conditioned phenomena, and a subsequent detachment that is nevertheless peaceful and loving, the radiant natural state of the mind freed from defilements.

One may start practice with a pure concentration exercise and then change to awareness of process. Initially some teachers prefer using a concentration technique to enable the meditator to still his wandering, undisciplined mind. Later they direct this concentration to the mind-body process to develop wisdom. Other teachers attempt to start directly watching the process, by focusing on changing sensations, feelings, or thoughts. This approach must still concern itself with the development of the mental qualities of tranquility and concentration before any insight will develop. Buddha taught both approaches at different times according to the needs of his students.

Although people disagree over the merits of the various approaches, we must remember these are only tools to be used and then discarded. In fact almost all meditation practices are good when practiced with discipline, sincerity, and perseverance, and holding on to any method or comparing this to that is only another attachment that leads to further suffering.

MINDFULNESS

In the development of wisdom, one quality of mind above all others is the key to practice. This quality is mindfulness, attention or self-recollection. The most direct way to understand our life situation, who we are and how our mind and body operate, is to observe with a mind that simply notices all events equally. This attitude of non-judgmental, direct observation allows all events to occur in a natural way. By keeping the attention in the present moment, we can see more and more clearly the true characteristics of our mind and body process.

13

Buddhism starts from the known. What is the world? The world is objects of sight, hearing, taste, smell, and touch; objects of mind; and the knowing (or consciousness) of these objects. It is through the quality of choiceless awareness that we can best penetrate and understand the nature of our world. For example, when one is mindful of seeing, the attention is not on evaluating the object of sight, forming concepts of good or bad, pretty or ugly, familiar or unfamiliar in regard to it. Rather the attention becomes an awareness of the process of seeing, the fact of seeing, rather than the facts associated with seeing. The concepts follow the experience. Mindfulness focuses on the moment of the process rather than on the reflection of it in concepts. Awareness is directed at the present moment, to the process itself, the only place where the understanding of reality's true nature can be gained. This awareness brings an understanding which will result in wisdom, freedom, and an end to suffering. Not only does developing mindfulness allow us to penetrate the nature of our world and understand the cause of suffering; when developed, mindfulness has other power. Mindfulness brings us to a moment-to-moment purity of mind. Each moment we are mindful, the mind is pure, free of clinging, hating, and delusion. For that moment, the mind is cool because it is filled with attention for what is without the coloration of judgment. Developing mindfulness also balances the other factors of mind such as energy and concentration that are needed for our spiritual development. In fact, coming to a perfect balance of mind is the whole development of the spiritual path. When well-established, mindfulness can allay all fears, for when the mind is free of clinging, condemning, and identifying, all objects in samsara, the chain of becoming, are equal. Nothing to be gained, nothing to be feared. 'No praise, no blame'. Ultimately, we see there is no one there to gain anything. Simply the natural flow of the process, empty of self.

One of the last instructions of the Buddha before his final nirvana was 'strive on with mindfulness'. To strive does not mean to make the effort to change things, but simply to make the effort to be clearly aware at all moments. Right here. Now. Mindfully.

14 COMPASSION AND LOVING-KINDNESS

The basic teachings of the Buddha can be expressed by two words: wisdom and compassion. Wisdom in its passive aspect is that penetrating insight into the nature of all existence and the balance of mind this illumination brings. Compassion and loving-kindness are the active aspects of this wisdom, the expression in the world of a deep understanding of the Dharma, the laws of nature.

The practices and meditations in this book emphasize the cultivation of insight, letting compassion grow naturally from this understanding. Most of these masters direct their teaching toward understanding of the characteristics of the mind-body process, knowing that to experience directly the truth of impermanence, unsatisfactoriness, and emptiness will bear the fruit of love and compassion. Seeing clearly the suffering in one's own life brings great caring to ease the suffering of others. Feeling the freedom of liberation grow as the empty nature of the world is revealed, one naturally shares this lightness and love with all other beings. Universal love comes from total unselfishness, and all Buddhist practice aims at the elimination of greed, hatred, and ignorance, the elimination of the roots of selfishness in the mind. The cultivation of mindfulness, essential to all insight meditation, is actually the cultivation of loving-kindness because mindfulness means allowing things to be as they are. Seeing clearly without judging, without reacting, without selfishness in relation to all experience is the space of both wisdom and love.

Although the teachings expressed in this book stress the path of insight, Buddhist tradition emphasizes insight and loving-kindness meditations as complementary practices ... some teachers work more with insight, others with loving-kindness. It is often very helpful to directly cultivate loving thoughts and mind states as a daily meditation. Without the balance of compassion, the path of wisdom can become dry and analytical, while love cultivated without wisdom is apt to be superficial or misguided. Although at times the path of insight and that of love may seem separate, they must unite for practice to be complete.

True understanding was the root of the Buddha's own practice and what he taught all who followed. That is, to attain liberation for the sake of all beings. Whatever helps in putting an end to selfishness: charity, kind actions in the world, loving-kindness meditation (and these are the practices stressed in most Buddhist temples), or the path of insight leading to the deepest wisdom, all are part of the path of the Buddha. As practice continues, it becomes clear that it is not possible to liberate less than all beings because to do so would be to still live in the delusion of a self separate from others. Coming to the understanding of non-duality and of emptiness, the most profound wisdom brings one back to the deepest love and the clearest expression of compassion in the world.

15

GOALS/NO GOALS

Two different attitudes to practice are represented in this book. Most meditation practice is approached from one or the other.

Strive very hard to achieve concentration of mind and enlightenment. You are extremely fortunate to be born a human and to hear the Dharma. Don't waste this chance. Work, meditate vigorously. This is one approach.

In the second approach, there is nothing to gain, nowhere to go. The very effort you make to be enlightened will prevent wisdom from arising, for wisdom can never arise from desire. Simply be, let go and watch. Naturally. Right here, right now. That is all there is.

As understanding deepens in the practice of meditation, we begin to experience the unity that underlies the various forms in samsara. Paradoxes become acceptable when the mind becomes silent, open to inner experience.

The path of trying to gain enlightenment and the path of just being in the moment lead to the same place. Each is an outward form, a representation of how to practice. From one perspective, we can say that wisdom is developed from concentration and insight in meditation. Equally, we can say that wisdom is the natural state of the mind. When we have let go of our habits, desires, distractions, those things that blind us, wisdom automatically appears.

Choosing an approach is much a matter of one's personal style and karma. For some, a strict teacher, rigorous discipline, and goal-oriented practice are right. Often this approach balances with their own internal lack of discipline. For others, particularly goal-oriented individuals whose predominant expression is attainment in the world, the practices of letting go, just sitting, just watching, are a balance for their habitual striving.

Bringing the mind into balance is the essence of meditation. Striving, not striving: Both can bring balance. Eventually, whatever practice one follows must be let go of, even the practice of letting go.

INTENSIVE / NON-INTENSIVE PRACTICE

Two other contrasting approaches to meditation are the intensive retreat style and a complementary non-intensive approach. These may be pursued separately or combined to suit a meditator's needs and lifestyle.

The non-intensive approach stresses practice which fits into daily life to help develop wisdom in normal activities at a natural pace. It emphasizes that meditation is practicing a way of being and does not require an intensive, isolated setting. The non-intensive approach allows for the gradual deepening of wisdom through daily sitting and natural mindfulness. It is a path without flashy insights and extremes of bliss and high concentration. This can be a difficult path to follow without supplementary intensive practice. Because insight grows slowly we may get discouraged. It is hard to maintain awareness in the midst of a busy life. At times, our desires, boredom, and day-to-day pain make it hard to continue practice. The tranquility and highs of strong concentration are slow in coming. But the non-intensive approach has great strengths. Wisdom developed is lasting and strong. Attachment to highs and bliss or excessive concentration is avoided. And, since ultimately there is nothing to gain and no time but *right now*, daily moment-to-moment practice is where it all leads.

Intensive practice of many hours daily in special retreats can develop strong concentration and deep insights quickly. In these intensive sessions, for days or months meditators will spend fifteen or more hours each day sitting and walking in meditation continuously. The mind becomes tranquil and as the power of concentration and awareness deepens, sharp insights arise. Often meditators in retreats will experience intense pain or bliss and various phenomena or distractions. For example, they may see lights or visions, feel their bodies floating and shrinking, or may experience spontaneous body movement. The high concentration and bliss which often result from continuous intensive practice combine with deep insight into the Dharma (the nature of things) to strengthen practice and faith. This experience in itself is of enormous importance. It provides a solid basis for daily meditation in the world after the retreat. Indeed, there are some teachers who stress that only through intensive retreats can one expect to penetrate and experience the true Dharma and the final peace of nirvana.

Both intensive and natural daily practice were recommended by the Buddha. They are both valid paths, and we in the West now have the special opportunity to experience the best of both approaches. We can spend time in periodic intensive retreats and combine this with daily practice of mindfulness. Both help balance our lives, deepen our wisdom, and allow us to let go. Retreats are important, but wherever we are right now is the time and place to begin/continue our practice.

THE FACTORS OF ENLIGHTENMENT

One of the clearest and most useful ways to describe practice is in terms of the seven factors of enlightenment. These are the natural qualities of mind that the Buddha described as the constituents of a proper spiritual practice. A mind in which these factors are fully developed and balanced experiences freedom.

Three of these factors are passive elements. They are concentration, or one-pointedness of mind; tranquility, or quietness of mind; and equanimity, or detachment and balance of mind in the face of change. Three other factors are energetic elements. These are effort, which means the volition to be mindful; investigation, or silent observation of what is happening; and rapture, which manifests as bliss and an intense interest in the spiritual practice.

The seventh factor is mindfulness, the key to practice. The development of this particular quality of mind automatically develops all of the other factors. Mindfulness, noticing the object in the present moment, also has the function of bringing these factors into proper balance.

Using the factors of enlightenment, one can evaluate the whole range of meditation techniques and spiritual paths. All of the approaches to practice discussed in this book may be considered in the light of the development of these seven qualities of mind. Some will develop the energy factors more rapidly or strongly. Others strengthen concentration or equanimity more quickly. No need to be concerned with the form of the practice or the words or style of the teaching. Simply see if it will lead to the development of the factors of enlightenment.

It all comes back to mind. Mind is the start and end of all spiritual work. One can examine a path to see what qualities of mind are developed and see if that path will help to bring the factors of enlightenment further into balance. If so, then use it, remembering that getting caught in further opinions and comparisons of various practices can be a great obstacle to liberation. Relax. Do your own practice and honor those around you with love.

WHY WRITE / READ DHARMA BOOKS

At one point in my meditation, I vowed that I would never write a book. What a waste of time! What a way to fool myself and others! There are more than enough books on Buddhism, meditation, spiritual practice. And not one of them tells the truth anyway, for the truth cannot be captured by words.

I like to think of books on meditation as spiritual garbage. However, eggshells and grapefruit rinds do indicate that somewhere nearby there has been nourishment. A discourse of the Buddha to a passing yogi is only the eggshell of the exchange. If the yogi understood, he got the nourishment. The essence is not in the words, it is in the experience.

Yet here is this book: a record, a pointing. It is an attempt to make available contemporary Theravada teachings to seekers of understanding in the West. In the past, much of Buddhism has been portrayed through stilted translations of ancient texts. But these teachings are still alive and are represented here in the words of some of this tradition's most important masters. I only hope that this may help lead readers to their own inner Dharma.

The teachings in this book may seem confusing and contradictory. One master will prescribe a particular approach to practice, only to be contradicted in the following chapter by another. The point of representing this paradox is to show that there are many valid approaches to the same fundamental truths. If the reader gains the understanding that the Dharma cannot be found in the contrasting forms and techniques of Buddhism but only in the underlying experience, then he is really ready to practice. Don't think too much about which is better or clearer or faster. Pick a practice, a teacher, and do it.

One day a famous woman lecturer on Buddhist metaphysics, came to see my Lao master. This woman gave periodic teachings in Bangkok on the Abhidharma and complex Buddhist psychology. In talking to the master she detailed how important it was for people to understand Buddhist psychology and how much her students benefited from their study with her. She asked my teacher whether he agreed with the importance of understanding Buddhist psychology and metaphysics. Yes, very important, he agreed. Delighted, she further questioned whether he had his own students learn Abhidharma. Oh yes, of course. And where, she asked, did he recommend they start, which books and studies were best?

"Only here," he said, pointing to his heart, "only here."

19

MEDITATION IN BURMA, LAOS, AND THAILAND

CHAPTER
TWO

There are many facets to the Buddhism currently found in Burma, Thailand, and the rest of Southeast Asia. First, there is the popular religion of the majority of people which involves the performance of meritorious deeds, such as alms-giving and the observance of rituals, to gain a good rebirth in lives to come. Then there is the traditional practice of many dedicated to the scholarly study of the Sanskrit and Pali languages and the Buddhist scriptures. Also there is the tradition of social service in which monks teach and assist in village daily life. Altogether, Buddhism in Southeast Asia functions in much the same way as organized religion in other parts of the world.

In addition, there is the tradition of monks and lay people concerned with spiritual development through practicing the paths of purification outlined by the Buddha. Although there have been a number of meditation centers and monasteries in Laos and Cambodia, they aren't available to Westerners because of the current political situation, and may not exist at all in the near future. Out of thousands of monasteries in Thailand, several hundred are particularly concerned with meditation. Of these, several dozen are large centers run by well-known masters with many disciples. We see then that meditation involves only a small part of the society and the religion. However, it plays an extremely important part in preserving the essential truths taught by the Buddha.

Buddhism in Burma is perhaps stronger than Buddhism in Thailand. The Burmese people are more concerned about their religion and spend more time at the temples. Here too, though, the tradition of self-development through meditation includes only a small percentage of the monks and general populace. The rest of Buddhism is concerned with rites, rituals, and scholarship or social endeavors. In Burma, too, only a minority of the more than ten thousand temples and centers are meditation monasteries. Of these meditation monasteries, there are several types. Some serve lay people in particular, some only monks, while others are open to both.

There are some important differences between meditation centers and meditation monasteries. Meditation centers are designed primarily for intensive retreats, either by monks or lay people. It is not uncommon in Burma for someone to take their yearly vacation at a meditation center. At these centers, people spend anywhere from ten days to several months or longer doing extremely intensive practice. They strive to develop rapidly high levels of concentration and awareness leading to insight and wisdom.

The tradition of meditation centers is most firmly established in Burma, although there are also a number to be found in Thailand. These centers are extremely quiet, special environments where there is either very limited or no social interaction, except with the teacher. One practices mostly in solitude, or perhaps for some part of the day in a group, devoting all of the time to meditation. The environment at these centers is tailored for a particular task, formal sitting and walking meditation, and all distractions are carefully minimized.

In contrast, meditation monasteries are places to live for long periods of time as a monk or a nun (there are many nuns in Southeast Asia). In the monasteries, meditation is taught as an integral part of the lifestyle, to be practiced all times of the day. The teaching is concerned with developing awareness of every aspect of one's daily life—eating, dressing, sewing, walking, cleaning, as well as the social interactions in the community. Meditation in these monasteries becomes a way of life rather than a particular exercise. Yet the teaching also includes regular daily sitting and walking practice. The best monasteries are extremely harmonious communities functioning under the rules of conduct for monks and nuns set down by the Buddha. This lifestyle is designed to develop the factors of enlightenment through careful attention to all daily activities. In fact, one of the masters of a monastic community said that he had learned as much Dharma from cultivating awareness and compassion in receiving the many visitors who came, responding to their problems, as he did from any other meditation exercise. Although he encouraged many hours of formal sitting meditation each day, he felt that social interaction meditation was equally important, learning to develop wisdom in all situations.

Both meditation centers for short-term intensive practice, and resident monasteries for developing a meditative way of life, provide an especially conducive environment for spiritual growth. They both offer the presence of a teacher, the quiet of a setting with limited distractions, a simple lifestyle with not much to do but explore one's own mind, and a community whose values are all directed toward spiritual development.

In the meditation center, the activities of the day consist almost entirely of spending one's time practicing meditation (alone or in a silent group), perhaps twelve to twenty hours per day. Generally, this means alternating sitting and walking; one does not sit for twenty hours straight. Usually, there is an interview once a day or every other day with the teacher, and only minimal time is spent taking care of the necessities of life. These few other activities include collecting alms if you are a monk, eating one or two meals in the morning, bathing, and finally sleeping perhaps four hours a night. In the practice at a center, all is directed at intensive development of concentration and mindfulness.

The daily life in the monastery, by contrast, is much fuller. One arises very early in the morning, sits in group meditation while it is still dark, and perhaps chants the Pali scriptures. Then the monks go out on alms rounds with a bowl, collecting food the lay people have prepared to offer them. Later the whole monastery eats either one or, as in some monasteries, two meals a day. All food must be eaten before noontime. After the meal cleanup there may be a short talk by the teacher. For the rest of the day, one's time is spent meditating, studying, or performing a number of tasks that are part of the community. Drawing water from the well, helping to build new structures that are necessary, repairing fences around the monastery, cleaning, washing, and sweeping. These tasks are generally apportioned evenly among all of the monks so that during the day one might spend several hours meditating, an hour or two reading or studying, and several hours involved in work for the community. In addition, some monks may receive lay people to teach and give meditation instruction. In a forest monastery, one also sews and dyes one's own robes. The monks take care of all the basic necessities of life in a very self-sufficient manner. Finally, in the evening time, the monks reconvene, with lay people as well, for chanting, group meditation for an hour or longer, and an evening Dharma talk delivered by the teacher. Questions and discussions of community business follow. Then all return to their cottages or living quarters to meditate

23

until sleep time. It is stressed that all the activities of the daily life of the community are part of meditation. Whether formally sitting doing a meditation exercise such as following the breath, or working at drawing water from the wells, or talking over community business, one is urged to do so with as much mindfulness and concentration as possible.

Another difference between the intensive meditation center tradition and the monastery is in the use of teacher interviews. With intensive practice in the meditation centers, one is encouraged to have an interview daily or every other day, sometimes even more frequently. One meets with the teacher to report the events of one's meditation and to allow the teacher to help guide and balance the practice. Because of the intensive nature of practice in such places, this is an important aspect of the teaching. By contrast, in monasteries and Dharma communities, interviews are infrequent although teachers are usually open to questions. Rather, teaching is done by Dharma talks to the whole community, and because practice is not necessarily so intensive the need for interviews is not stressed. In fact, in some monasteries it is felt that it is much more valuable as part of the lifestyle that the yogis or meditators learn to answer their own questions, to deal with their own doubts, to watch the process of doubting and questioning in their own mind. In this way they are directed back to their own experience and learn to resolve their questions as a part of their practice without being attached to a daily interview and needing such direct guidance from their teacher. Again, we can see that both approaches to teacher interviews are valid ways of development on the spiritual path. What is appropriate depends on where you're starting from and where you are.

What are other benefits of such carefully tailored environments as these centers and monasteries? In addition to creating the outer stillness necessary for high states of concentration, the absence of distraction prevents us from running away from ourselves. We must face our thoughts and our changing mind-states. Attention is forced inward. Our minds are revealed to us. Even in the simple lifestyle of a monk, one finds, interestingly enough, that the habit of clinging to things in the environment is so strong that it continues nonetheless. Even with but three or four possessions, one can become extremely attached to one's bowl or one's robes, thinking them more beautiful or in some way better than another's. One can become fearful of losing them. It is astonishing to discover that even in the simplest life, the mind will find new things to hold on

24

to and continue the process of clinging. It is only through seeing this process clearly, though, that we can become liberated from it.

Although meditation masters are few in contrast to the hundreds of thousands of other Buddhist monks in Southeast Asia, they are still among the best-known and the most highly respected members of their society. They are revered for their qualities of mind, their purity and saintliness, and in many cases for the powers that they are believed to possess. In this book, I have made almost no mention of the powers developed through meditation. This is in keeping with the meditation tradition of Southeast Asia, where even the most powerful and highly developed teachers do not particularly talk about or bother with magic, mystical energies or powers. Infatuation with power and mystery tends to sidetrack the development of compassion and wisdom, and all of these masters are concerned with only one thing—the deepening of insight leading to the full liberation of all beings.

25

Since Westerners now cannot get visas to stay in Burma for more than two weeks, and since Laos and Cambodia are still involved in great political change, most Westerners involved in the Theravadin Buddhist practice taught in Southeast Asia go to the country of Thailand. There are now more than fifty, perhaps as many as eighty, Western bhikkus or monks in Thailand. This number has doubled over the past few years.

There are difficulties in going to Thailand to become a bhikku. Visas are not easy to obtain, and they require that one ordain rather quickly or else periodically leave the country. There is also a language problem. One might go to Burma for a week's practice in an intensive center; there, many people speak English, since Burma was once a British colony. In Thailand however few meditation teachers speak English. One must either learn Thai or find a center where a translator is available, and translators are often difficult to find.

Sincere Westerners are allowed, and in fact encouraged, to ordain as monks. In the best temples one must first serve a period as a templeboy and then as a novice, learning the rules of the order, the proper social conventions, and behavior of a monk, becoming acquainted with the importance of strictly following the lifestyle and the precepts of monks after ordination.

In the meditation centers and monasteries of Southeast Asia you will find a very open Dharma; the teachers are willing to impart their entire meditation system to whoever comes to them. Aside from the initiations of ordinations into the order of bhikkus, there are no other initiations, no secrets, no observation of the mystical

JACK KORNFIELD

adition. Everything is openhanded, very direct and
 instructed how to practice and is encouraged to do
so. A Westerner coming to a temple or a center will often have a
special reception, as the Burmese and Thais are extremely pleased
at the recent growing interest of Westerners in Buddhism and are
particularly happy to help someone who has come so far to receive
the teaching. The lay people often feel a kind of awe, for they,
especially the simple villagers, see in the West their vision of
heaven, because we have televisions, cars, refrigerators, and beautiful houses. Someone who has given up heaven to come and live so
simply in a meditation center is most admirable to them. (In my
later years as a monk I often stressed to the villagers that the
heaven of the West isn't all it would seem to be and that, in fact,
any kind of happiness that comes through the senses is ultimately
unsatisfactory. It arises and ceases and comes and goes and can
never bring the satisfaction of inner peace and wisdom.)

As a lay person in a monastery or center, you will generally be
expected to follow the eight precepts. These include not killing, not
lying, not stealing, abstaining from sex (while a member of the
community), abstaining from drugs and alcohol intoxicants. You
are also often expected to abstain from using money, from wearing
perfume and fancy dress, and from using high and luxurious beds.
And finally there is a precept of no eating after mid-day. One or
perhaps two meals are served, early in the morning and then again
at noon. These precepts are used to simplify life, to make the outward form simple and harmonious within the community, and to
allow you to get on with the practice.

The question of how to pick a teacher, a center, and a method is a
problem for many people. There is a story in the Buddhist tradition that may help in understanding the answer to this question.
The Buddha is seated in a garden, surrounded by a large number of
his disciples. A man comes up to him, pays his respects, and begins
to praise the Sangha, the community of monks that the Buddha
has ordained. And after this fellow has praised it, the Buddha
himself continues the praise of the Sangha, pointing out the various groups of monks situated in various places in the garden. He
praises their virtue and says, "See there, those people who are
most inclined toward practice using powers are gathered with my
disciple, the great MahaMoggallana (who was known as the monk
with the great psychic powers in the time of the Buddha). And
those whose natural karma takes them to develop their path
through wisdom you see gathered over there with my great disci-

ple, Sariputtra (who was known as the monk with the greatest
wisdom, next only to the Buddha). And those, my friend, whose
karma or whose character makes them most inclined to develop
their spiritual path through the rules of discipline of the order are
over there with my great disciple, Upali, the master of the Vinaya.
And those who are most inclined to use absorptions or jhanas as a
path are there with another great disciple of mine," and so on.

Even in the time of the Buddha, then, there were many meditation techniques and approaches to spiritual development that he
taught; his various disciples who naturally inclined in one way
taught those people who also naturally inclined toward that practice. So we see that it is not a question of which practice is better,
but rather which is the most natural, which will suit one's own
personality and bring one most quickly into the balance and harmony that are the result of spiritual development.

Picking a teacher or a center involves several factors. One is
intuition. You may meet a teacher and intuitively, immediately
feel that he or she is someone you wish to learn from, that you have
a strong bond with him, that his method is just right for you. On
the other hand, this may not happen. In that case, it is wise to visit
several teachers, several centers, in this country or in Asia, to determine which environment, which kind of discipline, which sort
of practice feel the best for you. Trust your own heart and your
intuition, but also give yourself enough experience and data from
which to make the choice. You will have to decide whether you
want to go to a place where the mediation is integrated into part of
a greater lifestyle and where you can spend a long time, or to a
center for a short period of intensive development. Do you want to
practice with a teacher who enforces some very strict rules of discipline or a teacher for whom that form is not an essential part of
the teaching?

Not only are there different techniques and approaches in the
various centers and monasteries, there are also differences in the
personalities and teaching styles. In teaching styles, it is traditionally said that different teachers will have gained liberation
through the door which emphasizes predominance of one of the
three characteristics (although they are actually three aspects of
the same deep insight), and that this also will affect how they
teach. Some teachers have gained understanding through penetrating the characteristic of emptiness (anatta) of all phenomena
and are inclined to stress wisdom, clear seeing in their teaching.
The chapter of Achaan Buddhadasa follows this approach. Other
teachers have understood the truth through penetrating the

characteristic of suffering and they are inclined to stress effort in the practice. Sunlun Sayadaw emphasizes this approach. Some teachers have penetrated through the characteristic of impermanence and it is said that they tend to stress faith in practice. U Ba Khin is an example of this type of teaching. Of course, these qualities do not always hold true, and a skillful teacher will stress that which is most helpful to each individual student.

28   Personalities and styles of teachers may differ in other ways. The teacher of Achaan Maha Boowa and Achaan Chaa was Achaan Mun, one of the greatest Thai masters of this century. He used a great deal of force in his teaching. He was fierce, ferocious, and very strict with his disciples. There are other teachers such as Achaan Jumnien who are extremely loving, kind, and open. Neither of these is better than the other; the difference simply reflects the karma or the personality of the particular teacher, his own practice, and the way that he is best able to teach other people. Again, deciding which type of teacher feels right or best when you are selecting a place to practice is largely an intuitive process.

There are several important methods a teacher uses in his teaching. One way he teaches is through his love and acceptance of those who come to see him, which allows them to love and accept themselves. This is an important quality of mind to be developed in the spiritual path. Another method is using balance. A teacher will often prescribe a particular meditation to counterbalance a difficulty facing a disciple. For example, someone who has a great deal of anger might be asked to do a loving-kindness meditation; for someone who has a great deal of lust, a teacher might prescribe a meditation on the repulsiveness of the body. A teacher may see that one's energy and concentration are out of equilibrium and prescribe that one spend more time doing walking or energetic practice to correct the imbalance. Or, he may notice that one's faith and widsom are out of balance—that with too much faith one is not developing the quality of mind of investigation, not looking clearly to see what is the true nature of the mind and body process. To reestablish that balance, he might use a story to point out to his disciple that he really doesn't understand, that he needs to cut down some of his reliance on faith and increase his questioning or wisdom. The whole of spiritual development is a balancing act. And the teacher's function is to help balance the practice of his student.

Another key function of the teacher is to point out our latest attachments. As meditation progresses and the mind becomes more subtle, attachments go from outward forms of sense desires of a gross nature to more refined attachments, such as the attachment to certain kinds of bliss, or the lights, or the calm, that may come from meditation. Whatever it is that is happening when we come to see a teacher will emerge. He will see where we are stuck, what we are attached to, and help us to let go, to allow the natural process of non-attachment that will lead to our liberation. Non-attachment can be taught by telling stories, by changing the direction of meditation, or even, in the Zen meditation style, by hitting the student at just the right moment. In all of these ways of teaching, however, it is the meditator himself who is doing the work. The teacher is only assisting him in staying on the right track and keeping in balance.

It is important not to get too hung up on judging a teacher or a center by appearance. It was my experience to go first to a very strict and well-disciplined ascetic monastery. The teacher Achaan Chaa was a very precise, proper, and exquisite example of a monk living a very simple life. Then I went to a Burmese temple with a very different sort of teacher. At the Burmese temple I found a very famous meditation teacher who had had ten thousand disciples before me; yet when I saw him he appeared sloppy, his robe dragged on the ground, he smoked Burmese cigars, and he spent much of his day sitting around talking with the women in the temple in a very un-monkish way, unlike my former teacher. Sometimes he appeared to get angry and to be concerned with petty things. For the first two months of my intensive practice there I suffered a great deal making comparisons between these two teachers. The Burmese teacher was kind to me and gave me one of the nicest meditation cottages right near his own. As a result every day I would see him sitting around smoking his cigars and talking with the ladies. It upset my practice terribly. I would think to myself, "What am I doing learning from this man? I'm working so hard in meditating and he's out there like that, he doesn't have anything to teach me. Why doesn't he behave like a monk the way Achaan Chaa did?" It took me a couple of months to realize that his outward form did not detract from the value I was getting from the meditation. And that to judge and compare outward form, to look for the Buddha in the teacher, was simply creating more suffering for myself. The mind that judges creates suffering. Finally, when I was able to let go, I was able to benefit greatly from his instruction and teaching, and he was a very good teacher of this meditation technique. (And what wasn't useful, I left for him.) It took a lot of suffering to come to understand how the discriminating mind creates difficulties; but seeing, I was able to let go.

Many people in Theravada Buddhism (and in fact in every spiritual tradition) get caught up in judging and comparing teachers methods. Their teacher, their method, is the best, the right, the pure method or tradition. This sort of discrimination leads people to see the world increasingly in terms of good and evil. This is good, that is evil. This wrong understanding causes much fear and much pain.

There is no such thing as good or evil forces in the world. The only 'evil' that exists is within our own mind, the painful states of greed, hatred, and delusion. There is no difficulty outside of this, and for a mind purified of all these painful reactions, no other evil exists, nor can such a mind be shaken or moved by the arising and passing of any experience—for it sees the world with wisdom, as empty, as not self.

Similarly, those who cling to or claim to have established or follow 'pure' traditions and 'pure' sects can sometimes allow people to misunderstand the basic teaching of the Buddha. Purity does not exist within a tradition, nor within a method, or within a religion. There is only one basic purity that was taught by the Buddha, the purity which liberates, and that is purity of mind, freedom from greed, hatred, and delusion. Apart from this inner purification, even well-meaning claims to purity only increase clinging and discrimination. The essence of all practice is to get beyond all clinging and selfishness. Use any or all of these tools well, but do not get caught up in the tool or the teacher mistaking them for the truth of the Buddha. Practice diligently and let go of all that binds, settle for nothing less than tasting freedom for yourself.

As you continue meditating, your own practice will become your reference point. Before his death the Buddha asked his disciples to follow the *Dharma*, not any teacher or tradition. He put no one over the community of monks and nuns. The Dharma was to guide them. So for us, there is no blind belief or blind faith in Buddhism. We simply believe enough in the possibility of liberation and we are wise enough to see the suffering in our existence to have the faith to begin practice. And in the practice we see for ourselves the truth of the Dharma. The Buddha encouraged people with the words, "Be a lamp unto yourself, be a light unto yourself." Out of this practice will come freedom.

THE ENTIRE TEACHING

CHAPTER
THREE

I have reserved a whole chapter to make a simple statement.

The entire teaching of Buddhism can be summed up in this way:

Nothing is worth holding on to.

If you let go of everything,
    Objects
    Concepts
    Teachers
    Buddha
    Self
    Senses
    Memories
    Life
    Death
    Freedom

Let go and all suffering will cease. The world will appear in its pristine self-existing nature, and you will experience the freedom of the Buddha.

The rest that follows in this book are useful approaches and techniques for learning to let go.

ACHAAN CHAA

CHAPTER
FOUR

Achaan Chaa was born into a large and comfortable family in a rural village in the Lao area of northeast Thailand. He ordained as a novice in early youth and on reaching the age of twenty took higher ordination as a bhikku. Beyond the fourth grade education standard in the village schools, he studied some basic Dharma and scriptures as a young monk. Later he practiced meditation under the guidance of several of the local forest teachers in the Lao-speaking ascetic tradition. He walked for a number of years in the style of an ascetic monk, sleeping under the forest trees and spent a short but enlightening period with Achaan Mun, one of the most famous and powerful Thai-Lao meditation masters of this century. After many years of travel and practice he returned to settle in a thick forest grove near the village of his birth. This grove was uninhabited, known as a place of cobras, tigers, and ghosts and, as he said, the perfect location for a forest monk. Around Achaan Chaa a large monastery formed as more and more monks, nuns, and lay people came to hear his teaching and stay on with him. Now there are disciples teaching in more than thirty mountain and forest branch temples throughout northeast Thailand.

On entering Wat Ba Pong one is apt first to encounter monks drawing water from a well, and a sign on the path that says "You there, be quiet, we're trying to meditate." Although there is group meditation and chanting twice a day and usually an evening talk by Achaan Chaa, the heart of the meditation is the way of life. Monks work sewing robes and sweeping the forest paths and live extremely simply. Monks here follow the ascetic precepts limiting meals to one a day and limiting their number of possessions, robes, and living places. They live in individual cottages spread throughout the forest, and practice their walking meditation on cleared paths under the trees. Many of his Western disciples now choose to live at a huge new forest preserve monastery with scattered cottages built into caves in the hillside.

The simple regimen of the forest monastery provides the setting for the development of wisdom. Achaan Chaa stresses that "Each person has his own natural pace," and that we should not worry about the length of our path or destination. "Simply stick to the present moment," he advises, and, "eventually the mind will reach its natural balance where practice is automatic." He rarely speaks of attaining any special state of mind or states of concentration and enlightenment. Instead, when questioned on this topic he will ask the questioner if he has fully let go of all attachment and is totally free from suffering. With the usual reply of "Not yet," he will direct him to simply continue his practice of watching the mind and not clinging even to deep insights or enlightenment experiences, only continue this not-clinging from moment to moment.

Daily life in the monastery becomes as much the focus of practice as the formal sitting and walking. Washing robes, cleaning spittoons, sweeping the hall, collecting morning alms are all meditation, and as Achaan Chaa reminds us, in ". . . cleaning a toilet don't feel you are doing it as a favor for anyone else." There is Dharma there too. Meditation means mindfulness in whatever we do. At times the lifestyle seems strict and harsh and the struggle to find comfort and security becomes a great lesson in the meditation. "When you get angry or feel sorry for yourself it is a great opportunity to understand the mind." In surrendering to the rules that create a harmonious community, we see clearly how desires and images we hold conflict with this flow. The strict discipline helps us cut away at the ego-needs for outward display of individuality.

35

Achaan Chaa does not emphasize any special meditation techniques nor does he encourage crash courses to attain quick insights and enlightenment. In formal sitting one may watch the breath until the mind is still, and then continue practice by observing the flow of the mind-body process. Live simply, be natural, and watch the mind are the keys to his practice. Patience is stressed. As a new monk at his monastery I became frustrated by the difficulties of practice and the seeming arbitrary rules of conduct I had to follow. I began to criticize other monks for sloppy practice, and to doubt the wisdom of Achaan Chaa's teaching. At one point I went to him and complained, noting that even he was inconsistent and seemed to be contradicting himself often in an unenlightened way. He laughed and pointed out how much I was suffering by trying to judge the others around me. Then he explained that in fact his teaching was just a balance. "It is as though I see people walking down a road I know well," he said. "I look up and see someone about to fall in a ditch on the right-hand side of the road or get off on a side track on the right so I call out to him 'Go left, go left'. Similarly if I see someone about to go off on a sidetrack to the left, or to fall in the left-hand ditch, I call out 'Go right, go right'. All of practice is simply developing a balance of mind, not clinging, unselfishness." Sitting in meditation or working at our daily activities are all part of practice and watching patiently allows the unfolding of wisdom and peace in a natural way. This is Achaan Chaa's path.

Achaan Chaa welcomes Westerners and more than two dozen have lived and studied with him, often for many months or years. Wisdom is a way of living and being, and Achaan Chaa has preserved the special, simple lifestyle of the monks as organized by the Buddha for learning Dharma today.

Notes From a Session of Questions and Answers

4   *with Achaan Chaa of Wat Ba Pong*

Question: I'm trying very hard in my practice but I don't seem to be getting anywhere.
Answer: This is very important. Don't try to get anywhere in the practice. The very desire to be free or to be enlightened will be the desire that prevents your freedom. You can try as hard as you wish, practice ardently night and day, but if it is still with the desire to achieve in mind you will never find peace. The energy from this desire will be cause for doubt and restlessness. No matter how long or hard you practice, wisdom will not arise from desire. So, simply let go. Watch the mind and body mindfully but don't try to achieve anything. Don't cling even to the practice or to enlightenment.

Q: What about sleep? How much should I sleep?
A: Don't ask me; I can't tell you. A good average for some is four hours a night. What is important, though, is that you watch and know yourself. If you try to go with too little sleep the body will feel uncomfortable and mindfulness will be difficult to sustain.

Too much sleep leads to a dull or a restless mind. Find the natural balance for yourself. Carefully watch the mind and body and keep track of sleep needs until you find the optimum. If you wake up and then roll over for a snooze this is defilement. Establish mindfulness as soon as you open your eyes.

Q: How about eating? How much should I eat?
A: Eating is the same as sleeping. You must know yourself. Food must be consumed to meet bodily needs. Look at your food as medicine. Are you eating so much that you only feel sleepy after the meal and are you getting fatter every day? Stop. Examine your own body and mind. There is no need to fast. Instead experiment with the amount of food you take. Find the natural balance for your body. Put all of your food together in your bowl, following the ascetic practice. Then you can easily judge the amount you take. Watch yourself carefully as you eat. Know yourself. The essence of our practice is just this. There is nothing special you must do. Only watch. Examine yourself. Watch the mind. Then you will know what is the natural balance for your own practice.

Q: Are the minds of Asians and Westerners different?
A: Basically there is no difference. Outer customs and language may appear different, but the human mind has natural characteristics that are the same for all people. Greed and hatred are the same in an Eastern mind or a Western mind. Suffering and the cessation of suffering are the same for all people.

Q: Is it advisable to read a lot or study the scriptures as a part of practice?
A: The Dharma of the Buddha is not found in books. If you want to really see for yourself what the Buddha was talking about you don't need to bother with books. Watch your own mind. Examine to see how feelings come and go, how thoughts come and go. Don't be attached to anything, just be mindful of whatever there is to see. This is the way to the truths of the Buddha. Be natural. Everything you do in your life here is a chance to practice. It is all Dharma. When you do your chores try to be mindful. If you are emptying a spittoon or cleaning a toilet don't feel you are doing it as a favor for anyone else. There is Dharma in emptying spittoons. Don't feel you are practicing only when sitting still cross-legged. Some of you have complained that there is not enough time to meditate. Is there enough time to breathe? This is your meditation: mindfulness, naturalness in whatever you do.

Q: *Why don't we have daily interviews with the teacher?*
A: If you have questions you are welcome to come and ask them any time. But we don't need daily interviews here. If I answer your every little question you will never understand the process of doubt in your own mind. It is essential that you learn to examine yourself, to interview yourself. Listen carefully to the lectures every few days, then use this teaching to compare with your own practice. Is it the same? Is it different? Why do you have doubts? Who is it that doubts? Only through self-examination can you understand.

Q: *Sometimes I worry about monk's discipline. If I kill insects accidentally is this bad?*
A: Sila or discipline and morality are essential to our practice but you must not cling to the rules blindly. In not killing animals or in following other rules the important thing is intention. Know your own mind. You should not be excessively concerned about the monk's discipline. If used properly it supports the practice, but some monks are so worried about the petty rules that they can't sleep well. Discipline is not to be carried as a burden. In our practice here, the foundation is discipline. Good discipline plus the ascetic rules and practice. Being mindful and careful of even the many supporting rules as well as the basic 227 precepts has great benefit. It makes life very simple. There need be no wondering about how to act, so you can avoid thinking and instead just be simply mindful. The discipline enables us to live together harmniously, the community runs smoothly. Outwardly everyone looks and acts the same. Discipline and morality are the stepping stones for further concentration and wisdom. By proper use of the monk's discipline and the ascetic precepts we are forced to live simply, to limit our possessions. So here we have the complete practice of the Buddha: Refrain from evil and do good. Live simply keeping to basic needs. Purify the mind. That is, be watchful of your mind and body in all postures. Sitting, standing, walking, or lying, know yourself.

Q: *What can I do about doubts? Some days I'm plagued with doubts about the practice or my own progress, or the teacher.*
A: Doubting is natural. Everyone starts out with doubts. You can learn a great deal from them. What is important is that you don't identify with your doubts. That is, don't get caught up in them. This will spin your mind in endless circles. Instead, watch the

whole process of doubting, of wondering. See who it is that doubts. See how doubts come and go. Then you will no longer be victimized by your doubts. You will step outside of them and your mind will be quiet. You can see how all things come and go. Just let go of what you are attached to. Let go of your doubts and simply watch. This is how to end doubting.

Q: *What about other methods of practice? These days there seem to be so many teachers and so many different systems of meditation that it is confusing.*
A: It is like going into town. One can approach from the north, from the southeast, from many roads. Often these systems just differ outwardly. Whether you walk one way or another, fast or slow, if you are mindful it is all the same. There is one essential point that all good practice must eventually come to. That is not clinging. In the end all meditation systems must be let go of. Also, one cannot cling to the teacher. If a system leads to relinquishment, to not clinging, then it is correct practice.

You may wish to travel, to visit other teachers and try other systems. Some of you have done so already. This is a natural desire. You will find out that a thousand questions asked and knowledge of many systems will not bring you to the truth. Eventually you will get bored. You will see that only by stopping and examining your own mind can you find out what the Buddha talked about. No need to go searching outside yourself. Eventually you must return to face your own true nature. Here is where you can understand the Dharma.

Q: *A lot of times it seems that many monks here are not practicing. They look sloppy or unmindful. This disturbs me.*
A: It is not proper to watch other people. This will not help your practice. If you are annoyed, watch the annoyance in your own mind. If others' discipline is bad or they are not good monks, this is not for you to judge. You will not discover wisdom watching others. Monk's discipline is a tool to use for your own meditation. It is not a weapon to use to criticize or to find fault. No one can do your practice for you, nor can you do practice for anyone else. Just be mindful of your own doings. This is the way to practice.

Q: *I have been extremely careful to practice sense restraint. I always keep my eyes lowered and am mindful of every little action I do. When eating, for example, I take a long time and try to see each touch—*

chewing, tasting, swallowing, etc. I take each step very deliberately and carefully. Am I practicing properly?
A: Sense restraint is proper practice. We should be mindful of it throughout the day. But don't overdo it! Walk and eat and act naturally. And then develop natural mindfulness of what is going on with yourself. Don't force your meditation or force yourself into awkward patterns. This is another form of craving. Be patient. Patience and endurance are necessary. If you act naturally and are mindful, wisdom will come naturally too.

Q: *Is it necessary to sit for very long stretches?*
A: No, sitting for hours on end is not necessary. Some people think that the longer you can sit, the wiser you must be. I have seen chickens sit on their nests for days on end. Wisdom comes from being mindful in all postures. Your practice should begin as soon as you awaken in the morning. It should continue until you fall asleep. Don't be concerned about how long you can sit. What is important is only that you keep watchful whether you are working or sitting or going to the bathroom.

Each person has his own natural pace. Some of you will die at age fifty. Some at age sixty-five and some at age ninety. So too, your practices will not be all identical. Don't think or worry about this. Try to be mindful and let things take their natural course. Then your mind will become quieter and quieter in any surroundings. It will become still like a clear forest pool. Then all kinds of wonderful and rare animals will come to drink at the pool. You will see clearly the nature of all things in the world. You will see many wonderful and strange things come and go. But you will be still. Problems will arise and you will see through them immediately. This is the happiness of the Buddha.

Q: *I still have many thoughts. My mind wanders a lot even though I am trying to be mindful.*
A: Don't worry about this. Try to keep your mind in the present. Whatever there is that arises in the mind, just watch it. Let go of it. Don't even wish to be rid of thoughts. Then the mind will reach its natural state. No discriminating between good and bad, hot and cold, fast and slow. No me and no you, no self at all. Just what there is. When you walk on alms round no need to do anything special. Simply walk and see what there is. No need to cling to isolation or seclusion. Wherever you are, know yourself by being natural and watching. If doubts arise, watch them come and go.

It's very simple. Hold on to nothing.

It is as though you are walking down a road. Periodically you will run into obstacles. When you meet defilements just see them and just overcome them by letting go of them. Don't think about the obstacles you have passed already. Don't worry about those you have not yet seen. Stick to the present. Don't be concerned about the length of the road or about a destination. Everything is changing. Whatever you pass, do not cling to it. Eventually the mind will reach its natural balance where practice is automatic. All things will come and go of themselves.

Q: Have you ever looked at the Altar Sutra of the Sixth Patriarch, Hui Neng?
A: Hui Neng's wisdom is very keen. It is very profound teaching, not easy for beginners to understand. But if you practice with our discipline and with patience, if you practice not clinging, you will eventually understand. Once I had a disciple who stayed in a grass-roofed hut. It rained often that rainy season and one day a strong wind blew off half the roof. He did not bother to fix it, just let it rain in. Several days passed and I asked him about his hut. He said he was practicing not clinging. This is not clinging without wisdom. It is about the same as the equanimity of a water buffalo. If you live a good life and live simply, if you are patient and unselfish you will understand the wisdom of Hui Neng.

Q: You have said that Samatha and Vipassana or concentration and insight are the same. Could you explain this further?
A: It is quite simple. Concentration (Samatha) and wisdom (Vipassana) work together. First the mind becomes still by holding on to a meditation object. It is quiet only while you are sitting with your eyes closed. This is Samatha and eventually this concentration is the cause for wisdom or Vipassana to arise. Then the mind is still whether you sit with your eyes closed or walk around in a busy city. It's like this. Once you were a child. Now you are an adult. Are the child and the adult the same person? You can say that they are or looking at it another way you can say that they are different. In this way Samatha and Vipassana could also be looked at as separate. Or it is like food and feces. Food and feces could be called the same. Don't just believe what I say, do your practice and see for yourself. Nothing special is needed. If you examine how concentration and wisdom arise, you will know the truth for yourself. These days many people cling to the words. They call their practice

Vipassana. Samatha is looked down on. Or they call their practice Samatha. It is essential to do Samatha before Vipassana, they say. All this is silly. Don't bother to think about it in this way. Simply do the practice and you'll see for yourself.

Q: Is it necessary to be able to enter absorption in our practice?
A: No, absorption is not necessary. You must establish a modicum of tranquility and one-pointedness of mind. Then use this to examine yourself. Nothing special is needed. If absorption comes in your practice this is OK too. Just don't hold onto it. Some people get hung up with absorption. It can be great fun to play with. You must know proper limits. If you are wise then you will know the uses and limitations of absorption, just as you know the limitations of children versus grown men.

Q: Why do we follow the ascetic rules such as only eating out of our bowls?
A: The ascetic precepts are to help us cut defilement. By following the ones such as eating out of our bowls we can be more mindful of our food as medicine. If we have no defilements then it does not matter how we eat. But here we use the form to make our practice simple. The Buddha did not make the ascetic precepts necessary for all monks. But he allowed them for those who wished to practice strictly. They add to our outward discipline and thereby help increase our mental resolve and strength. These rules are to be kept for yourself. Don't watch how others practice. Watch your own mind and see what is beneficial for you. The rule that we must take whatever meditation cottage is assigned to us is similarly helpful discipline. It keeps monks from being attached to their dwelling place. If they go away and return they must take a new dwelling. This is our practice—not to cling to anything.

Q: If putting everything together in our bowls is important, why don't you as a teacher do it yourself? Don't you feel it is important for the teacher to set an example?
A: Yes, it is true, a teacher should set an example for his disciples. I don't mind that you criticize me. Ask whatever you wish. But it is important that you do not cling to the teacher. If I were absolutely perfect in outward form it would be terrible. You would all be too attached to me. Even the Buddha would sometimes tell his disciples to do one thing and then do another himself. Your doubts in your teacher can help you. You should watch your own reactions.

Do you think it is possible that I keep some food out of my bowl in dishes to feed the laymen who work around the temple?

Wisdom is for yourself to watch and develop. Take from the teacher what is good. Be aware of your own practice. If I am resting while you all must sit up does this make you angry? If I call the color blue red or say that male is female, don't follow me blindly.

One of my teachers ate very fast. He made noises as he ate. Yet he told us to eat slowly and mindfully. I used to watch him and get very upset. I suffered, but he didn't! I watched the outside. Later I learned. Some people drive fast but carefully. Others drive slowly and have many accidents. Don't cling to rules, to outer form. If you watch others at most ten percent of the time and watch yourself ninety percent, this is proper practice. At first I used to watch my teacher Achaan Tong Rath and had many doubts. People even thought he was mad. He would do strange things or get very fierce with his disciples. Outside he was angry but inside there was nothing. Nobody there. He was remarkable. He stayed clear and mindful until the moment he died.

Looking outside the self is comparing, discriminating. You will not find happiness that way. Nor will you find peace if you spend your time looking for the perfect man or the perfect teacher. The Buddha taught us to look at the Dharma, the truth, not to look at other people.

Q: How can we overcome lust in our practice? Sometimes I feel as if I am really a slave to my sexual desire.
A: Lust should be balanced by contemplation of loathsomeness. Attachment to bodily form is one extreme and one should keep in mind the opposite. Examine the body as a corpse and see the process of decay or think of the parts of the body such as lungs, spleen, fat, feces, and so forth. Remember these and visualize this loathsome aspect of the body when lust arises. This will free you from lust.

Q: How about anger? What should I do when I feel anger arising?
A: You must use loving-kindness. When angry states of mind arise in meditation, balance them by developing loving-kindness feelings. If someone does something bad or gets angry don't get angry yourself. If you do, you are being more ignorant than he. Be wise. Keep in mind compassion, for that person is suffering. Fill your mind with loving-kindness as if he were a dear brother. Concentrate on the feeling of loving-kindness as a meditation subject.

Spread it to all beings in the world. Only through loving-kindness is hatred overcome.

Sometimes you may see other monks behaving badly. You may get annoyed. This is suffering unnecessarily. It is not yet our Dharma. You may think like this: "They are not as strict as I am. They are not serious meditators like us. Those monks are not good monks." This is a great defilement on your part. Do not make comparisons. Do not discriminate. Let go of your opinions and watch yourself. This is our Dharma. You can't possibly make everyone act as you wish, or to be like you. This wish will only make you suffer. It is a common mistake for meditators to make, but watching other people won't develop wisdom. Don't worry. Simply examine yourself, your feelings. This is how you will understand.

Q: I feel sleepy a great deal. It makes it hard to meditate.
A: There are many ways to overcome sleepiness. If you are sitting in the dark move to a lighted place. Open your eyes. Get up and wash your face, slap your face, or take a bath. If you are sleepy, change postures. Walk a lot. Walk backward. The fear of running into things will keep you awake. If this fails, stand still, clear the mind, and imagine it is full daylight. Or sit on the edge of a high cliff or deep well. You won't dare sleep. If nothing works, then just go to sleep. Lie down carefully and try to be aware until the moment you fall asleep. Then as soon as you awaken, get right up. Don't look at the clock or roll over. Start mindfulness from the moment you awaken.

If you find yourself sleepy every day, try to eat less. Examine yourself. As soon as five more spoonfuls will make you full, stop. Then take water until just properly full. Go and sit. Watch your sleepiness and your hunger. You must learn to balance your eating. As your practice goes on you will feel naturally more energetic and eat less. But you must adjust yourself.

Q: Why must we do so much bowing here?
A: Bowing is very important. It is an outward form that is part of practice. This form should be done correctly. Bring the forehead all the way to the floor. Have elbows near knees and knees about eight inches apart. Bow slowly, mindful of your body. It is a good remedy for our conceit. We should bow often. When you bow three times you can keep in mind the qualities of the Buddha, Dharma, and Sangha. That is, the qualities of mind of purity, radiance, and

peace. So we use the outward form to train ourselves. Body and mind become harmonious. Don't make the mistake of watching how others bow. If the young novices are sloppy or the aged monks appear unmindful, this is not for you to judge. People can be difficult to train. Some learn fast but others learn slowly. Judging others will only increase your pride. Watch yourself instead. Bow often, get rid of your pride.

Those who have really become harmonious with the Dharma get   45
far beyond outward form. Everything they do is a way of bowing. Walking, they bow; eating, they bow; defecating, they bow. This is because they have got beyond selfishness.

Q: What is the biggest problem of your new disciples?
A: Opinions. Views and ideas about all things. About themselves, about practice, about the teachings of the Buddha. Many of those who come here have a high rank in the community. These are wealthy merchants or college graduates, teachers, and government officials. Their minds are filled with opinions about things. They are too clever to listen to others. It is like water in a cup. If a cup is filled with dirty, stale water it is useless. Only after the old water is thrown out can the cup become useful. You must empty your minds of opinions, then you will see. Our practice goes beyond cleverness and beyond stupidity. If you think to yourself, 'I am clever, I am wealthy, I am important, I understand all about Buddhism,' you cover up the truth of anatta or non-self. All you will see is self, I, mine. But Buddhism is letting go of self. Voidness. Emptiness. Nirvana.

Q: Are defilements such as greed or anger merely illusory or are they real?
A: They are both. The defilements we call lust or greed or anger or delusion; these are just outward names, appearance. Just as we can call a bowl large, small, pretty, or whatever. This is not reality. It is the concept we create from craving. If we want a big bowl we call this one small. Craving causes us to discriminate. The truth, though, is merely what is. Look at it this way. Are you a man? You can say yes. This is the appearance of things. But really you are only a combination of elements or a group of changing aggregates. If the mind is free it does not discriminate. No big and small, no you and me. There is nothing. Anatta, we say, or non-self. Really, in the end there is neither atta nor anatta.

Q: Could you explain a little more about karma?
A: Karma is action. Karma is clinging. Body, speech, or mind all make karma when we cling. We make habits. These can make us suffer in the future. This is the fruit of our clinging, of our past defilement. All attachment leads to making karma. Suppose you were a thief before you became a monk. You stole, you made others unhappy, made your parents unhappy. Now you are a monk but when you remember how you made others unhappy you feel bad and suffer yourself even today. Remember not only body, but speech and mental action can make conditions for future results. If you did some act of kindness in the past and remember it today you will be happy. This happy state of mind is a result of past karma. All things are conditioned by causes, both long term and, when examined, moment to moment. But you need not bother to figure out past, present, or future. Merely watch the body and mind. You can then understand karma in yourself. Watch your mind, practice, and you will see clearly. Make sure, however, that you leave the karma of others to them. Don't cling to and don't watch others. If I take poison, I suffer. No need for you to share it with me! Take what is good that your teacher offers. Then you can become peaceful, your mind will become like that of your teacher. If you will examine it you will see. Even if now you don't understand, when you first practice it will become clear. You will know by yourself. This is called practicing the Dharma.

When we were young our parents used to discipline us and get angry. Really they wanted to help us. You must see it over the long term. Parents and teachers criticize us and we get upset. Later on we can see why. After long practice you will know. Those who are too clever leave after a short time. They never learn. You must get rid of your cleverness. If you think yourself better than others you will only suffer. What a pity. No need to get upset. Just watch.

Q: Sometimes it seems that since becoming a monk I have increased my hardships and suffering.
A: I know that some of you have had a background of material comfort and outward freedom. By comparison, now you live an austere existence. Then, in the practice I often make you sit and wait for long hours. Food and climate are different from your home. But everyone must go through some of this. This is the suffering that leads to the end of suffering. This is how you learn. When you get angry or feel sorry for yourself it is a great opportunity to understand the mind. The Buddha called defilements our teachers.

All my disciples are like my children. I have only loving-kindness and their welfare in mind. If I appear to make you suffer it is for your own good. I know some of you are well educated and very knowledgeable. People with little education and worldly knowledge can practice easily. But it is as if you Westerners have a very large house to clean. When you have cleaned the house you will then have a big living space. You can use the kitchen, the library. You must be patient. Patience and endurance are essential to our practice. When I was a young monk I did not have it as hard as you. I knew the language and was eating my native food. Even so, some days I despaired. I wanted to disrobe or even commit suicide. This kind of suffering comes from wrong views. When you have seen the truth, though, you are freed from views and opinions. Everything becomes peaceful.

47

Q: I have been developing very peaceful states of mind from meditation. What should I do now?
A: This is good. Make the mind peaceful, concentrated. Use this concentration to examine the mind and body. When the mind is not peaceful you should watch also. Then you will know true peace. Why? Because you will see impermanence. Even peace must be seen as impermanent. If you are attached to peaceful states of mind you will suffer when you do not have them. Give up everything, even peace.

Q: Did I hear you sat that you were afraid of very diligent disciples?
A: Yes, that's right. I am afraid. I am afraid that they are too serious. They try too hard, but without wisdom. They push themselves into unnecessary suffering. Some of you are determined to become enlightened. You grit your teeth and struggle all the time. This is trying too hard. People are all the same. They don't know the nature of things. All formations, mind and body, are impermanent. Simply watch and don't cling.

Others think they know. They criticize, they watch, they judge. That's OK. Leave their opinions to them. This discrimination is dangerous. It is like a road with a very sharp curve. If we think others are worse or better or the same as us we go off the curve. If we discriminate, we will only suffer.

Q: I have been meditating many years now. My mind is open and peaceful in almost all circumstances. Now I would like to try to backtrack and practice high states of concentration or mind absorption.

A: This is fine. It is beneficial mental exercise. If you have wisdom you will not get hung up on concentrated states of mind. It is the same as wanting to sit for long periods. This is fine for training. But really, practice is separate from any posture. It is a matter of directly looking at the mind. This is wisdom. When you have examined and understood the mind, then you have the wisdom to know the limitations of concentration. Or of books. If you have practiced and understand not-clinging you can then return to the books. They will be like a sweet dessert. They can help you to teach others. Or you can go back to practice absorption. You have the wisdom to know not to hold on to anything.

Q: Would you review some of the main points of our discussion?
A: You must examine yourself. Know who you are. Know your body and mind by simply watching. In sitting, in sleeping, in eating, know your limits. Use wisdom. The practice is not to try to achieve anything. Just be mindful of what is. Our whole meditation is looking directly at the mind. You will see suffering, its cause and its end. But you must have patience. Much patience and endurance. Gradually you will learn. The Buddha taught his disciples to stay with their teachers for at least five years. You must learn the values of giving, of patience, and of devotion.

Don't practice too strictly. Don't get caught up with outward form. Watching others is bad practice. Simply be natural and watch that. Our monk's discipline and monastic rules are very important. They create a simple and harmonious environment. Use them well. But remember the essence of monk's discipline is watching intention. Examining the mind. You must have wisdom. Don't discriminate. Would you get upset at a small tree in the forest for not being tall and straight like some of the others? This is silly. Don't judge other people. There are all varieties. No need to carry the burden of wishing to change them all.

So, be patient. Practice morality. Live simply and be natural. Watch the mind. This is our practice. It will lead you to unselfishness. To peace.

48

MAHASI SAYADAW

CHAPTER
FIVE

Mahasi Sayadaw has had a far-reaching effect on the practice of insight meditation in Therevada Buddhist countries. His scholastic studies at a village monastery began at age six and culminated several years after his full bhikku ordination with highest honors in government-sponsored Pali and scholastic examinations. After teaching the scriptures for many years he set out with robe and bowl in search of a clear and effective meditation practice. On reaching Thaton, he met and began study under U Narada, Mungun Sayadaw, who instructed him in intensive insight meditation practice. After extensive meditation and continued study, Mahasi returned to his home village to begin systematic instruction in mindfulness practice.

Shortly after Burma gained her independence from Britain, the new Prime Minister, U Nu, requested that the venerable Mahasi Sayadaw come to Rangoon to teach in a large center provided for him. Since that time, more than 100 meditation centers have been opened by his disciples in Burma alone, and his method has spread widely in Thailand and Ceylon.

An extraordinary honor was given to Mahasi at the World Buddhist Council in 1956, twenty-five hundred years after the first teachings of the Buddha. He took the role of chief questioner, the central role in clarifying and preserving the Buddhist teachings for generations to come.

Thathana Yeiktha, Mahasi's center in Rangoon, has many large halls and cells for meditation training. The center is usually filled with hundreds of meditators who are practicing intensive Vipassana. The visitor can see halls of yogis doing the walking exercises and many rooms of people sitting or having group interviews with the teachers. It is not uncommon for devout Burmese laymen to take their vacations by going to meditation centers for intensive retreats.

In Mahasi's system, practice is continuous, alternating sitting and walking for sixteen hours a day. In this intensive setting, concentration and mindfulness develop quickly even for inexperienced laymen. Besides intensive continuous practice, Mahasi's approach to mindfulness is developed strictly as an insight practice from the first. There is no special preparatory development of concentration on one object. Instead, from the very beginning, one establishes awareness of the moment-to-moment change of body and mind. This is facilitated by the technique of making mental notes of each impersonal aspect of body or mind as it comes to consciousness. These mental notes help to direct even the thinking process of mind into the meditation. This helps the yogi keep from identifying or getting involved with the content of different experiences. Mahasi emphasizes that awareness should focus on direct experience each moment and that mental notes are simply a peripheral aid to seeing more clearly. To characterize this in other terms, 95 percent of one's effort should go to perceive the process directly and 5 percent to making the mental notes as described.

Although Mahasi Sayadaw recommends the use of the rise and fall of the abdomen as a central meditation object, his teaching disciples also allow the use of the in-and-out breath felt at the nose tip as an alternative way to practice. In this system what is essential is not which object is observed but the quality of clear, detached awareness used to see its true nature.

As this talk continues, Mahasi Sayadaw uses great detail to explain in a clear, non-mystical way what one may experience with the deepening of awareness and the power of noticing. This is an expansion of the classical stages of the progress of insight as described in some traditional Buddhist texts. It must be remembered that not all meditators will experience practice in exactly this way, even when following Mahasi's exercises precisely.   53

Although sometimes insight will develop as Mahasi describes, often meditators' experiences will seem quite different. What is absolutely essential to remember is that it is dangerous to develop any expectations in practice. One must simply develop clearer and deeper awareness of what is actually experienced moment to moment. Then practice will deepen and insight and wisdom will develop in the most profound and natural way.

In the late 1950s and early 60s many Westerners studied Vipassana at the center, and a number of them were trained as teachers. Although Mahasi and some of his chief disciples speak English, the current two-week visa limitation on visits to Burma makes study at the center limited for Westerners. However, Kandaboda Temple in Ceylon; the Venerable Anagarika Munindra in Bodh Gaya, India; and Achaan Asabha at Wat Wiwake Asrom in Thailand all make the teachings of Mahasi available outside Burma.

In addition, several of Mahasi Sayadaw's important Burmese works have been published in English, including the *Progress of Insight* and *Practical Insight Meditation*, which contain further instruction beyond the materials presented in this chapter.

Insight Meditation:
Basic and Progressive Stages

5

by Mahasi Sayadaw

It is a truism to say that nobody likes suffering and everybody seeks happiness. In this world of ours, human beings are making all possible efforts for prevention and alleviation of suffering and enjoyment of happiness. Nevertheless, their efforts are mainly directed to the physical well-being by material means. Happiness is, after all, conditioned by attitudes of mind, and yet only a few persons give real thought to mental development; fewer still practice mind-training in earnest.

To illustrate this point, attention may be drawn to the commonplace habits of cleaning and tidying up one's body; the endless pursuits of food, clothing, and shelter; and the tremendous technological progress achieved for raising the material standard of living, for improving the means of transport and communications, and for prevention and cure of diseases and ailments. All these strivings are, in the main, concerned with the care and nourishment of the body. It must be recognized that they are essential. However, these human efforts and achievements cannot possibly bring about the alleviation or eradication of suffering associated with old age and disease, domestic infelicity and economic troubles; in short, with non-satisfaction of wants and desires. Sufferings of this nature are not overcome by material means; they can be overcome only by mind-training and mental development.

Therefore, it becomes clear that the right way must be sought for training, stabilizing, and purifying the mind. This way is found in the Maha Satipatthana Sutta, a well-known discourse of the Buddha, delivered well over twenty-five hundred years ago. The Buddha declared thus:

> *This is the sole way for the purification of beings, for the overcoming of sorrow and lamentation, for the destroy-*

*ing of pain and grief, for reaching the right path, for the
realization of nirvana, namely the Four Foundations of
Mindfulness.*

BASIC PRACTICE

Preparatory Stage If you sincerely desire to develop contemplation
and attain insight in this your present life, you must give up
worldly thoughts and actions during training. This course of action is for the purification of conduct, the essential preliminary
step toward the proper development of contemplation. You must
also observe the rules of discipline prescribed for laymen (or for
monks, as the case may be), for they are important in gaining
insight. For layfolk, these rules comprise the eight precepts which
Buddhist devotees observe on holidays and during periods of
meditation. These voluntary precepts are abstention from (1)
killing, (2) stealing, (3) sexual intercourse, (4) lying, (5) intoxicants,
(6) eating solid foods after noon, (7) dance, shows, wearing flowers,
perfume, and adornments, and (8) high and luxurious beds. An
additional rule is not to speak with contempt, in jest, or malice to
or about any of the noble ones who have attained states of
enlightenment.

The old masters of Buddhist tradition suggest that you entrust
yourself to the enlightened one, the Buddha, during the training
period, for you may be alarmed if it happens that your own state of
mind produces unwholesome or frightening visions during contemplation. Also place yourself under the guidance of your meditation instructor, for he can talk to you frankly about your work in
contemplation and give you the guidance he thinks necessary.

The aim of this practice and its greatest benefit is release from
greed, hatred, and delusion, which are the roots of all evil and
suffering. This intensive course in insight training can lead you to
such release. So work ardently with this end in view so that your
training will be successfully completed. This kind of training in
contemplation, based on the foundations of mindfulness (satipatthana), is that taken by all Buddhas and noble ones, for attaining
enlightenment. You are to be congratulated on having the opportunity to take the same kind of training.

It is also important for you to begin your training with a brief
contemplation on the 'four protections' which the Buddha offers

you for reflection. It is helpful for your psychological welfare at this stage to reflect on them. The subjects of these four protective reflections are the Buddha himself, loving-kindness, the loathsome aspects of the body, and death.

First, devote yourself to the Buddha by sincerely appreciating his nine chief qualities in this way:

56

> *Truly, the Buddha is holy, fully enlightened, perfect in knowledge and conduct, a welfarer, world-knower, the incomparable leader of men to be tamed, teacher of gods and mankind, the awakened and exalted One.*

Second, reflect upon all sentient beings as the receivers of your loving-kindness, be fortified by your thoughts of loving-kindness and identify yourself with all sentient beings without distinction, thus:

> *May I be free from enmity, disease and grief .... As I am, so also may my parents, preceptors, teachers, intimate, unknown, indeed all other beings be free from enmity, disease, and grief. May they be released from suffering.*

Third, reflect upon the repulsive nature of the body to assist you in diminishing the unwholesome attachment that so many people have for the body. Dwell upon some of its impurities, such as stomach, intestines, phlegm, pus, blood. Ponder these impurities so that the absurd fondness of the body may be eliminated.

The fourth protection for your psychological benefit is to reflect on the phenomenon of ever-approaching death. Buddhist teachings stress that life is uncertain but death is certain, life is precarious but death is sure. Life has death as its goal. There is birth, disease, suffering, old age, and eventual death. These are all aspects of the process of existence.

To begin training, take the sitting posture, sit erect with legs crossed. You might feel more comfortable if the legs are not interlocked but evenly placed on the ground, without pressing one against the other. Have your meditation teacher explain the sitting posture in detail. If you find that sitting on the floor interferes with contemplation, then obtain a more comfortable way of sitting. Now proceed with each exercise in contemplation as described.

Basic Exercise I Try to keep your mind (but not your eyes) on the abdomen. You will thereby come to know the movements of rising and falling, the expansion and contraction of this organ. If these movements are not clear to you in the beginning, then place both hands on the abdomen to feel these rising and falling movements. After a short time the outward movement of inhalation and the inward movement of exhalation will become clear. Then make a mental note, *rising* for the outward movement, *falling* for the inward movement. Your mental note of each movement must be made while it occurs. From this exercise you learn the actual manner of the movements of the abdomen. You are not concerned with the form of the abdomen. What you actually perceive is the bodily sensation of pressure caused by the heaving movement of the abdomen. So do not dwell on the form of the abdomen but proceed with the exercise.

For the beginner it is a very effective method of developing the facilities of attention, concentration of mind and insight in contemplation. As practice increases, the manner of movement will be clearer. The ability to know each successive occurrence of the mental and physical processes at each of the six sense-organs is acquired only when insight contemplation is fully developed. Since you are a beginner whose attentiveness and power of concentration are still weak, you may find it difficult to keep the mind on each successive rising movement and falling movement as it occurs. In view of this difficulty, you may be inclined to think: "I just don't know how to keep my mind on each of these movements." Then simply remember that this is a learning process. The rising and falling movements of the abdomen are always present, and therefore there is no need to look for them. Actually with practice it becomes easy for a beginner to keep his mind on these two simple movements. Continue with this exercise in full awareness of the abdomen's rising and falling movements. Never verbally repeat the words *rising, falling,* although you may make a mental note *rising* and *falling* in the mind silently as they occur. Be clearly aware only of the actual process of the rising and falling movement of the abdomen. Avoid deep or rapid breathing for the purpose of making the abdominal movements more distinct, because this procedure causes fatigue that interferes with the practice. Just be totally aware of the movements of rising and falling as they occur in the course of normal breathing.

57

Basic Exercise II While occupied with the exercise of observing each of the abdominal movements, other mental activities may occur between the noting of each rising and falling. Thoughts or other mental functions, such as intentions, ideas, imaginings, etc., are likely to occur between each mental note of rising and falling. They cannot be disregarded. A mental note must be made of each as it occurs.

58   If you imagine something, you must know that you have done so and make a mental note *imagining*. If you simply think of something, mentally note *thinking*. If you reflect, *reflecting*. If you intend to do something, *intending*. When the mind wanders from the object of meditation, which is the rising and falling of the abdomen, mentally note *wandering*. Should you imagine you are going to a certain place, mentally note *going*. When you arrive, *arriving*. When, in your thoughts, you meet a person, note *meeting*. Should you speak to him or her, note *speaking*. If you imaginatively argue with that person, *arguing*. If you envision and imagine a light or color, be sure to note *seeing*. A mental vision must be noted on each occurrence of its appearance until it passes away. After its disappearance, continue with Basic Exercise I by being fully aware of each movement of the rising and falling abdomen. Proceed carefully, without slackening. If you intend to swallow saliva while thus engaged, make a mental note *intending*. While in the act of swallowing, *swallowing*. If you intend to spit, *spitting*. Then return to the exercise of rising and falling. Suppose you intend to bend the neck, *intending*. In the act of bending, *bending*. When you intend to straighten the neck, *intending*. In the act of straightening the neck, *straightening*. The neck movements of bending and straightening must be done slowly. After mentally making a note of each of these actions, proceed in full awareness with noticing the movements of the rising and falling abdomen.

Basic Exercise III Since you must continue contemplating for a long time while in one position, that of sitting or lying down, you are likely to experience an intense feeling of fatigue, stiffness in the body or in the arms and legs. Should this happen, simply keep the knowing mind on that part of the body where such feeling occurs and carry on the contemplation, noting *tired* or *stiff*. Do this naturally, that is, neither too fast nor too slow. These feelings gradually become fainter and finally cease altogether. Should one of these feelings become more intense until the bodily fatigue or stiffness of joints is unbearable, then change your position. However, do not forget to make a mental note of *intending*, before you proceed to change position. Each detailed movement must be contemplated in its respective order.

If you intend to lift the hand or leg, make a mental note, *intending*. In the act of lifting the hand or leg, *lifting*. Stretching either the hand or leg, *stretching*. When you bend, *bending*. When putting down, *putting*. Should either the hand or leg touch, *touching*. Perform all these actions in a slow, deliberate manner. As soon as you are settled in the new position, continue with the contemplation of the abdominal movements. If you become uncomfortably warm in the new position, resume contemplation in another position keeping to the procedure as described in this paragraph.

Should an itching sensation be felt in any part of the body, keep the mind on that part and make a mental note, *itching*. Do this in a regulated manner, neither too fast nor too slow. When the itching sensation disappears in the course of full awareness, continue with the exercise of noticing the rising and falling of the abdomen. Should the itching continue and become too strong and you intend to rub the itching part, be sure to make a mental note, *intending*. Slowly lift the hand, simultaneously noting the action of *lifting*, and *touching* when the hand touches the part that itches. Rub slowly in complete awareness of *rubbing*. When the itching sensation has disappeared and you intend to discontinue the rubbing, be mindful by making the usual mental note of the action, *withdrawing*. When the hand rests in its usual place touching the leg, *touching*. Then again devote your time to observing the abdominal movements.

If there is pain or discomfort, keep the knowing mind on that part of the body where the sensation arises. Make a mental note of the specific sensation as it occurs, such as *painful, aching, pressing, piercing, tired, giddy*. It must be stressed that the mental note must not be forced nor delayed but made in a calm and natural manner. The pain may eventually cease or increase. Do not be alarmed if it increases. Firmly continue the contemplation. If you do so, you will find that the pain will almost always cease. But if, after a time, the pain has increased and becomes almost unbearable, you must ignore the pain and continue with the contemplation of rising and falling.

As you progress in mindfulnesss you may experience sensations of intense pain: stifling or choking sensations such as pain from the slash of a knife, the thrust of a sharp-pointed instrument, unpleasant sensations of being pricked by sharp needles, or small insects crawling over the body. You might experience sensations of itching, biting, intense cold. As soon as you discontinue the contemplation you may also feel that these painful sensations cease. When you resume contemplation you will have them again as soon as you gain in mindfulness. These painful sensations are not to be considered as something serious. They are not manifestations of disease but are common factors always present in the body and are usually obscured when the mind is normally occupied with more conspicuous objects. When the mental faculties become keener you are more aware of these sensations. With the continued development of contemplation the time will arrive when you can overcome them and they cease altogether. If you continue contemplation, firm in purpose, you will not come to any harm. Should you lose courage, become irresolute in contemplation, and discontinue for a time, you may encounter these unpleasant sensations again and again as your contemplation proceeds. If you continue with determination you will most likely overcome these painful sensations and may never again experience them in the course of contemplation.

Should you intend to sway the body, then knowingly note *intending*. While in the act of swaying, *swaying*. When contemplating you may occasionally discover the body swaying back and forth. Do not be alarmed; neither be pleased nor wish to continue to sway. The swaying will cease if you keep the knowing mind on the action of swaying and continue to note *swaying* until the action ceases. If swaying increases in spite of your making a mental note of it, then lean against a wall or post or lie down for a while. Thereafter proceed with contemplation. Follow the same procedure if you find yourself shaking or trembling. When contemplation is developed you may sometimes feel a thrill or chill pass through the back or the entire body. This is a symptom of the feeling of intense interest, enthusiasm, or rapture. It occurs naturally in the course of good contemplation. When your mind is fixed in contemplation you may be startled at the slightest sound. This takes place because you feel more intensely the effect of sensorial impression while in the state of good concentration.

If you are thirsty while contemplating, notice the feeling, *thirsty*. When you intend to stand, *intending*. Then make a mental note of each movement in preparation for standing. Keep the mind intently on the act of standing up, and mentally note, *standing*. When you look forward after standing up straight, note *looking, seeing*. Should you intend to walk forward, *intending*. When you begin to step forward, mentally note each step as *walking, walking* or *left, right*. It is important for you to be aware of every moment in each step from beginning to end when you walk. Adhere to the same procedure when strolling or when taking a walking exercise. Try to make a mental note of each step in two sections as follows: *lifting, putting; lifting, putting*. When you have obtained sufficient practice in this manner of walking, then try to make a mental note of each step in three sections: *lifting, moving, placing;* or *up, forward, down*.

When you look at the water faucet, or water pot, on arriving at the place where you are to take a drink, be sure to make a mental note *looking, seeing*.

When you stop walking, *stopping*.

When you stretch the hand, *stretching*.

When the hand touches the cup, *touching*.

When the hand takes the cup, *taking*.

When the hand dips the cup into the water, *dipping*.

When the hand brings the cup to the lips, *bringing*.

When the cup touches the lips, *touching*.

Should you feel cold at the touch, *cold*.

When you swallow, *swallowing*.

When returning the cup, *returning*.

Withdrawing the hand, *withdrawing*.

When you bring down your hand, *bringing*.

When the hand touches the side of the body, *touching*.

If you intend to turn back, *intending*.

When you turn around, *turning*.

When you walk forward, *walking*.

On arriving at the place where you intend to stop, *intending*.

When you stop, *stopping*.

If you remain standing for some time continue the contemplation of rising and falling. But if you intend to sit down, *intending*. When you go forward to sit down, *walking*. On arriving at the place where you will sit, *arriving*. When you turn to sit, *turning*. While in the act of sitting, *sitting*. Sit down slowly, and keep the mind on the downward movement of the body. You must notice every movement in bringing hands and legs into position. Then resume the prescribed exercise of contemplating the abdominal movements.

Should you intend to lie down, *intending*. Then proceed with the contemplation of every movement in the course of lying down: *lifting, stretching, leaving, touching, lying*. Then make as the object of contemplation every movement in bringing hands, legs, and

61

body into position. Perform these actions slowly. Thereafter continue with rising and falling. Should pain, fatigue, itching, or any other sensation be felt, be sure to notice each of these sensations. Notice all feelings, thoughts, ideas, considerations, reflections, all movements of hands, legs, arms, and body. If there is nothing in particular to note, put the mind on the rising and falling of the abdomen. Make a mental note of *drowsy*, when drowsy, and *sleepy*, when sleepy. After you have gained sufficient concentration in contemplating you will be able to overcome drowsiness and sleepiness and feel refreshed as a result. Take up again the usual contemplation of the basic object. Suppose you are unable to overcome a drowsy feeling, you must then continue to contemplate until you fall asleep.

The state of sleep is the continuity of subconsciousness. It is similar to the first state of rebirth consciousness and the last state of consciousness at the moment of death. This state of consciousness is feeble and therefore unable to be aware of an object. When you are awake the continuity of subconsciousness occurs regularly between moments of seeing, hearing, tasting, smelling, touching, and thinking. Because these occurrences are of brief duration they are usually not clear and therefore not noticeable. Continuity of subconsciousness remains during sleep—a fact which becomes obvious when you wake up; for it is in the state of wakefulness that thoughts and dense objects become distinct.

Contemplation should start at the moment you wake up. Since you are a beginner, it may not yet be possible for you to start contemplating at the very first moment of wakefulness. But you should start with it from the moment when you remember that you are to contemplate. For example, if on awakening you reflect on something, you should become aware of the fact and begin your contemplation by a mental note, *reflecting*. Then proceed with the contemplation of rising and falling. When getting up from the bed, mindfulness should be directed to every detail of the body's activity. Each movement of the hands, legs, and body must be performed in complete awareness. Are you thinking of the time of the day when awakening? If so, note *thinking*. Do you intend to get out of bed? If so, note *intending*. If you prepare to move the body into position for rising, note *preparing*. As you slowly rise, *rising*. When you are in the sitting position, *sitting*. Should you remain sitting for any length of time, revert to contemplating the abdominal movements of rising and falling.

Perform the acts of washing the face or taking a bath in their order and in complete awareness of every detailed movement; for instance, *looking, seeing, stretching, holding, touching, feeling cold, rubbing.* In the acts of dressing, making the bed, opening and closing doors and windows, handling objects, be occupied with every detail of these actions in their order.

You must attend to the contemplation of every detail in the action of eating:

When you look at the food, *looking, seeing.*   63

When you arrange the food, *arranging.*

When you bring the food to mouth, *bringing.*

When you bend the neck forward, *bending.*

When the food touches the mouth, *touching.*

When placing the food in the mouth, *placing.*

When the mouth closes, *closing.*

When withdrawing the hand, *withdrawing.*

Should the hand touch the plate, *touching.*

When straightening the neck, *straightening.*

When in the act of chewing, *chewing.*

When you are aware of the taste, *tasting.*

When swallowing the food, *swallowing.*

Should, while swallowing, the food be felt touching the sides of the gullet, *touching.*

Perform contemplation in this manner each time you partake of a morsel of food until you finish the meal. In the beginning of the practice there will be many omissions. Never mind. Do not waver in your effort. You will make fewer omissions if you persist in your practice. When you reach an advanced stage of the practice, you will also be able to notice more details than those mentioned here.

Basic Walking Exercise Between sessions of the sitting practice which may last from forty to ninety minutes you can alternate with a walking meditation. This will help serve to balance the factors of concentration and energy and overcome sleepiness. On a quiet stretch of ground or in a room you can do this practice. It is best for this exercise if you walk deliberately much slower than usual. Something about the speed of a good slow march is ideal, but nevertheless you should walk in as simple and natural a manner as speed allows. During this walking exercise, you should focus attention on the movement of the feet and legs. You should note as the right foot begins to rise from the ground, *lifting;* as it moves forward, *moving;* and as it places again on the ground, *placing.* Similarly for the left foot, and so on.

In exactly the same manner as during the sitting breathing practice, all distracting thoughts or sensations should be noted in the
opposite manner. If you happen to look up at something while
walking, you should immediately register *looking* and revert to the
movement of the feet. Looking about and noticing the details of
objects, even those on your path is not a part of the practice. If you
inadvertently do, then note *looking*.

64 On reaching the end of the path the need will arise to turn and
walk in the opposite direction. You will become aware of this fact a
pace or two before reaching the end. This intention to turn should
be noted as *intending*. Intention may be hard to note at first but if
concentration is strong, it will be seen. After noting the intention
to turn, note all other details of the thoughts and movements involved in the turn. As the last step forward is taken and you begin
actually to turn the body, you should note *turning*, as the other foot
raises, *lifting, turning, placing*, and so on. Then as you step out
again on the return path, *lifting, moving, placing*. There is often a
temptation on coming to the end of your 'tether' to look up and
glance around for something interesting. If this undisciplined im-
pulse occurs it should be noted as *intending*, and the attention can
revert naturally to the movement of the feet again.

It is normally best for beginners to develop this walking exercise
with a three-stage noting technique as indicated. *Lifting, moving,
placing*. Depending on your capacity, your instructor may recommend either fewer or more stages to register. At times walking too
slowly is inconvenient, especially outside of your meditation surroundings, so a simple *left, right, left, right*, will suffice for these
cases. The important point is not how many or how few points of
noting you make, but whether you are really aware of them as they
occur, or whether your mind is off 'wool gathering'.

Advancement in Contemplation After having practiced for a while,
you may find your contemplation considerably improved and that
you are able to prolong the basic exercise of noticing the abdominal rising and falling. At this time you will notice that there is
generally a break between the movements of rising and falling. If
you are in the sitting posture fill in the pause with a mental note on
the act of sitting, in this way: *rising, falling, sitting*. When you make
a mental note of sitting, keep your mind on the erect position of the
upper body. When you are lying down you should proceed with full
awareness as follows: *rising, falling, lying*. If you find this easy,
continue with noticing these three sections. Should you notice that

a pause occurs at the end of the rising as well as the falling movement, then continue in this manner: *rising, sitting, falling, sitting.* Or when lying down: *rising, lying, falling, lying.* Suppose you no longer find it easy to make a mental note of three or four objects in the above manner. Then revert to the initial procedure of noting only the two sections, *rising* and *falling.*

While engaged in the regular practice of contemplating bodily movements you need not be concerned with objects of seeing and hearing. As long as you are able to keep your mind on the abdominal movements of rising and falling it is assumed that the purpose of noticing the acts and objects of seeing and hearing is also served. However, you may intentionally look at an object, then simultaneously make a mental note, two or three times, *seeing.* Thereafter return to the awareness of the abdominal movements.. Suppose some person comes into your view, make a mental note of *seeing,* two or three times, and then resume attention to the rising and falling movements of the abdomen. Did you happen to hear the sound of a voice? Did you listen to it? If so make the mental note of *hearing, listening* while it is happening, and having done so, revert to *rising* and *falling.* But suppose you heard loud sounds, such as the barking of dogs, loud talking, or singing. If so, immediately make a mental note two or three times, *hearing.* Then return to your basic exercise of attending to *rising* and *falling.* If you fail to note and dismiss such distinctive sights and sounds as they occur, you may inadvertently fall into reflections about them instead of proceeding with intense attention to rising and falling, which may then become less distinct and clear. It is by such weakened attention that mind-defiling passions breed and multiply. If such reflections do occur, make two or three times the mental note, *reflecting,* and again take up the contemplation of rising and falling. Should you forget to make a mental note of body, leg, or arm movements, then mentally note *forgetting,* and resume your usual contemplation of the abdominal movements. You may feel at times that breathing is slow or that the rising and falling movements of the abdomen are not clearly perceived. When this happens, and you are in the sitting position, simply carry on the attention to *sitting, touching;* if you are lying down, *lying, touching.* While contemplating touching, your mind should not be kept on the same part of the body, but on different parts successively. There are several places of touch, and at least six or seven should be contemplated. Some of these points are where the thigh and knee touch, or the hands are placed together, or finger to finger, thumb to thumb, closing of the eyelids, tongue inside the mouth, or lips touching together.

65

Basic Exercise IV Up to this point you have devoted quite some time to the training course. You might begin to feel lazy after deciding that you have made inadequate progress. By no means give up. Simply note the fact, *lazy*. Before you gain sufficient strength in attention, concentration, and insight, you may doubt the correctness or usefulness of this method of training. In such a circumstance, turn to contemplation of the thought, *doubtful*. Do you anticipate or wish for good results? If so, make such thoughts the subject of your contemplation, *anticipating* or *wishing*. Are you attempting to recall the manner in which this training was conducted up to this point? Yes? Then take up contemplation on *recollecting*. Are there occasions when you examine the object of contemplation to determine whether it is mind or matter? If so, then be aware of *examining*. Do you regret that there is no improvement in your contemplation? If so, then attend to that feeling of *regret*. Conversely, are you happy that your contemplation is improving? If you are, then contemplate the feeling of being *happy*. This is the way in which you make a mental note of every item of mental behavior as it occurs, and if there are no intervening thoughts or perceptions to note, you should revert to the contemplation of rising and falling.

During a strict course of meditation, the time of practice is from the first moment you wake up until you fall asleep. To repeat, you must be constantly occupied either with the basic exercise or with mindful attention throughout the day and during those night hours when you are not asleep. There must be no relaxation. Upon reaching a certain stage of progress in contemplation you will not feel sleepy in spite of these prolonged hours of practice. On the contrary, you will be able to continue the contemplation day and night.

Summary It has been emphasized during this brief outline of the training that you must contemplate on each mental occurrence good or bad, on each bodily movement large or small, on every sensation (bodily or mental feeling) pleasant or unpleasant, and so on. If, during the course of training, occasions arise when there is nothing special to contemplate upon, be fully occupied with attention to the rising and falling of the abdomen. When you have to attend to any kind of activity that necessitates walking, then, in complete awareness, each step should be briefly noted as *walking, walking* or *left, right*. But when you are taking a walking exercise, contemplate each step in three sections, *lifting, moving, placing*.

The student who thus dedicates himself to the training during day and night, will be able in not too long a time to develop concentration to the initial stage of the fourth degree of insight (knowledge of arising and passing away) and onward to higher stages of insight meditation.

PROGRESSIVE PRACTICE 67

When, as mentioned above, by dint of diligent practice, mindfulness and concentration have improved, the meditator will notice the pairwise occurrence of an object and the knowing of it, such as the rising and awareness of it, the falling and awareness of it, sitting and awareness of it, bending and awareness of it, stretching and awareness of it, lifting and awareness of it, putting down and awareness of it. Through concentrated attention (mindfulness), he knows how to distinguish each bodily and mental process: "The rising movement is one process, the knowing of it is another; the falling is one process, the knowing of it is another." He realizes that each act of knowing has the nature of 'going toward an object.' Such a realization refers to the characteristic function of the mind as inclining toward an object, or cognizing an object. One should know that the more clearly a material object is noticed, the clearer becomes the mental process of knowing it. This fact is stated thus in the ancient *Path of Purification (Visuddhi Magga):*

> *For in proportion as materiality becomes quite definite, disentangled and quite clear to him, so the immaterial states that have that materiality as their object become plain of themselves too.*

When the meditator comes to know the difference between a bodily process and a mental process, should he be a simple man, he would reflect from direct experience thus: "There is the rising and knowing it, the falling and knowing it, and so on and so forth. There is nothing else besides them. The words *man* or *woman* refer to the same process; there is no *person* or *soul.*" Should he be a well-informed man, he would reflect from direct knowledge of the difference between a material process as object and a mental process of knowing it, thus: "It is true that there are only body and mind. Besides them there are no such entities as man or woman.

While contemplating, one notices a material process as object and a mental process of knowing it, and it is to that pair alone that the terms of conventional usage—*being, person,* or *soul, man* or *woman*—refer. But apart from that dual process, there is no separate person or being, I or another, man or woman." When such reflections occur, the meditator must note *reflecting, reflecting* and go on observing the rising of the abdomen, its falling, etc.

68   With further progress in meditation, the conscious state of an intention is evident before a bodily movement occurs. The meditator first notices that intention. Though also at the start of his practice, he does notice *intending, intending* (for instance, to bend an arm), yet he cannot notice that state of consciousness distinctly. Now, at this more advanced stage, he clearly notices the consciousness consisting of the intention to bend. So he notices first the conscious state of an intention to make a bodily movement, then he notices the particular bodily movement. At the beginning, because of omission to notice an intention, he thinks that bodily movement is quicker than the mind knowing it. Now, at this advanced stage, mind appears to be the forerunner. The meditator readily notices the intention of bending, stretching, sitting, standing, going, and so on. He also clearly notices the actual bending, stretching, etc. So he realizes the fact that mind knowing a bodily process is quicker than the material process. He experiences directly that a bodily process takes place after a preceding intention. Again he knows from direct experience that the intensity of heat or cold increases while he is noticing *hot, hot* or *cold, cold.* In contemplating regular and spontaneous bodily movements such as the rising and falling of the abdomen, he notices one after another continuously. He also notices the arising in him of various mental images such as the Buddha, a pagoda, bodies, or objects of nature. He notices as well any kind of sensation that arises in his body (such as itch, ache, heat) with attention directed on the particular spot where the sensation occurs. One sensation has hardly disappeared, then another arises, and he notices them all accordingly. While noticing every object as it arises he is aware that a mental process of knowing depends on an object. Sometimes, the rising and falling of the abdomen is so faint that he finds nothing to notice. Then, it occurs to him that there can be no knowing without an object. When no noticing of the rising and falling is possible one should be aware of sitting and touching or lying and touching. *Touching* is to be noticed alternatively. For example, after noticing *sitting,* notice the touch sensation at the right foot

(caused by its contact with the ground or seat). Then, after noticing *sitting*, notice the touch sensation at the left foot. In the same manner, notice the touch sensation at several places. Again, in noticing seeing, hearing, and so on, the meditator comes to know clearly that seeing arises from the contact of eye and visual object, hearing arises from the contact of ear and sound, and so on.

Further he sees: "Material processes of bending, stretching, and so on, follow mental processes of intending to bend, stretch, and so forth." He goes on to reflect: "One's body becomes hot or cold because of the element of heat or cold; the body exists on food and nourishment; consciousness arises because there are objects to notice; seeing arises through visual objects; hearing through sounds, etc.; and also because there are the sense organs, eye, ear, etc., as conditioning factors. Intention and noticing result from previous experiences; feeling (sensations) of all kinds are the consequences of previous karma. There is nobody to create this body and mind, and all that happens has causal factors." Such reflections come to the meditator while he is noticing any object as it arises. He does not stop doing so to take time to reflect. While noticing objects as they arise, he experiences these reflections so quickly that they appear to be automatic. The meditator, then, must note: *reflecting, reflecting, recognizing, recognizing* and continue noticing objects as usual. After having reflected that material processes and mental processes being noticed are conditioned by the previous processes of the same nature, the meditator reflects further that body and mind in the former existences were conditioned by the preceding causes, that in the following existences body and mind will result from the same causes, and apart from this dual process there is no separate 'being' or 'person,' only causes and effects taking place. Such reflections must also be noticed and then contemplation should go on as usual. Such reflections will be many in the case of persons with a strong intellectual bent and less in the case of those with no such bent. Be that as it may, energetic noticing must be made of all these reflections. Noticing them will result in their reduction to a minimum, allowing insight to progress unimpeded by an excess of such reflections. It should be taken for granted that a minimum of reflections will suffice here.

As practice is continued in an intensive manner, the meditator may experience almost unbearable sensations, such as itching, aches, heat, dullness, and stiffness. If mindful noticing is stopped, such sensations will disappear. When noticing is resumed, they

69

will reappear. Such sensations arise as previously stated in consequence of the body's natural sensitivity and are not the symptoms of a disease. If they are noticed with energetic concentration they fade away gradually.

Again, the meditator sometimes sees images of all kinds as if seeing them with his own eyes. For example, the Buddha comes into the scene in glorious radiance; a procession of monks in the sky; pagodas and images of the Buddha; meeting with beloved ones; trees or woods, hills or mountains, gardens, buildings; finding oneself face to face with bloated, dead bodies or skeletons; the destruction of buildings and dissolution of human bodies; swelling of one's body, covered with blood, falling into pieces and reduced to a mere skeleton; seeing in one's body the entrails and vital organs and even germs; seeing the denizens of the hells and heavens, etc. These are nothing but creatures of one's imagination sharpened by intense concentration. They are similar to what one comes across in dreams. They are not to be welcomed and enjoyed, nor need one be afraid of them. These objects seen in the course of contemplation are not real; they are mere images or imaginations, whereas the mind that sees those objects is a reality. But mind as purely mental processes, unconnected with fivefold sense-impressions, cannot easily be noticed with sufficient clarity and detail. Hence principal attention should be given to sense-objects which can be noticed easily, and to those mental processes which arise in connection with sense perceptions. So whatever object appears, the meditator should notice it, saying mentally, *seeing, seeing* until it disappears. It will either move away, fade away, or break asunder. At the outset, this will take several noticings, say about five to ten. But when insight develops, the object will disappear after a couple of noticings. However, if the meditator wishes to enjoy the sight, or to look closely into the matter, or gets scared of it, then it is likely to linger on. If the object be one induced deliberately, then through delight it will last a long time. So care must be taken not to think of or incline toward extraneous matters while one's concentration is good. If such thoughts come in, they must be instantly noticed and dispelled. In the case of persons who experience no extraordinary objects or feelings while contemplating as usual, they may become lazy. They must notice this laziness thus: *lazy, lazy,* until they overcome it. At this stage, whether or not the meditators come across extraordinary objects of feelings, they know clearly the initial, the intermediate, and the final phases of every noticing. At the beginning of the practice, while noticing one object, they had to switch onto a different object that arose, but they did not notice clearly the disappearance of the previous object. Now, only after cognizing the disappearance of an object, will they notice the new object that arises. Thus they have a clear knowledge of the initial, the intermediate, and the final phases of the object noticed.

At this stage, when the meditator becomes more practiced, he perceives in every act of noticing that an object appears suddenly and disappears instantly. His perception is so clear that he reflects thus: "All comes to an end; all disappears. Nothing is permanent; it is truly impermanent." His reflection is quite in line with what is stated in the commentary to the Pali text: "All is impermanent, in the sense of destruction, non-existence after having been." He reflects further: "It is through ignorance that we enjoy life. But in truth, there is nothing to enjoy. There is a continuous arising and disappearing by which we are harassed ever and anon. This is dreadful indeed. At any moment we may die and everything is sure to come to an end. This universal impermanence is truly frightful and terrible." His reflection agrees with the commentarial statement: "What is permanent is painful, painful in the sense of terror; painful because of oppression by rise and fall." Again, experiencing severe pains he reflects thus: "All is pain, all is bad." This reflection agrees with what the scripture commentary states: "He looks on pain as a barb; as a boil; as a dart." He further reflects: "This is a mass of suffering, suffering that is unavoidable. Arising and disappearing, it is worthless. One cannot stop its process. It is beyond one's power. It takes its natural course." This reflection is quite in agreement with the commentary: "What is painful is not self, not self in the sense of having no core, because there is no exercising of power over it." The meditator must notice all these reflections and go on contemplating as usual.

Having thus seen the three characteristics by direct experience, the meditator, by inference from the direct experience of the objects noticed, comprehends all the objects not yet noticed as being impermanent, subject to suffering, and without a self.

In respect to objects not personally experienced he concludes: "They too are constituted in the same way: impermanent, painful, and without a self." This is an inference from his present direct experience. Such a comprehension is not clear enough in the case of one with less intellectual capacity or limited knowledge who pays no attention to a reflection but simply goes on noticing objects. But such a comprehension occurs often to one who yields to

71

reflection, which, in some cases, may occur at every act of noticing. Such excessive reflecting, however, is an impediment to the progress of insight. Even if no such reflections occur at this stage, comprehension will nevertheless become increasingly clear at the higher stages. Hence, no special attention should be given to reflections. While giving more attention to the bare noticing of objects, the meditator must, however, also notice these reflections if they occur, but he should not dwell on them.

72

After comprehending the three characteristics, the meditator no longer reflects, but goes on with noticing those bodily and mental objects which present themselves continuously. Then, at the moment when the five mental faculties—namely, faith, energy, mindfulness, concentration, and knowledge—are properly balanced, the mental process of noticing accelerates as if it becomes uplifted, and the bodily and mental processes to be noticed also arise much quicker. In a moment of in-breathing, the rising of the abdomen presents itself in quick succession, and the falling also becomes correspondingly quicker. Quick succession is also evident in the process of bending and stretching. Slight movements are felt spreading all over the body. In several cases, prickly sensations and itching appear in quick succession momentarily. By and large, these are feelings hard to bear. The meditator cannot possibly keep pace with that quick succession of varied experiences if he attempts to notice them by name. Noticing has here to be done in a general manner, but with mindfulness. At this stage one need not try to notice details of the objects arising in quick succession, but one should notice them generally. If one wishes to name them, a collective designation will be sufficient. If one attempts to follow them in a detailed manner, one will get tired soon. The important thing is to notice clearly and to comprehend what arises. At this stage, the usual contemplation focused on a few selected objects should be set aside and mindful noticing should attend to every object that arises at the six sense-doors. Only when one is not keen on this sort of noticing, should one revert to the usual contemplation.

Bodily and mental processes are many times swifter than a wink of an eye or a flash of lightning. Yet, if the meditator goes on simply noticing these processes he can fully comprehend them as they happen. The mindfulness becomes very strong. As a result, mindfulness seems as if plunging into an object that arises. The object too seems as if alighting on mindfulness. One comprehends each object clearly and singly. Therefore the meditator then believes: "Bodily and mental processes are very swift indeed. They are as fast as a machine or an engine. And yet, they all can be noticed and comprehended. Perhaps there is nothing more to know. What is to be known has been known." He believes so because he knows by direct experience what he has not even dreamt of before.

Again, as a result of insight, a brilliant light will appear to the meditator. There arises also in him rapture, causing 'gooseflesh,' falling of tears, tremor in the limbs. It produces in him a subtle thrill and exhilaration. He feels as if on a swing. He even wonders whether he is just giddy. Then, there arises tranquility of mind and along with it appears mental agility, etc. When sitting, lying, walking, or standing, he feels quite at ease. Both body and mind are agile in functioning swiftly, they are pliant in being able to attend to any object desired for any length of time desired. He is free from stiffness, heat, or pain. Insight penetrates objects with ease. Mind becomes sound and straight, and he wishes to avoid all evil. Through firm faith, mind is very bright. At times, when there is no object to be noticed, the mind remains tranquil for a long time. There arise in him thoughts like these: "Verily, the Buddha is omniscient. Truly, the body-and-mind process is impermanent, painful, and without self." While noticing objects he comprehends lucidly the three characteristics. He wishes to advise others to practice meditation. He is free from sloth and torpor; his energy is neither lax nor tense. There arises in him equanimity associated with insight. His happiness exceeds his former experiences. So he wishes to communicate his feelings and experiences to others. There arises further a subtle attachment of a calm nature that enjoys the insight associated with the brilliant light, mindfulness, and rapture. He comes to experience all this as the bliss of meditation.

The meditator should not reflect on these happenings. As each arises, he should notice them accordingly: *brilliant light, faith, rapture, tranquility, happiness,* and so on. When there is brightness, one should notice it as *bright,* until it disappears. Similar acts of noticing should be made in the other cases too. When brilliant light appears, at the beginning one tends to forget noticing and enjoys seeing the light. Even if the meditator applies mindful noticing to the light, it will be mixed with feelings of rapture and happiness, and it is likely to linger on. However, one later gets used to such phenomena and will continue to notice them clearly until they disappear. Sometimes the light is so brilliant that one finds it

73

difficult to make it vanish by the mere act of noticing it mindfully. Then one should cease to pay attention to it and turn energetically to the noticing of any object that arises in one's body. The meditator should not ponder as to whether the light is still there. If one does so, one is likely to see it. If such a thought arises, one should disperse it by vigorously directing attention to that very thought. While concentration is intense, not only a brilliant light but also other extraordinary objects may arise and will continue if one inclines to one or the other of them. If such inclination happens to arise, the meditator must notice it quickly. In some cases, even if there is no such inclination toward any object in particular, faint objects appear one after the other like a train of railway carriages. The meditator should then respond to such visual images simply by *seeing, seeing,* and each object will disappear. When the meditator's insight becomes weaker, the objects may become more distinct. Then each of them must be noticed until the whole train of objects disappears finally.

One must recognize the fact that cherishing an inclination toward phenomena such as brilliant lights and being attached to them is a wrong attitude. The correct response that is in conformity with the path of insight, is to notice these objects mindfully and with detachment until they disappear. When the meditator continues to apply mindfulness to body-and-mind, his insight will grow in clarity. He will come to perceive more distinctly the arising and disappearing of the bodily and mental processes. He will come to know that each object arises at one place and on that very place it disappears. He will know that the previous occurrence is one thing and the succeeding occurrence is another. So, at every act of noticing, he comprehends the characteristics of impermanence, painfulness, and egolessness. After thus contemplating for a considerable time, he may come to believe: "This is surely the best that can be attained. It can't be better," and he becomes so satisfied with his progress that he is likely to pause and relax. He should, however, not relax at this stage, but go ahead with his practice of noticing the bodily and mental processes continuously for a still longer time.

With the improvement of practice, and when knowledge becomes more mature, the arising of the objects is no longer apparent to the meditator; he notices only their ceasing. They pass away swiftly. So also do the mental processes of noticing them. For instance, while noticing the rising of the abdomen, that movement vanishes in no time. And in the same manner vanishes also the mental process of noticing that movement. Thus it will be clearly known to the meditator that both the rising and the noticing vanish immediately one after another. The same applies in the case of the falling of the abdomen, of sitting, bending, or stretching of an arm or leg, stiffness in the limbs, and so on. The noticing of an object and the knowledge of its ceasing occur in quick succession. Some meditators perceive distinctly three phases: noticing an object, its ceasing, and the passing away of the consciousness that cognizes that ceasing—all in quick succession. However, it is sufficient to know, in pairwise sequence, the dissolution of an object and the passing away of the consciousness of noticing that dissolution.

When a meditator can clearly notice these pairs uninterruptedly, the particular features such as body, head, hand, leg are no longer apparent to him, and there appears to him the idea that everything is ceasing and vanishing. At this stage he is likely to feel that his contemplation is not up to the mark. But in fact, it is not so. Mind as a rule takes delight in dwelling on the sight of particular features and forms. When they are absent, mind is wanting in satisfaction. But as a matter of fact, this is a manifestation of the progress of insight. At the beginning, it is the features and names of objects that are clearly noticed first, but now the disappearance of objects is noticed first, because of the progress. Only on repeated reflection do features appear again, but if they are not noticed the fact of dissolution reappears most strongly. So one comes to know by direct experience the truth of the wise saying: "when a name or designation arises, a reality lies hidden; when a reality reveals itself, a name or designation disappears."

When the meditator notices the objects clearly, he thinks that his noticings are not close enough. This is because the insight is so swift and clear that he comes to know even the momentary subconsciousness in between the processes of cognition. He intends to do something, for instance bending or stretching an arm, and he readily notices that intention which thereby tends to fade away, with the result that he cannot bend or stretch for some time. In that event, he should continue and simply switch his attention to contemplating the present occurrences at one of the six sensedoors.

If the meditator extends his contemplation over the whole body, as usual, beginning with the noticing of the rising and falling of the abdomen, he will soon gain momentum, and then he should continue noticing touching and knowing, or seeing and knowing, or

75

hearing and knowing, and so on, as one or the other occurs. While so doing, if he feels that he is either restless or tired, he should revert to noticing the rising and falling of the abdomen. After some time, when he gains momentum, he should notice any object that arises in the whole body.

When he can contemplate well in such a spread-out manner, even if he does not notice an object with vigor, he knows what he hears fades away, what he sees dissolves in broken parts, with no continuation between them. This is seeing things as they really are. Some meditators do not see clearly what is happening because the vanishing is so swift that they feel their eyesight is getting poorer or they are giddy. It is not so. They are simply lacking the power of cognition to notice what happens before and after, with the result that they do not see the features or forms. At such a time, they should relax and stop contemplating. But the bodily and mental processes continue to appear to them, and consciousness, of its own accord, continues to notice them. The meditator may decide to sleep, but he does not fall asleep and remains fit and alert. He need not worry about the loss of sleep; because of his concentration he will not feel unwell or fall ill. He should go ahead with noticing energetically and he will see that his mind is quite capable to perceive the objects fully and clearly.

When engaged in noticing continuously both the dissolution of the objects and the act of knowing it, he reflects: "Even for the wink of an eye or a flash of lightning nothing lasts. I did not realize this before. As it ceased and vanished in the past so will it cease and vanish in the future." He must notice such a reflection. Besides, in the midst of contemplations, the meditator is likely to have an awareness of fearfulness. He reflects: "One enjoys life, not knowing the truth. Now that one knows the truth of continuous dissolution it is truly fearful. At every moment of dissolution one can die. The beginning of this life itself is fearful. So are the endless repetitions of the arisings. So the efforts to arrest the changing phenomena for the sake of well-being and happiness are futile. To be reborn is fearful in that it entails living with a recurrence of objects that are ceasing and vanishing always. Fearful indeed it is to be old, to die, to experience sorrow, lamentation, pain, grief, and despair." Such reflection should be noticed and then dismissed.

Then the meditator sees nothing to depend on and becomes as it were weakened in mind as well as in body. He is seized with dejection. He is no longer bright and spirited. But he should not despair. This condition of his is a sign of the progress of insight. It is nothing more than being unhappy at the awareness of fearfulness. He must notice such a reflection and as he continues to notice objects as they arise, one after another, this unhappy feeling will disappear. However, if he fails to contemplate for some time, then grief will assert itself and fear will overpower him. This kind of fear is not associated with insight. Therefore, care must be taken to prevent the oncoming of such undesirable fear by energetic contemplation.

Again in the midst of noticing objects, he is likely to find faults, in this manner: "This body-and-mind process, being impermanent, is unsatisfactory. It was not a good thing to have been born. It is not good either to continue in existence. It is disappointing to see the appearance of seemingly definite features and forms of objects while in fact they are not realities. It is in vain that one makes efforts to seek well-being and happiness. Birth is not desirable. Dreadful are old age, death, lamentation, pain, grief, and despair." A reflection of this nature must likewise be noticed.

Then, one tends to feel that body-and-mind as the object and the consciousness of noticing it are very crude, low, or worthless. By noticing their arising and disappearing, he gets sick of them. He might see his own body decaying and decomposing. He looks upon it as being very fragile.

At this stage, while the meditator is noticing all that arises in his body-and-mind, he is getting disgusted with it. Although he cognizes clearly their dissolution by a series of good noticings he is no longer alert and bright. His contemplation is associated with disgust. So he becomes lazy. But nevertheless he cannot refrain from contemplating. For example, it is like one who feels disgusted at every step when he has to walk on a muddy and dirty path and yet he cannot stop going. He cannot help but go on. At this time, he sees the human abode as being subject to the process of dissolution, and he does not relish the prospect of being reborn as a human being, man or woman, king or multimillionaire. He has the same feelings toward the celestial abodes.

When through this knowledge he feels disgusted with regard to every formation noticed, there will arise in him a desire to forsake these formations or be delivered from them. Seeing, hearing, touching, reflecting, standing, sitting, bending, stretching, noticing—he wishes to get rid of them all. He should notice this wishing. He now longs for the liberation from bodily and mental processes. He reflects: "Every time I notice them, I am meeting with repetitions, which are all bad. I had better stop noticing them." He should take notice of such a reflection.

Some meditators, when so reflecting, actually stop noticing the formations. Although they do so, the formations do not stop taking place, namely: rising, falling, bending, stretching, intending, and so on. They go on as ever. Noticing of the distinct formations also continues. So, reflecting thus, he feels pleased: "Although I stop noticing the body-and-mind, formations are taking place all the same. They are arising, and consciousness of them is there, by itself. So liberation from them cannot be achieved by mere stopping noticing them. They cannot be forsaken in this way. Noticing them as usual, the three characteristics of life will be fully comprehended and then no heed being given to them, equanimity will be gained. The end of these formations, nirvana, will be realized. Peace and bliss will come." So reflecting with delight, he continues to notice the formations. In the case of those meditators who are not capable of reflecting in this way, they continue their meditation once they become satisfied with the explanation of their teachers.

Soon after continuing meditation they gain momentum and at that time, in some cases, various painful feelings arise. This need not cause despair. It is only the manifestation of the characteristic inherent in this mass of suffering, as stated in the commentary thus: "Seeing the five aggregates as painful, as a disease, a boil, as a dart, a calamity, an affliction, etc." Even if such painful feelings are not experienced, one of the characteristics of impermanence, suffering or no-self will be apparent at every noticing. Although the meditator is properly noticing, he feels that he is not doing well. He thinks that the consciousness of noticing and the object noticed are not close enough. This is because he is too eager to comprehend fully the nature of the three characteristics. Not satisfied with his contemplation he changes his posture often. While sitting, he thinks he will do better walking. While walking he wants to resume sitting. After he has sat down he changes the position of his limbs. He wants to go to another place; he wants to lie down. Although he makes these changes he cannot remain long in one particular position. Again, he becomes restless. But he should not despair. All this happens because he has come to realize the true nature of the formations, and also because he has not yet acquired the knowledge of equanimity about formations. He is doing well and yet he feels otherwise. He should try to adhere to one posture, and he will find that he is then comfortable in that posture. Continuing to notice the formations energetically, his mind will gradually become composed and bright. In the end his restless feelings will disappear totally.

When the knowledge of equanimity about formations becomes mature, the mind will be very clear and able to notice the formations very lucidly. Noticing runs smoothly as if no effort is required. Subtle formations, too, are noticed without effort. The true characteristics of impermanence, pain, and no-self are becoming evident without any reflection. Attention is directed to a particular spot at any part of the body wherever a sensation occurs, but the feeling of touch is as smooth as that of cotton-wool. Sometimes the objects to be noticed in the whole body are so many that noticing has to be accelerated. Both body and mind appear to be pulling upwards. The objects being noticed become sparse and one can notice them easily and calmly. Sometimes the bodily formations disappear altogether, leaving only the mental formations. Then the meditator will experience within himself a feeling of rapture as if enjoying a shower of tiny particles of water. He is also suffused with serenity. He might also see brightness like a clear sky. These marked experiences, however, do not influence him excessively. He is not overjoyed. But he still enjoys them. He must notice this enjoyment. He must also notice rapture, serenity, and bright lights. If they do not vanish when being noticed, he should pay no heed to them and notice any other object that arises.

At this stage he becomes satisfied with the knowledge that there is no I, mine, self, and that only formations arise; formations only are cognizing other formations. He also finds delight in noticing the objects one after another. He is not tired of noticing them for a long time. He is free from painful feelings. So whatever posture he chooses he can retain it long. Either sitting or lying he can go on contemplating for two or three hours without experiencing any discomfort, spending his time tirelessly. Even after that time, his posture is as firm as before.

At times formations arise swiftly and he is noticing them well. Then he may become anxious as to what will happen to him. He should notice such an anxiety. He feels he is doing well. He should notice this feeling. He looks forward to the progress of insight. He should notice this anticipation. He should notice steadily whatever arises. He should not put forth a special effort nor relax. In some cases, because of the anxiety, joy, attachment, or anticipation, noticing becomes lax and retrogressive. Some who think that the goal is very near contemplate with great energy. While doing so, noticing becomes lax and retrogression sets in. This happens be-

79

cause a restless mind cannot concentrate properly on formations. So when noticing is in good swing the meditator must go on steadily, which means he should neither relax nor put forth special effort. If he does go on steadily, he will rapidly gain insight into the end of all the formations and realize nirvana. In the case of some meditators, they may, at this stage, rise higher and again fall several times. They should not give way to despair but instead hold fast to determination. Heed must be paid to noticing whatever arises at all the six sense-doors. However, when noticing is not going on smoothly and calmly, contemplation in such a spread-out manner is not possible.

If the meditator begins either with the rising and falling of the abdomen or with any other bodily and mental object, he will find that he is gaining momentum. And then the noticing will go on of its own accord, smoothly and calmly. It will appear to him that he is watching with ease the ceasing and vanishing of all formations in a clear manner. At this point, his mind is quite free from all defilements. However pleasant and inviting an object may be, it is no longer attractive to him. Again, however loathsome an object may be, it no longer bothers him. He simply sees, hears, smells, tastes, feels a touch, or cognizes. With six kinds of equanimity described in the texts, he notices all the formations. He is not even aware of the length of time he is engaged in contemplation. As soon as the five faculties (indriya) of faith, energy, mindfulness, concentration, and wisdom are developed in an even manner, he will realize nirvana.[1]

One who has attained the knowledge of nirvana is aware of the distinct change of his temperament and mental attitude and feels that his life has changed. His faith or trustful confidence in the Buddha, Dharma, and Sangha becomes very strong and firm. Due to his strengthened faith he also gains rapture and serenity. There arises spontaneous happiness. Because of these ecstatic experiences, he cannot notice the objects in a distinct manner although he endeavors to do so right after the experience of nirvana. However, these experiences wane gradually after some hours or days, and he will then be able again to notice the formations distinctly. In some cases, the meditators, having attained nirvana, feel re-

[1] *At this point, Mahasi details how one experiences nirvana, but this explanation is not helpful to most meditators. There is a danger of knowing too much and developing expectations instead of seeing clearly what is happening for oneself in the present moment.*

lieved of a great burden, free and easy, and do not wish to go on contemplating. Their object has been achieved and their hearts' content is understandable. They may then go on to the higher stages of practice.

A Special Note The technique of insight meditation outlined in this treatise is quite sufficient for persons of fair intelligence. Such persons, having read it, should practice these contemplations with firm faith, keen desire, and great diligence in a methodical manner, and they can be sure of progress. It must, however, be pointed out that the details of the experiences and the progressive stages of insight gone through by meditators cannot possibly be described in full in this short treatise. There still remains much that is worthy of description. On the other hand, what has been described here is not experienced in toto by every meditator. There are bound to be differences according to one's capabilities and karma. Again, one's faith, desire, and diligence do not remain constant always. Furthermore, a meditator, having no instructor and being entirely dependent on book knowledge, will be as cautious and hesitant as a traveler who has never been on a particular journey. Therefore, it is obviously not very easy for such a person to attain the paths and fruitions of nirvana if he goes on striving without a teacher to guide and encourage him. This being so, one who is really keen to meditate until he attains his goal, nirvana, must find a teacher who is fully qualified by his own attainments to guide him all along the way from the lowest stage of insight to the highest knowledges of the path and the fruition of nirvana. This advice is quite in accord with what is stated in the scriptures: "A teacher should be sought for knowledge about decay-and-death as it really is."

SUNLUN SAYADAW

CHAPTER
SIX

Sunlun Sayadaw was so named because he came from the cave monasteries of Sunlun Village near Myingyan in middle Burma. He was born in 1878 and was named U Kyaw Din. He was sent to a monastery school but learned little. At the age of fifteen he entered employment as an office boy in the district commissioner's office at Myingyan. He married Ma Shwe Yi of the same village. At the age of thirty he resigned from his post and returned to his native village to become a farmer. He found that his fields prospered while other fields failed. In 1919 there was an epidemic. U Kyaw Din's fields were still prospering. There is a belief among Burmese people that if one's worldly possessions rise rapidly then one will die soon. Anxious because of his rising prosperity, U Kyaw Din consulted an astrologer. He was told that a two-legged being would soon leave his house. This was tantamount to saying that he would die.

In great fear, U Kyaw Din decided to accomplish one great act of charity. He erected a pavilion in front of his house and invited people to meals for three days. On the third day a certain mill clerk turned up uninvited at the feast. He began to converse about the practice of Vipassana and, on hearing these words, U Kyaw Din became greatly affected. He could not sleep that night. He felt that he wanted to undertake the practice but was afraid to mention his wish because of his lack of knowledge of scriptural texts. The next day he asked the clerk whether a man ignorant of the texts could undertake the practice. The clerk replied that the practice of insight meditation did not require doctrinal knowledge but only deep interest and assiduity. He told U Kyaw Din to practice in-breathing and out-breathing. So from that day, whenever he could find the time, U Kyaw Din would direct breath in and breath out. One day he met a friend who told him that directing breathing in and out alone was not sufficient; he had also to be aware of the touch of breath at the nostril tip.

U Kyaw Din practiced awareness of the touch of breath. Then as his practice became more intense, he tried to be aware not only of the touch of breath but also of the touch of his hand on the handle of the knife as he chopped corn cobs, the touch of rope on the hand as he drew water, the touch of his feet on the ground as he walked. He tried to be aware of touch in everything he did. As he tended his cattle he would sit under a tree and practice mindfulness of breathing. During the practice he began to see colored lights and geometrical patterns. He did not know what they were but felt that they were the fruit of practice. This greatly encouraged him and he began to practice more assiduously. With more intensive practice, sensations were sometimes intensely unpleasant. But they did not deter him. He believed that they were the fruit of the practice and that if he desired to win greater fruit he would have to overcome and get beyond them. Therefore he generated more energy and developed a more rigorous mindfulness until he overcame the unpleasant sensations and passed beyond to the higher stages of the practice.

Endeavoring in this zealous manner, U Kyaw Din attained the stage of stream entry, the first taste of nirvana, in mid-1920. The next month he won the second stage of liberation. In the third month he won the third stage. He asked permission of his wife to let him become a monk; after much resistance, the wife agreed. But even then she asked him to sow a final crop of peas before he left. U Kyaw Din set out for the fields. But even as he was broadcasting the seeds he felt the great urge to renounce the world. Setting his cattle free, he put the yoke up against a tree, went to the village monastery, and begged the monk there to accept him as a novice in the order. He next betook himself to the caves nearby and practiced diligently, until in October, 1920, he attained the final stage of freedom, arahatship. His achievement became known among the monks and many came to test him. Though he was a barely literate man, his answers satisfied even the most learned monks. Very often they disagreed with his replies but when his answers were checked against the texts they found many important passages in the scriptures to support his statements. Many learned monks from various parts of the world went to practice mindfulness under him, including one very learned monk, the Nyaung Sayadaw, who also became fully enlightened after intense practice. Sunlun Sayadaw performed the act of leaving the body (parinirvana)[1] in 1952.

Sunlun Sayadaw was an intrinsically honest man, laconic and precise in speech, and possessed of great strength and determination. Photographs of him reveal a sturdily built man with a steady gaze, clear eyes, and a firmly set jaw. One senses in these photographs a quality of great courage, the attribute of the truly enlightened man.

Currently there are a number of meditation masters teaching the practices of Sunlun Sayadaw throughout Burma, and several Sunlun centers can be found in and around Rangoon. One of the largest, the Sunlun Monastery of S. Okkalapa has two resident Sayadaws, U

[1] *See Glossary.*

Tiloka and U Thondera, both senior disciples of Sunlun. Only twenty monks or so reside here, for the large compound of cottages and halls is more oriented toward serving lay people. Group sittings take place four and five times daily, after a fiery and inspirational talk by the Sayadaw. "You are lucky to be born a human and even luckier to hear the Dharma. Take advantage of this special opportunity to really practice, be diligent, and work hard to win liberation."

The huge, mirrored hall is often filled with several hundred meditators of every age. The sittings can last two or more hours. During the first forty-five minutes the entire hall is engaged in intensely practicing the heavy breathing concentration exercise. On the Sayadaw's instruction, the yogis then turn to mindfulness of sensation in the body, continuing to sit motionless until the end of a two- or three-hour period.

Although the teachers of Sunlun Sayadaw's meditation recognize other ways of practice as possible, they emphasize that theirs is the clearest, most simple and direct path. They would find the natural method of Achaan Chaa and Buddhadasa too slow and indirect, and criticize other techniques such as Mahasi Sayadaw and Taungpulu Sayadaw as developing concentration through concepts but not direct insight.

Special emphasis on intense effort, concentrated on direct perception of sensation (especially pain), is the key to Sunlun practice. Walking into a hall full of heavily breathing Sunlun meditators is like finding oneself in the middle of a steam calliope. This enormous effort made to concentrate the mind by watching heavy breathing is then deepened in insight practice while sitting rigid, motionless, fully experiencing the pains of the body. The use of sensation, especially pain, is what most characterizes Sunlun practice. It is strongly goal-oriented, directing total effort in each sitting to the development of concentration and insight that will lead to nirvana and liberation. There is emphasis on long, motionless sitting. While practicing as a monk at the Sunlun center, I was given a beautiful set of Burmese beads. The devout lay supporter offered them to me along with the fervent wish that I might soon be sitting all night without moving, and thereby sooner realize nirvana.

Total effort to overcome pain and distraction is the way of Sunlun Sayadaw. The power of the concentrated heavy breathing and the pain that follows is suitable for overcoming many of the hindrances that normally distract a meditator. No matter how sleepy you feel, a session of hard breathing concentrating only on sensations at the nostrils will wake you right up. The technique is equally valuable for quieting an agitated, distracted mind, for in the face of the enormous effort in hard breathing, most thoughts are blasted away like clouds before a wind.

Sunlun practice clears the mind of sleepiness and distraction, leaving the meditator clear and concentrated. Further mindfulness of pain and changing sensations strengthens the mindful, observing quality of mind. In a short time with this practice one may experience the power of a calm, concentrated mind which, when applied to observing the mind-body process, leads to clear insight, wisdom, and liberation.

This Sunlun center of S. Okkalapa is very receptive to Western meditators. Here as elsewhere in Burma, the hospitality and support for visiting yogis is overwhelming. Although the Sayadaws do not speak English, there are a number of articulate and fluent English-speaking disciples who are able to translate for visitors. The Sayadaws are available for questions but the emphasis is primarily on strong sustained practice, the only way really to answer Dharma doubts.

The following chapter is a talk given in Rangoon several years ago by one of the chief teaching disciples of Sunlun Sayadaw.

The Yogi and Insight Meditation

6

as taught by Sunlun Sayadaw

I propose to take a practical approach to meditation for you this evening. I shall consider the matter from the point of view of the yogi, his propensities and inclinations, his encounters with the problems and difficulties of execution, his small concerns and clingings, and his subtle self-deceptions. While doing this I shall attempt to weave in the teachings of the Sunlun Sayadaw on the practice of Vipassana to illustrate my points.

The first essential equipment of the yogi is a concentrated mind. For only a concentrated mind is a cleansed mind. And only the mind which is cleansed of the five elements of sensual lust, ill will, sloth, agitation, and doubt can function properly to realize Vipassana insight.

For the initiation of the cleansing process, the normal, everyday mind requires an object to grasp. This object can be one of two types: external to the corporeal-mental system of the yogi or belonging to it. Those objects which are external to the yogi belong to the environment, such as color discs, corpses, or the food which he eats daily. Those objects which belong to the corporeal-mental organization of the yogi are his body and his thoughts. Any of these can be taken as an object of meditation to establish concentration.

For example, color discs can be employed. The yogi takes, let us say, a colored disc or spot and places it at an appropriate distance, about three yards. He sits down with legs crossed under him, faces the disc, and holding the body erect he gazes on the disc with eyes opened neither too wide nor too narrow. He lets his mind dwell with earnestness on the disc in order to gain fixity of mind. He does this until at last, even with closed eyes, he perceives a mental reflex image of the disc. This is the acquired sign or image. As he continues to direct attention to this image there may arise a clearer counter-image. This counter-image appears together with the concentrated mind. If he wills to see it far, he sees it far. If he wills to see it near, to the left, to the right, within, without, above, and below, he sees it accordingly. After acquiring the counter-image, the yogi protects it with reverence through constant endeavor. Thereby he acquires facility in the practice, and after due practice he gains high and controlled concentration. Fixed meditation absorption follows. These exercises can produce all stages of fixed meditation.

Likewise he can practice the earth element meditation, the water meditation, the fire meditation, and so on. One of the benefits acquired through the ardent practice of the earth meditation is that a man, acquiring supernormal power, is able to walk on water just as on earth. If he gains supernormal power through the practice of the water meditation he can bring down rain or cause water to gush from his body. If he gains supernormal power through the practice of the fire meditation he is able to produce smoke and flame. But somehow it is not possible easily to acquire these powers in our day. Sunlun Sayadaw once said that the times were no more opportune. One might be able to gain absorption level concentration through such practices, but the supernormal benefits of the practices can hardly be acquired. Let us say that one practices the earth element exercise. He gains mastery of the signs. Let us say he goes to a pond and, seating himself near it, he arouses in himself the elements of the earth meditation. Then looking upon the waters of the pond he endeavors to turn them into earth so that he may walk upon them. He will find at the most that the water thickens to a slushy earth which cannot uphold his feet when he attempts to walk upon it. Perhaps yogis in other countries have done better but I believe it may be taken as a general rule that the acquisition of the total benefits of the element and color exercises are difficult to achieve in our time.

Another set of objects of meditation can be the loathsome ones, the corpses, or death. These exercises are not without their risk, as may be recounted in an anecdote of the Sunlun Sayadaw and a monk. The monk was in the habit of crossing the creek which separated the monastery from the burial grounds, to meditate on corpses. One morning the Sunlun Sayadaw met him as he was setting out to meditate for the day. The Sunlun Sayadaw smiled at him and and said: "The anapana breathing exercise is free of dangers." The monk did not act on the suggestion, but continued in the practice of gazing on corpses. One evening he returned to his cell. As he opened the door and looked inside he gave a yell of terror. He had seen a corpse lying on the threshold. Actually that corpse was only the acquired image of his object of meditation. When the Sunlun Sayadaw heard the story he smiled and said: "Meditation on breath is free of dangers."

Meditation may be practiced through the analysis of the four elements. The essence of earth is the nature of hardness, strength, thickness immobility, security, and supporting. The essence of water is the nature of oozing, humidity, fluidity, trickling, permeation, increasing, and flowing cohesion. The essence of fire is the nature of heating, warmth, evaporation, maturing, consuming, and grasping. The essence of air is the nature of supporting, coldness, ingress and egress, easy movement, reaching low, and grasping. The yogi grasps the elements briefly and in detail through consideration and reflection. But as will be noticed through a recounting of the essential natures of the four elements, they are difficult to distinguish within the body; they are hard to grasp directly; they have to be approached through indirection, through the repetition by word of mouth of the essential characteristics and a forcing of understanding of their natures. This understanding normally takes place first in the realm of concepts. And a yogi who arrives at such an understanding is often led too much to believe for himself that this is the peak requirement of the practice. This is not true, of course. The understanding that is required is not of the elements as they are made for us but of the elements as they are in their essentiality, as they are in themselves. And this, their nature, is beyond the realm of concept and logical thought.

The postures of the body can be good subjects leading to the proper establishment of concentration. The yogi attempts to be mindful of going, standing, sitting, lying, bending, stretching, eating, drinking, chewing, savoring, defecating, and urinating. The postures are dynamic, the going-on of the process is unmistakable, and when the postures are really grasped for what they are, the mind can be considered to be pretty well cleansed. However, the yogi should consider whether the postures serve better as the primary object of meditation or as a secondary one to be taken up in those moments of comparative relaxation when the primary object is being set aside for a while.

All of the methods mentioned are traditional Buddhist objects of meditation. They are all contained either in the list of forty subjects for concentration or in the *Great Discourse on Awareness*

(Maha Satipatthana Sutta), most of them in both. They all lead the yogi toward the establishment of concentration, some more, some less. The yogi may legitimately employ them to gain the concentration he needs. But perhaps it would be a wise approach for the yogi to seek to employ and practice that exercise which will lead him all the way to the final goal he seeks. That goal is liberating Vipassana insight knowledge.

Now, there are two forms of the practice of mental culture. These are known as Samatha, or concentration practice, and Vipassana, or insight practice. Samatha leads to calm and tranquility and Vipassana leads to intuitive knowledge of the true nature of phenomena and consequent liberation. Samatha is concerned with the universe as it is for us; Vipassana is concerned with the universe as it is in itself. Since the realm of Samatha is the universe as it is for us, the objects of meditation which lead to Samatha are accordingly those objects which we have made for ourselves. The colored visualization disc is something we have made for ourselves. The thought of the loathsomeness is something we have brought up in ourselves. The stability of earth, the cohesion of water, the maturing of fire, the interception of air are qualities of the four elements which have been conceptualized by us to help us in grasping them. Even the thought of walking in the fact of walking, the thought of bending in the fact of bending, the thought of touching in the fact of touching are ideas which we have created in our minds so that we can better get at the actualities, the postures as they are. But whatever makes the universe for us leads to Samatha; whatever artifact we construct, whatever idea, image, thought, or concept we create leads to Samatha. There is nothing wrong in Samatha in itself. The practice of Samatha is legitimate; there are many reasons why it should even be recommended. But concentration is not insight. Therefore he who would gather the fruits of concentration may practice concentration, but he who desires to gather the fruits of insight will have to practice insight. This he will have to do sooner or later, either after the practice of concentration or directly by selecting an exercise which sets him at once on the high road to insight. Whether he wishes to practice concentration now only to switch to Vipassana later, or alternatively to take up the practice of Vipassana immediately, is a matter of personal choice. And I as a practitioner of Vipassana should not be too eager to prompt him on that choice. Sunlun Sayadaw once said: "Man does what he likes to do, and the doing of what he likes does not bother him."

Questions arise: If we normally conceptualize the four elements to grasp them, if we commonly make thoughts about walking, bending, and touching to help us get at them better, if our minds are ever so prone to create images and ideas, can we possibly attempt to get at processes as they are in themselves? Is it not necessary that we handle the processes with the gloves of concepts and ideas? This is the answer: If it were true that it is necessary to handle the processes with the gloves of concepts and thoughts, that processes can never be got at directly, then there could be no path to freedom and no liberating knowledge. But because it is possible to get at processes directly as they are in themselves there is Vipassana and the winning of intuitive liberating knowledge.

Let us take an exercise, awareness of in-breathing and out-breathing. It is said to be a suitable exercise for all types of personalities. If a man practices mindfulness of respiration, he attains the peaceful life. He causes evil and unwholesome states to be overcome. His body and mind do not tremble. He fulfills the four foundations of mindfulness[2] and the seven enlightenment factors[3] and realizes wisdom and freedom. Mindfulness of breathing was practiced by the Buddha. Furthermore, watching the breath is said to be unadulterated, not requiring any addition to make it complete.

This exercise may be practiced in the simple concentration (Samatha) way or performed so as to realize insight (Vipassana). Breathe in and out. As the breath goes in and out it will touch the nostril tip or upper lip or some other places within that region. Fixing the mind on that point of touch, count the in-going and out-going breaths. This is one method. Breathe in and out again. Fix the mind on the point of touch of breath. Thus fixing the mind, know a short breath to be short and a long breath to be long. This is the second method. Breathe in and out again. Fixing the mind on the point of touch of breath, follow the breath in and out. In doing this, you should not follow the breath into the pit of the stomach or out into the beyond. The breath-body should be experienced going in and out. It is like a saw. The teeth of the saw are always at one point of contact with the wood but that point of wood experiences the whole length of the saw because the whole length of the saw passes across that point. This is the third method. Notice that in all three methods the yogi looks for the in-breaths and out-breaths

---

[2] See "Achaan Dhammadaro."
[3] See Chapter One.

nowhere else than at the point of touch. This is true also for the fourth method. Breathe in and out. Fix the mind on the point of touch of breath. Be aware of the touch. Do not count, do not know the degree of length, do not follow the breath in and out.

Of these four methods of mindfulness of breathing, the first three are simple concentration-type exercises while the fourth is an insight exercise. In the first method, there is counting. Numbers are concepts. In the second method, the form of the breath is noted. Form is an image. In the third method, the going in and out of the breath is noted. This is achieved through the creation of an idea. Concepts, images, and ideas belong to the universe as it is for us and therefore are concerned with Samatha. Only the fourth method, where the touch alone is taken in its bareness, performs the insight practice. Yet even this practice can be adulterated with concentration. If instead of being aware of the touch in its bare actuality, if instead of guarding this awareness with mindfulness, the yogi makes a mental note of it, then for that moment he has slipped into the old habit of forming a concept or an idea and practices Samatha instead of the intended Vipassana.

93

Mental noting tends to take place at a much slower pace than the actual processes of phenomena. Thus, instead of being able to take these processes as they are, it tends to keep slipping into a past where the processes are reconstructed by an intervening reasoning mind. To be able to keep up with the natural processes the yogi need only be mindful. This is not difficult to perform. The initial requirement is awareness. Be aware of the touch or sensation. *Then ward and watch this awareness with mindfulness.* When the awareness is guarded with mindfulness, thoughts are locked out, they cannot intrude. No opportunity is offered for the formation of concepts, images, or ideas. Thereby the processes are got at directly in the very moment of occurrence, as they are in themselves without the distortion of thought. This is true insight practice.

Thoughts always tend to intrude. Ideas and images stand just beyond the threshold, ready to enter at the least weakening of mindfulness. The only way to keep up with the processes, to be mindful of them, is to exercise vigilance through a rigor of effort. That is why in a motto the Sunlun Sayadaw said: "Be rigorously mindful of the awareness of touch."

He emphasized rigorousness as an essential element because he understood the yogi. The yogi is much inclined to sit loosely and to meditate in a relaxed, leisurely way. He tends to be reflective and considerate. Reflective in the sense of reflecting and thinking about the task to be done rather than doing it. Considerate in the sense of sympathizing with himself, taking great care to see that he is neither overexerted nor hurt. The yogi has a great love for himself and therefore prefers to let his thoughts run away with him, to drift rather than to pull himself together. To pull himself together needs exertion and that is anathema to the yogi. That is why when he is told to breathe harder he is ready to quote chapter and verse to prove that he does not need to exert himself. Perhaps he takes a few lines from the famous meditation manual, the *Visuddhi Magga*, and says: "The yogi should not essay too strenuously. If he essays too strenuously he will become restless."

This statement is true. The yogi who essays too strenuously will become restless. But why does he become restless? It is because instead of being mindful of touch or sensation the yogi has his mind on the effort he is making. The effort should not be allowed to draw the attention away from the object of meditation. To keep the attention on the object and yet to generate effort, the yogi should first make sure that the attention is fixed on the object. When the object has been grasped with full awareness and this awareness guarded with mindfulness, the yogi should step up the effort. When he proceeds in this manner, he will find that the generated effort serves to fix the attention more on the object instead of distracting it away into the effort itself. Furthermore, a greater intentness of the mind will have been developed by the increased effort.

The full text of the above quotation from the *Visuddhi Magga* in fact reads thus:

> He, the yogi, should be mindful and should not let the
> mind be distracted. He should not essay too strenuously
> nor too laxly. If he essays too laxly he will fall into rigid-
> ity and torpor. If he essays too strenuously he will be-
> come restless.

This means then that the effort should be just enough for the purpose of mindfulness and knowledge. But how much is enough? I think it was William Blake who said this: "One never knows what is enough until one knows what is more than enough." And a measure of what is enough may perhaps be supplied by the words of the Buddha when he spoke on how a monk should endeavor.

> Monks, if his turban or hair were on fire he would make

*an intense desire, effort, endeavor, exertion, struggle,
mindfulness, and attentiveness to extinguish the fire.
Even so, an intense desire, effort, endeavor, exertion,
struggle, mindfulness, and attentiveness is to be made by
him so as to give up every evil and wrong state.*

Because he knew how much effort was required, because he was
familiar with the propensity to slackness on the part of the yogi,
the Sunlun Sayadaw instructed: "Be rigorously mindful." To be
mindful rigorously is to mobilize all of one's resources, to grasp the
processes as they are without thinking or reflecting. Rigorousness
calls forth the element of energy or right effort.

Another inclination of the yogi is to fidget. He likes to scratch, to
shift, or, if he is breathing, he likes to stop, then start and stop
again. These are signs of distraction. These indicate that mindfulness has not been thoroughly established. To remind the yogi that
the distraction is to be avoided and the agitation stilled, Sunlun
Sayadaw instructed: "Do not scratch when itched, nor shift when
cramped, nor pause when tired." He required the yogi who feels
the itch, cramp, or tiredness to breathe harder if he is breathing or
to plunge the mind deeper into the sensation if he is watching the
sensation, and thereby, with increased attention to the performance of the task, to develop more intense mindfulness. The
Visuddhi Magga meditation manual says that by getting up and so
disturbing the posture, the meditator has to start the meditation
anew. The yogi who sits down to meditate, then an hour later gets
up to walk away the sensations of sitting, then another hour later
sits down to think away the sensations of walking, keeps disturbing the posture. Whatever sensation arises in the sitting posture
has to be watched in the sitting posture until it has phased itself
out. Whatever sensation arises in the standing posture has to be
watched in the standing posture until it has phased itself out.

Remaining still with attention riveted to the awareness of touch
or sensation calls forth the element of mindfulness. It is the essential element in practice, right mindfulness.

There is a third behavior characteristic of the yogi. After the
lower hindrances have been removed, lights, colors, and geometrical patterns appear to the yogi. On the one hand, there is the
fascination of the yogi for these things which have never appeared
to him like this before. On the other hand, these lights, colors, and
patterns are attractive. Because of these two forces, the yogi begins
to turn his attention to the lights and patterns, he gazes on them,

he dwells in them. And with this turning away from the object of meditation, he abandons his original purpose.

In like manner, after a period of practice, when the yogi has cleansed his mind somewhat, he will begin to experience a measure of calm and tranquility. Since he has never before experienced such peace of mind he thinks that this is the best fruit of the practice. Because of this appreciation of the experience and because the measure of calm and tranquility attained is attractive in itself, the yogi begins to dwell in it, to savor the calmness to the full. He likes to sink in the sense of peace and hates to put forth the necessary effort to get back again onto the right path. Sunlun Sayadaw illustrated this with a local simile. Myingyan River beach is a stretch of sand a mile wide. A traveler to the river finds the sand exceedingly hot beneath his feet under the raging noonday sun. On the way he comes to a tree. He decides to rest in its shade for a moment. But when that moment has passed he finds that he cannot urge himself to get up to move out of that cool shade into the heat which rages above and beneath him. So he continues to dwell in the shade. But will this ever help him to reach the riverside? The destination can be reached only if he steps out again into the heat and urges his body forward. That is why the meditation masters warn the yogi not to let himself be drawn by the minor calm and tranquility he finds along the way. There was once a yogi who habitually drifted into this area of tranquility and would not budge out of it. The Sunlun Sayadaw said of him: "This man keeps lifting up the tail and patting the behind of the little iguana he has caught." I hope the distinguished yogis will not be satisfied with a mere iguana.

With a further increase in the clarity and purity of the mind the yogi sometimes becomes more perceptive to extrasensual things. It is not the true divine sight and divine hearing that he attains but it is a power somewhat similar to these. Because of this power the yogi can see what others cannot see, he can hear what others cannot hear. People come to consult him and his predictions come true. He becomes a sort of shaman. Thus has he degenerated from a Vipassana yogi to a shaman. But after some time, as the distractions of the new vocation grow more varied and the practice of meditation becomes less intense, the answers turn out to be less and less accurate, and gradually the clients go away, never to return. The yogi is left with an interrupted practice.

Many are the occasions in which the yogi indulges in self-deception. Though he should practice intensively, he deceives

96

himself that the goal of liberation can be won in a leisurely manner. Though he should sit still, he deceives himself that a slight shift or movement can do no harm. Perhaps he is right for the initial crude moments of the practice but for the peak in each phase of practice the smallest wavering of mindfulness can bring down the structure of meditation and the edifice will need to be set up again. Since he can deceive himself in these matters of the body, how much more so can he do it in the subtle mental matters? A strong inclination for the yogi is to take the first signs of progress on the path to be signs indicating the higher stages. For instance, unpleasant sensation can snap abruptly. For one moment there is the intense unpleasantness of the sensation; the next moment it is gone, snuffed out, and in its place there is a deep sense of calm and quiet. The yogi often likes to believe that this is the post-mental functioning of the enlightenment knowledge. And he notches for himself one stage of the four enlightened stages.

97

This wrong assignment of the phases of practice can be made also because the meditation master himself is not thoroughly versed in such matters or because his instructions and the teachings in the books are not understood well. However it is, the yogi likes to classify himself as having attained at least one or two of the enlightenment stages. And with this thought in mind he goes about seeking confirmation of his belief. And woe to the meditation master who, however gently and indirectly, makes his failings known to him. Sunlun Sayadaw would never pass judgment on anyone, whether or not that yogi had really attained the said phase or stage. His only remark would be: "If it is so, it is so." In any case, a true attainment would need no confirmation from another source. The yogi would know it himself. Likewise, a wrong sense of attainment would not need debunking; the yogi would realize it for himself.

The main danger of this form of self-deception is the wrong sense of achievement that it gives to the yogi. Satisfied with what he thinks has been his progress, he relaxes his practice and is thus stranded on the path without having gained any progress of real value.

There is one pet hate of the yogi, and that is unpleasant sensation. Let him face slight feelings of cramp, heat, or muscular tension, and he will try to be mindful of it for some time. But give him the pain within the marrow of the bone, the burning sensation, the sharp excruciating pain along the limbs, and he will abandon them in a few minutes. As usual, he is ready with his excuses and the quotation of chapter and verse. Who says one must employ unpleasant sensation as an object of meditation, he wants to know. Cannot a yogi attain whatever is to be attained by working on pleasant sensation? Who says one should suffer so much? Is this not self-mortification?

The answer is that if a yogi is so well blessed with karma to be one who can tread the pleasant path, one who can gain wisdom without undergoing pain, then he can work on pleasant sensation. But for the overwhelming majority of us, as may be observed, there is no choice but to tread the path of unpleasant sensation, for we are not blessed with such karma.

Actually there should be no cause for regret. Unpleasant sensation is an efficacious object of meditation which takes the yogi steadily up the path to the attainment of the final goal. The very fact that the yogi does not normally like unpleasant sensation can be employed by him to establish a deeper and more intense mindfulness. Made to work with an object he does not like, he will remember to arouse the necessary zeal to overcome the unpleasant sensation. It is different with pleasant sensation. Because he likes it, he will tend to sink in it, to suffuse himself with its pleasantness without trying to be mindful of it. When he does that, the greed and lust that are latent in pleasant sensation will overwhelm him. The yogi will not be able to hold on to sensation as sensation, but sensation will carry him forward to originate the next link of desire in the chain leading to further births.

It is as though a swimmer in a strong current were asked to grasp the bunch of flowers at the winning post. If he were swimming with the current and stretched out his hand to grasp the flowers and missed, he would be carried beyond the point by the force of the current. If he were swimming against the current and missed when he stretched out his hand to grasp the flowers, he would still be below them and thus have an opportunity to try again consciously and deliberately. The swimmer with the current is like the yogi who employs pleasant sensation. If he is unable to be mindful of pleasant sensation he will be carried beyond by clinging to it. The swimmer against the current is like the yogi who employs unpleasant sensation. If he is unable to be mindful of unpleasant sensation as it is in itself, he will still be conscious of it and will be able to summon up the energy and mindfulness to accomplish his mission.

---

[4] See "Mogok Sayadaw."

Pleasant sensation is like a hidden enemy; it catches the yogi unawares. Unpleasant sensation is like a conspicuous foe; the yogi can recognize it and take corrective action so that anger which is latent in unpleasant sensation does not get an opportunity to rise. Between natural dislike of unpleasant sensation and a zealous effort to establish mindfulness, the yogi will neither immerse himself in it nor flinch from it. He will be able to detach himself completely from the unpleasant sensation, dwelling within the sensation, watching the sensation, without thinking any thought connected with the sensation. Unpleasant sensation serves as a firm hitching post for the mind which inclines to wander. An unpleasant sensation will never deceive the yogi about the true nature of phenomena—unpleasantness.

99

Also, there should be no cause for fear of unpleasant sensation. There are techniques to arouse a sufficient depth and intensity of mindfulness to overcome the infliction and hurt of unpleasant sensation. This infliction is due to the identification of the yogi with the area of pain and the effect of unpleasant sensation. But when mindfulness has been established sufficiently to penetrate the sensation and eliminate the identification with the notion of a personality, an 'I' which can be hurt, then unpleasant sensation becomes only an unpleasant sensation and no more a source of pain.

The ultimate purpose of meditation is to eliminate the illusive notion of 'I'. A yogi has to chip at the notion of 'I' again and again in these struggles with unpleasant sensation. Let us say the unpleasant sensation rises. The yogi keeps mindful of it until the unpleasant sensation is consumed. Thereby, the cause is killed in the effect. He does it again and again until with perfect proficiency he finally manages to kill the cause in the cause, to end the cause in the cause, so that it can never again give rise to an effect which will only turn out to be another cause in the endless chain. This killing of the cause in the cause is enlightenment. And it is because of this quality of efficiency in eliminating the false notion of 'I', Sunlun Sayadaw stated: "The uncomfortable truly is the norm; the comfortable will set you all adrift on the currents of samsara." Unpleasant sensation is the yogi's internal enemy. Once the internal enemy can be overcome, the external sources of suffering cannot touch him anymore.

After a period of ardent practice, there comes a moment when the true liberating knowledge is offered to the yogi. These moments come only to the very few. To arrive at this moment, the yogi must have completely perfected the establishment of mindfulness of the body. He must have completely perfected the establishment of the foundation of mindfulness of the sensations. This means that he must have perfectly overcome the unpleasant sensation. Unpleasant sensations are the greatest obstacles confronting the yogi in his progress along the path. This is where he keeps falling back. To overcome them, he needs to possess unflinching energy, resolve, and intentness, as well as the right technique. Then these sensations equip the yogi with sufficient powers of concentration and mindfulness to deal with the subtle processes of the next phase, the establishment of mindfulness of consciousness. When mindfulness of consciousness has been completed perfectly, he will be offered the task of establishing the foundations of mindfulness of mental objects and fundamental principles. Here comes that awful moment of truth. If the yogi is not perfectly establishing mindfulness of the principles, when liberating knowledge is offered to him he will shy away from it, he will fail to grasp it. But if he has fully perfected the establishment of the four aspects of awareness,[5] and he has fully developed the seven factors of enlightenment, then in that very moment of perfecting and acquiring these seven there will arise in him the true liberating knowledge.

Unfortunately, less than perfect behavior characteristics are typical of the yogi. He is disinclined to endeavor ardently, is quick to fidget, eager to follow after lights and colors, prone to rest in areas of calm, ready to exaggerate minor successes, willing to misuse subsidiary power, liable to give himself the benefit of the doubt, afraid of unpleasant sensation, and terrified and clumsy when the real moment of truth is offered. We do not need to search for this yogi elsewhere; we are the prototype. It is us who would like to reap the benefits of meditation but are unwilling to sow the good seed; it is us who wish to gather the returns but who do not wish to lay down the investment. We wish to talk ourselves to a goal which can only be reached by high endeavor; we wish to deceive ourselves into a situation which will permit the entry of only the perfectly truthful.

Does this mean then that the goal will forever be beyond our reach? That is not so. Where Sunlun Sayadaw has trodden, we too can tread. We need only to follow his instructions faithfully. Sunlun Sayadaw instructed us:

Be rigorously mindful of the awareness of touch.

[5] *See "Achaan Dhammadaro."*

We should be rigorously, ardently, intensively mindful.
Do not rest when tired, scratch when itched, nor shift
when cramped.
We should keep our bodies and minds absolutely still and
strive till the end.
The uncomfortable truly is the norm; the comfortable
will set us adrift on the current of illusion.

101

We should penetrate unpleasant sensation; only he who has penetrated sensation will see processes as they are.

We should generate a willing suspension of disbelief, exert that extra ounce of effort, and be rigorously mindful. Have faith, energy, and awareness to purify ourselves, to overcome pain and grief, to reach the right path, to win nirvana.

DEVELOPING THE SUNLUN WAY OF MINDFULNESS

In this age, the objects of desire and aversion impinge upon the senses with increasing force and growing variety. There is a greater urge and opportunity for the gratification of the senses. The accelerating pace of living and the increasing pressure create stresses leading to anxiety and neurosis. City life is becoming noisier and noise is a thorn in the flesh of concentration. At the same time the people do not have enough leisure for a long and sustained practice of mindfulness. The result is an increasing diversion of the attention and diffusion of mental powers with less and less time even for minimum corrective action. To cap it all, people who are born in these days long after the Buddha are of sluggish intuition rather than of quick intuition. Therefore there is an urgent need for a way of mindfulness which takes into account the growing urges and commodities for sense-gratification, increasing noise and distraction, lack of time, and the meditator's own sluggish intuition.

Sunlun Sayadaw's way of mindfulness provides a technique to quickly overcome sloth and desires of the senses. It raises the threshold over which noise and distraction must pass to divert the attention of the meditator. For the man of sluggish intuition it provides an amazingly sure and rapid method for the complete and perfect establishment of the four foundations of mindfulness.

It is not a method fashioned out of the elements available in the books. It is a method forged in the struggle against self-love and ignorance. Sunlun Sayadaw was a barely literate man and was thus blessed by not being sicklied with the pale cast of thought. With earnestness, courage, and perseverance he became liberated in 1920. The technique is now available to the city man who is without the overwhelming courage and perseverance of the Sunlun Sayadaw. What follows is a very brief sketch of the method.

Posture Assume a meditative posture which can be maintained for some time without change. Do not lie in bed nor recline in a chair. The posture should be one which will permit the gathering together and assumption of all of one's resources. The posture should be one designed for hard work and not relaxation. A suitable posture is to sit with legs crossed. The back should be straight. The arms should be held close against the side of the body. The right fist should be held in the left hand. This is to facilitate the clenching of the fist as the meditator summons his strength to combat unpleasant sensation which may arise later. Do not mesh the fingers of the hands nor hold them lightly with each thumb against the other. Let the head be slightly bowed. Do not sit loosely. Assume a tight posture where the body provides a firm base, its circuit is closed and the meditator is alert.

Select a spot where the meditation session can be concluded without disturbance. It is better to select a quiet place out of the wind, but that is not essential. Meditation may be done individually or in a group. No elaborate preparation of the place is required nor should it be made a ritual.

There are no set periods for meditation. Time should be arranged to suit the meditator's convenience. But he should take care that the meditation hour or two is not sacrificed to some other purpose. Western books suggest that the beginner should start with a session of two or three minutes a day, the period to be gradually extended. Sunlun's experience is that an intensive initial session of an hour or so produces more beneficial results. A normal session should not be less than an hour or two. Those practicing intensively sit through the whole day or night.

After the posture has been selected and assumed it should not be changed or altered in any way. It will have to be kept up until the end of the session. Sunlun Sayadaw has said: "If cramped don't move, if itchy don't scratch, if fatigued don't rest."

Breathing Commence by inhaling. It will be noticed that the breath touches the nostril tip or upper lip. Be keenly mindful of the touch of breath. With mindfulness vigilantly maintained, breathe strongly, firmly, and rapidly. Strong, hard, and rapid breathing wards off external noises, helps to control the mind, quickly removes the hindrances, rapidly establishes concentration, and enables the meditator to cope with the unpleasant sensation which may arise later.

103

Strong, hard, and rapid breathing will cause inhaled and exhaled breath to touch with increased friction against the tips of the nostril holes, the upper lip, or some other part of the body in that region. Be mindful of that touch of breath.

"When the breath touches the nostril tip or upper lip you will be aware of it. Be mindful of that awareness," said the Sunlun Sayadaw. Let not a single touch pass without awareness. Be aware of every single touch. Mindfulness should be rigorous. It should not be relaxed. This means that there should be putting forth of energy, that the meditator should be ardent and zealous.

Do not let the awareness be of the breath-body. Do not follow it in and out of the body. Do not count its entrances and exits. Do not take note of the area of touch of breath whether it be the nostril tip or upper lip. Let awareness be only of the sensation of touch of breath. Be mindful only of the sensation of touch.

Breathe in air attentively and fully as though water were being drawn into a syringe. Exhale sharply. Full and hard drawing-in of breath helps to establish concentration rapidly. It helps the sensations to arise. It provides strength in the coming struggle with unpleasant sensation. Since most people have stronger exhalation it is necessary to pay greater attention in inhalation to realize a balance between inhalation and exhalation. When these two are balanced, the touch will be continuous. When they are balanced, the meditator will have reached the stage of smooth, effortless, self-compelled rhythmic breathing. Breathe without shaking the head and body. This will obtain concentration quickly.

Fatigue may set in at the early stages of strong, hard, rapid breathing but the meditator should neither stop nor reduce the strength and rapidity of breathing. "Don't rest when fatigued," said the Sunlun Sayadaw. The fatigue is probably due to either insufficient strength of inhalation or to excessive blowing on exhalation. The remedy is to increase the strength of inhalation. When inhalation and exhalation strengths are balanced at a high level, the fatigue will disappear. The meditator will then have broken

out of the zone of difficult breathing into the zone of smooth, effortless, self-compelled rhythmic breathing. Attention can then be addressed wholly to mindfulness of touch of breath. There are three
levels of breathing: high (very strong, hard, rapid breathing);
medium (strong, hard, rapid); and low (weak, soft, slow, or the
common way of breathing). Since man is not a machine he will
sometimes flag and falter. It is necessary to reach the high level
early so that later, when the pace falls, the meditator will reach the
balanced, medium level of respiration and be able to maintain it.

104

Do not preset the time for breathing. On firm, rapid breathing,
unpleasant sensations will rise within oneself. These unpleasant
sensations may assume the forms of pain, cramp, ache, numbness,
heat or cold, or some other sensation. Continue the breathing until
there is sufficient sensation to stop the strong respiration. Here
sensation is the clock to time the period of respiration. Alternatively, the meditator may preset the time for breathing, say three-
quarters of an hour or an hour, at which time he will proceed to the
second part of the meditation. But this is not as preferable as the
first method.

When it is about time to stop strong respiration, 50 or 100
strokes of breath should be made—this time with all the strength
at the meditator's command. Meanwhile, mindfulness of touch of
breath should be relentless. Then respiration should be stopped
suddenly on the inhaled breath and, collecting oneself, the whole
body should be watched internally.

Sensation Respiration should be stopped completely and suddenly
on inhaled breath. The body should be stilled, gathered together,
and watched rigorously. Sensations of pain, cramp, ache, numbness, or heat or cold will arise in the body. Be mindful of the most
pronounced sensation. Do not let it go. Do not switch the attention
to the navel, the solar plexus, nor any other region. It is natural for
the most pronounced sensation to demand one's attention. Turning to the other regions which do not have the most pronounced
sensation makes one lose grasp of the immediate present.

"If the sensation is weak, know the fact of its weakness. If the
sensation is strong, know the fact of its strength," said the Sunlun
Sayadaw. Know neither less nor more. Know it only as it is. Know
whatever arises, as it arises, when it arises, in the bare fact of its
arising. Be mindful of just this. Let no thoughts of 'me' and 'mine'
interfere. Do not think that this is one's foot or one's body or one's
hand. Do not reflect "this is body and mind." Do not consider "this

is impermanence, this sufferingness, and this non-self." All thinking, reflection, and consideration are conceptual. They are not insight practice.

Sunlun makes direct, immediate contact with reality. It cannot afford the time and effort required first to build a conceptual bridge to approach reality. Confronted with the elephant of its search, it does not follow the footprints backwards and then retrace them again to the elephant. When there arises an ache it immediately catches hold of the fact of the ache; it does not formulate the concept 'aching, aching' and then return to the fact of the ache. Therefore it tells the meditator: "Avoid name-calling; do not conceptualize reality."

Neither reach toward the sensation nor reach after it. Be mindful of the sensation in the immediacy of its arising or vanishing which is in the present time, the now. In the struggle with unpleasant sensation which may rage with extreme force and virulence the meditator takes care that he does not reach beyond the sensation. This is to say that the effort exerted should not exceed that which is necessary to maintain firm attention. When there is an excess of energy it is as though the meditator had placed his effort before the unpleasant sensation, with the result that the attention slips from the sensation itself and all that remains is the violence of his effort. This violence is none other than anger. And anger is one of the forces which turn the wheel of samsara.

The meditator should take care on the other hand that he does not fall short of the sensation. This is to say that the effort exerted should not fall short of that which is necessary to maintain firm attention. When the effort is inadequate the meditator slips back into torpor and sloth or is overwhelmed by the unpleasant sensation if the sensation is intense. Severe unpleasant sensation which is not held with mindfulness gives rise to fear, anxiety, and anger, which all constitute a force which turns the wheel of samsara. Torpor and sloth are the basis of ignorance, yet another force which conditions rebirth and delusion.

Therefore the meditator must take great care not to reach beyond nor fall short of the sensation. He must exert that forceful and vigilant attention necessary for knowledge and mindfulness. This means that the time relation of attention to sensation should not be one of future or past but of the simple, immediate present. This is realized when, instead of being passively attentive to the arising of the sensation and to its disintegrating future, the meditator tends actively to perceive the very birth of the sensation.

When dealing with the arising of many sensations simultaneously, such as in the head, the arm, the body, and the legs, the unguided meditator's mind will run helter-skelter after them and there will be no mindfulness of them right here and now. The result will be personal distress and suffering. To avoid this there should be mindfulness of only the most pronounced sensation. Vigorous awareness of it should be aroused and this awareness vigilantly watched by mindfulness. The meditator should be able to penetrate into the sensation to realize its nature. Effort is required to do this. The simile is of a nail being driven into wood. The wood is sensation, the nail is the mind, the finger which holds the nail straight is mindfulness, and the hammer is effort.

When the mind has penetrated into the sensation, the meditator will no longer feel the form of his foot, arm, or body; he will no longer feel that 'I' am suffering. These conceptual notions will be replaced by a simple, clear awareness of sensation alone. Because the idea of an 'I' which suffers has been removed, the meditator will not feel the discomfort of the unpleasant sensation. The sensation which a few moments ago was felt as pain or burning will now be felt by the meditator only as an intense sensation without the element of infliction.

Of the three sensations—unpleasant, pleasant, and neutral—the last is most subtle and not normally suitable for ordinary people as an initial object for the establishment of mindfulness. When it arises in the succeeding stages of development the meditator will have to be mindful of it as it arises and when it arises. But by then the meditator should have developed the power to grasp subtle neutral sensation.

As we have noted, unpleasant sensation is the greatest obstacle on the road of Vipassana. Only when the meditator is able to overcome that obstacle can he forge forward to attain the rewards beyond unpleasant sensation. It is possible to completely overcome and learn from unpleasant sensation. Since unpleasant sensation too is subject to the Law of Impermanence it must come to an end some time. This end can occur in various ways. Its intensity can subside; but this would not be a true ending. Some measure of unpleasant sensation would remain. The real overcoming of unpleasant sensation takes place when the meditator dwells in the sensation, watching the sensation without thinking any thought connected with the sensation, and it is consumed, it ends, it snaps, it is shed or extinguished. It is said to be consumed when it gradually subsides until there is no remainder. It ends when the

meditator follows it until there is no more of it, like a road followed to the end, like a length of string felt along the whole length
till no more is felt. It snaps when it breaks off suddenly, as when a
taut rope is snapped. It is shed like the skin of a snake. It is extinguished like a light which has used up its oil and wick.

Pain is unpleasant, ache is unpleasant, heat is unpleasant, cold is
unpleasant. Within the unpleasantness of all these there is an element of discomfort. It is this underlying element of discomfort   107
which is basic to all our experience. The meditator who feels
fatigue in his limbs and wishes to alter his position, or whose mind
being confined to the narrow point of touch wishes to be let loose
among sensual objects, desires escape from the discomfort of his
posture and confined mind. But how can one attain enlightenment
and escape from the pain of this mind-body process by hankering
after the delights and comforts of the senses? "The uncomfortable
truly is the norm; the comfortable will set you all adrift on the
current of samsara," said Sunlun Sayadaw. He was referring to the
efficacy of suffering to overcome suffering.

How should one be mindful of unpleasant sensation in order to
consume it, end it, snap it, shed it, extinguish it? The only answer
is that the meditator should be rigorously mindful of unpleasant
sensation as it arises, when it arises, in the here and now. But how
does one hold steadfast the mind which flinches from unpleasant
sensation? How does one catch unpleasant sensation in the very
moment of its arising in the very manner of its arising?

First, in being mindful of unpleasant sensation, collect the body
and mind together and keep both perfectly still. Watch the unpleasant sensation with bated breath. Hold the breath as long as
you can easily hold it. This is not an exercise in breath retention. It
is just the normal practice effected in carrying out the common
duties of life. Whenever something is done with great attention the
breath is naturally held back. For example, in putting a thread
through a needle hole, the operator normally holds his breath till
the task is accomplished. In like manner, the meditator should
watch unpleasant sensation with bated breath. This will enable
him to exercise greater awareness and more rigorous mindfulness.

If the unpleasant sensation is too intense for proper attention
with bated breath the meditator should stiffen himself against it.
He tenses his whole body against the sensation to support the work
of the mind. He holds his arms tighter against the sides of his body,
he closes his fists, he stiffens his neck and clenches his teeth. He
puts forth energy as he would in a physical struggle against a

strong opponent. All the time he keeps rigorously mindful of the sensation.

If the unpleasant sensation is excruciating and cannot be overcome by endeavor with bated breath and tensed body, the meditator should brace his mind against it. Just as in breathing he had respired strongly and firmly, so also in applying his mind to unpleasant sensation he should do it strongly and firmly. He should pit the resources of his breath, his body, and his mind against the sensation. With bated breath, tensed body, and fortified mind he should exert pressure against the pressure of the sensation until he is able to penetrate it, to dwell in it, watch it without thinking any thought connected with it, until finally the sensation is completely consumed or ended.

It will be noticed that the important element in the technique is intentness. The meditator should put forth unflinching energy; he should be ardent, zealous, earnest, and energetic. He should be all that the Buddha required of his disciples. Escape from delusion is not achieved through reflective, considerate, relaxed effort. It is achieved only through the most powerful and sustained thrust of all the physical and mental capabilities at the meditator's command. Sunlun calls for just this.

Though intentness is called for in regard to mental objects of meditation, it will not be necessary also to stir up physical force in being mindful of emotional feeling. However, it will still be necessary to stir up zeal and earnestness for unremitting mindfulness. For the meditator whose training with unpleasant sensation has helped him to develop those qualities, the practice of mindfulness of emotional feelings should not be difficult. Moreover, since emotional feeling is usually accompanied by unpleasant physical sensations, the meditator may turn his attention to those physical sensations and thus overcome attachment to emotions through the conquest of unpleasant physical sensation.

Beyond Sensation When the meditator perfectly dwells in sensation, watching the sensation without thinking any thought connected with the sensation, and the sensation snaps or is completely extinguished, the meditator's mind becomes cleansed, purged, firm, and serviceable. He becomes full of loving-kindness for all living things and he is able to suffuse them with true loving-kindness, which is not mere repetition of words, which is without craving and self-identification, and which is without differentiation between a person whom the meditator hates, one whom he likes, and one to whom he is indifferent.

With cleansed, purged, firm, and serviceable mind he contemplates consciousness in consciousness. He knows consciousness with lust as with lust; he knows consciousness without lust as without lust; he knows consciousness with hate as with hate; he knows consciousness without hate as without hate. He knows when lust and hate have arisen and keeps mindful of them so that they may not be the cause to further originate lust and hate and thus give another turn to the wheel of samsara. This is killing the causative force in the effect. When he comes into contact with an object which could arouse lust or hate he keeps rigorously mindful of it so that lust or hate cannot arise. This is killing the cause in cause.

With this last act of mindfulness he perfectly practices what the scriptures instruct: "In what is seen there should be only the seen; in what is heard only the heard; in what is sensed only the sensed; in what is thought only the thought." He is able to do this because he has cleansed his mind and made it firm and serviceable through ardent mindfulness of unpleasant sensation. For the common meditator with sluggish intuition, trying to see only the seen in what is seen is extremely difficult if practiced as the initial exercise in mindfulness. This is because consciousness is a subtle object of contemplation and not readily grasped or held with the impure, weak, and unmanageable mind. But when the mind of the meditator has been strengthened through mindfulness of unpleasant sensation he is able to hold the seen as the seen, the heard as the heard, the thought as the thought.

It has been suggested that if during the practice of mindfulness distractions should arise, the mind should follow after them to take note of them. Theoretically it should be possible to follow each distraction to grasp it mindfully. However, in practice, it is extremely difficult for the distracted mind to be mindful of whatever had distracted it. If it had been powerfully concentrated it would not at all have been distracted away from its originally selected object of meditation. Moreover, in taking note of the distraction, the meditator often runs the risk of believing that he is being mindful of the distraction whereas he is in fact being drawn along by it. Therefore the safest and most effective method is to generate additional zeal to be more mindful of the initial object of meditation, the touch or sensation.

With respect to the contemplation of mental elements, these are yet more subtle than consciousness. Contemplation of mental elements may be said to be a practice arising out of the ardent mindfulness of sensation. During the period of energetic mindfulness of sensation, the mental elements of the five hindrances[6] may arise. When sensation has been consumed or ended, the factors of enlightenment[7] may appear. The meditator will have to be mindful of these elements as they arise and disappear. If the hindrance of anger arises, the meditator does not make a mental note that it is 'anger'; he merely keeps vigilantly aware of the fact of anger. If the detachment factor of enlightenment arises, the meditator keeps vigilantly aware of the fact of detachment. Here again the meditator will be able to accomplish his mission well because he has developed a powerful concentration and a clear and firm mind from the practice of mindfulness of sensation.

In fact the four stations of mindfulness—body, sensation, consciousness, and mental elements do not arise independently of each other. They arise together in association. When the meditator is being mindful of the awareness of touch there is in it the station of the body, the station of sensation, the station of consciousness, and the station of the mental elements. Being mindful of one, the meditator is mindful of all the others. It is as in a glass of sherbet the four elements of water, lemon, sugar, and salt are present together in association. And when one element is dominant, the sherbet is called respectively watery, sour, sweet, or salty. When sensation is dominant it is called mindfulness of feeling; when consciousness is dominant it is called mindfulness of consciousness, and so on.

When mindfulness of the four stations are completed and perfected, the meditator develops fully the seven factors of enlightenment. When the seven factors of enlightenment are completely and perfectly developed, the meditator attains enlightenment. However this is a future result, and further consideration to this matter need not be given in this brief sketch of the Sunlun way of mindfulness. If a mango seed is sown, a mango tree will sprout. A man should give all his attention to sowing well the best mango seed he can obtain. The result will take care of itself.

Conclusion The Sunlun way of mindfulness is practiced by an ardent monk or layman throughout the day and night. For the less ardent meditator, the centers offer five to seven sessions a day,

[6] *See Glossary.*
[7] *See Chapter One.*

each session lasting from one to three hours. The man who is too busy with affairs of work or business should be able to practice it twice a day. Meanwhile, the mind should not be left unguarded in the hours between sessions. The meditator should endeavor to be continually mindful. He accomplishes this by being mindful of the sense of touch. At no moment of the day will his body not be in contact with an object. If he is sitting, his body will be in touch with the chair. If he is lying, his head will be in touch with the pillow. If he is walking, his feet will touch the ground on each step. If he is handling a tool or an object, his fingers will touch it. The meditator should be mindful of touch of body against chair, of head against pillow, of feet against ground, of fingers against tool or object. He should, if possible, be mindful of touch of visual object against the eye, of sound against ear, of taste against tongue, of smell against nose. "Be rigorously mindful of the awareness of touch," said the Sunlun Sayadaw.

Sunlun is a simple system; it is as simple as drawing a line or writing an O. Even the child's first attempts with paper and pencil are drawing lines or circles. But to draw a perfectly straight line and a perfectly round circle is extremely difficult. Yet when one practices it with sufficient earnestness and zeal, quick results can be obtained. Most other methods are difficult to describe, and though easy to perform, the results come slow. Sunlun is easy to describe. Literature on Sunlun is almost non-existent. There is in Burmese just a pamphlet describing the method and a small book on the life of the Sunlun Sayadaw. Since the method is easy to describe and there is very little theorizing, there has not been much use for books. Sunlun is difficult to perform. By this is not meant that the sequence of operations are complex; they are simple. This means only that it is not a relaxed, comfortable method. It calls for courage to face the discomfort of strong breathing and unpleasant sensation, zeal to pass beyond them, and unremitting mindfulness to accomplish the purpose. But when this is done well, and it can be done well, the results are rapidly gained because Sunlun makes immediate and direct contact with reality and also stirs up the meditator's zeal to help him move forward at an intense pace.

For the lazy man of today who has little time to spare for anything whatsoever, who with his conceptualization, logicalism, and rationalism is moving further away from the root source of reality and knowledge, Sunlun offers much. It makes him throw away his thought-systems to grasp directly and immediately the actuality of things. It pulls taut, mobilizes, and uses his great physical and mental reserves. It gives him the means and strength to withstand the vicissitudes of life. It strikes at the heart of that deceptive, self-loving illusive notion of 'I' which is the cause of all misery and unsatisfactoriness.

Sunlun is an intense, resolute, zealous method to establish the four foundations of mindfulness for "the purification of beings, for the overcoming of sorrow and misery, for the destruction of pain and grief, for reaching the right path, for the attainment of nirvana."

112

"Be rigorously mindful of the awareness of touch."

QUESTIONS AND ANSWERS

Question: Why is it that when we start the deep breathing, for the first few minutes we feel very tired; then when we breathe longer we no longer feel tired?
Answer: We feel tired when our breathing is not balanced; usually the out-breath tends to be stronger than the in-breath. Inhalation should be increased. Once we establish proper breathing balance, once our breathing becomes rhythmic, we no longer feel tired and in fact we can go on breathing for a long time.

Q: Why do we stop our breathing with an in-breath?
A: So that we can gather our energies together to grapple with the sensations. If we stop on an out-breath we are likely to be relaxed, which is not good for mindfulness.

Q: When we sit in certain positions we feel strong sensations such as cramps. Do we sit on until the sensations subside, and how long do such sensations last?
A: Yes, we should let all sensations subside. The length of time depends on individuals. Some take only a short time; others may take hours. Any sensation that arises is natural and we should not be afraid but should be mindful and patient. We should sit and not move, and should keep our mindfulness on the sensations until they disappear completely.

Q: Sometimes after the most pronounced sensation has worn off, there is left some numbness, say in the foot. Should we continue till this too has gone?

A: Yes, you should continue until all sensations have gone. You may have to sit a long time for all the sensations to go, but this is necessary. Of course, if you are able to establish rigorous and intense mindfulness it does not take so much time. Intentness is important.

113

Q: But if we do not have the time to sit so long, can we stop before the numbness disappears entirely?

A: You can, though it is not good; your body may feel heavy and your mind not fully purified. If you do not have enough time, you need not breathe for too long to start with. Your sensations may not then be too pronounced, and you may not have to sit for very long for all sensations to disappear. But then you are not really doing what you should and there may arise feelings of dissatisfaction with the practice or with yourself.

Q: I have found that I can make my sensations go by simply stretching my legs for example. Why do I then have to sit till they disappear?

A: The essence of meditation is to grapple with sensations to overcome them. We can of course make the sensations disappear by simply moving our legs, our arms, or our body, but in this way we are not grappling with our sensations. We are trying to escape from them, and in doing so we come up against new sensations. We have to know that we cannot escape from any sensation, that what we cannot escape from is the suffering inherent in our body, and that the only way is to face up to it and win through to insight, to liberation.

Q: What is meant by mindfulness? Is it, for example, meditation on the cause of the sensation that arises in us?

A: Certainly not. Mindfulness is alert awareness and holding rigorously on to this awareness without any conceptual notion, without any thought whatever.

Q: What is the difference between Samatha meditation and Vipassana meditation?

A: Samatha meditation is concentration on objects, ideas, and images. Vipassana meditation uses the power of concentration primarily on sensations within the body. Samatha makes the mind powerful, while Vipassana purifies the mind to enable it to gain insight. A person who succeeds with pure concentration will for example be very persuasive in arguments, and everybody will be influenced by him, but usually reaction will come later. With Vipassana it is different; a person who succeeds in Vipassana is so clearly full of insight and knowledge that he will be listened to without any doubt appearing either then or later.

114

Q: Is it possible for a person practicing Vipassana to go into Samatha?
A: Samatha uses concentration as its main support, while Vipassana uses the two legs of concentration and sensation. One who practices concentration can do so without Vipassana, but one who practices Vipassana uses concentration to some extent, to obtain the instant-to-instant concentration, and trains this concentration on the sensation. As long as you keep on this path you will not go into pure concentration. But if you lean entirely on the leg of concentration you can go into the path of Samatha. You may see colors, images, etc., and you may become distracted. The trouble is that those who go into Samatha may feel that they are achieving something, whereas in fact their experiences tend to become obstacles in the path of true liberation. It is difficult for a person who is well developed in Samatha to advance in Vipassana. The only way to help such a person is to teach him to lean on the leg of mindfulness as well.

Q: What should we do if the sensations are too intense to bear?
A: Patience, perseverance—these are the qualities required to stand up to sensations however intense they may be, and to overcome them. Be mindful, and sensation will disappear, even the most intense sensations. The more intense the sensation which has been overcome, the clearer will be the resultant mind.

Q: If firm attention is maintained on bodily sensations, that is, if we can be aware of the sensations without the mind intervening, how are we to be benefited in our mind?
A: It is not a question of the intervention of the mind, it is a matter of a way of functioning of the mind. The mind should continue to function through the operation of awareness. Its thinking function should not interfere; there should be no thinking of thoughts about the sensation. If we are mindful of whatever sensation, when the sensation subsides the mind becomes cleansed and firm; whence

arises loving-kindness and calm. Besides, sensations are not only bodily sensations; there are mental sensations as well, but these are better left to a later stage.

Q: How can we be mindful in our everyday life?
A: When we walk our feet touch the ground; be mindful of this touch. When we hold an object, there is the touch on the hand; when we see an object, there is the touch on the eyes; when we hear a sound, there is the touch on the ears; when we smell an odor, there is the touch on the nostrils; when we eat, there is the touch on the tip of the tongue. We can be mindful in these and in many other ways. But it is best to be mindful of touch on any part of the body. This is easier to grasp and hold.

115

Q: What are the benefits of this form of meditation?
A: The benefits of this form of meditation are the purification of oneself, the overcoming of sorrow and misery, the destruction of pain and grief, reaching the right path, and the attainment of nirvana. By purification is meant the cleansing of the mind and the strengthening of the moral sense. The mind is quieted through the removal of the five hindrances, namely, sloth and torpor, sensual lust, ill will, agitation, and distraction and doubting. The mind is purified—at least for a period—of greed, hatred, and ignorance. The moral sense is strengthened not through the acceptance of the social sanctions but through a greater awareness of what happens when one is immoral. Sorrow, misery, pain, and grief take two forms, physical and mental. Physical misery and pain arise when the body is ill or not functioning properly. Sorrow and grief arise when the mind is disturbed. This form of meditation helps the body to function properly. (I shall here only mention that there are many cases of cure of physical disorders and disease due to meditation but these are minor by-products gained in the pursuit of true liberation.) This form of meditation helps one to attain peace of mind. A peaceful mind is one in which there does not arise either attachment or revulsion and one is thus unaffected by sorrow or joy, grief or anger. It is a mind which refuses to identify itself with anything whatsoever and thus does not become involved in the suffering and joy around it. Reaching the right path is acquiring the sense of what is and what is not. And one can never truly know this until one has realized what is true in himself. Nirvana can be won only by deep courage and high endeavor.

ACHAAN BUDDHADASA

CHAPTER
SEVEN

Achaan Buddhadasa is perhaps the best-known Dharma master in Thailand at this time. In addition to being a great scholar of Buddhist tradition and scriptures, he is learned in many other fields. He has written numerous books in Thai and English on meditation, comparative religion and the application of Dharma to daily life. In one extensive work, *Annapanasati*, Buddhadasa details the practice of formal mindfulness of breathing from preliminary stages to final enlightenment. Although this was central to his own practice, he is more inclined these days to teach in a very open style, using meditation as a way to approach each activity of the day. He is a very ecumenical teacher who stresses that the heart or truth of all religions is the same, freely borrowing images and ways of teaching from all traditions. Through his numerous Dharma tracts and elegantly simple talks, Buddhadasa has become a leading voice in raising Thai Dharma from simply ritual to an understanding of how peace arises from non-attachment.

On entering Wat Suan Moke (The Garden of Liberation), one encounters a Zen-like feeling of peace and harmony with nature. Suan Moke is both a meditation temple for the few nuns and thirty to fifty resident monks and a center for lay visitors. It is surrounded by the beauty of a large, still pond and acres of southern Thai forest rolling up the hills with cottages scattered throughout. Achaan Buddhadasa has built a large 'museum' which displays Dharma through pictorial art and sculpture gleaned from the various Buddhist countries and from other religions as well. Some of the best art work in the 'museum' was done by a Westerner who came to Buddhadasa from a Japanese Zen temple and who later died while meditating in a cave on the coast of southern Thailand. His cave walls and notebook were found filled with exquisite pictures and exclamations on the joy of enlightenment.

In going to live with Buddhadasa, one is free to practice various methods. One may sit alone and pursue strict mindfulness of breathing as an intensive formal practice, or study the scriptures under Buddhadasa's guidance. Most often, however, the monks and nuns who live at Suan Moke practice a kind of meditation-in-action while working at various projects around the monastery. This is the chief focus of Buddhadasa's teaching—natural meditation done throughout one's daily activities. Although he does not deny that the strict intensive methods advocated by many other Theravada teachers may lead to insight and liberation, he warns us about the dangers of attachment to any formal practice, to concentration, or to any special states of mind.

In advocating the natural development of insight, Buddhadasa does not see himself as a meditation master who directs one's practice but as a good friend who provides a suitable place to live and some good advice on how to allow the natural development of wisdom to take place. A big part of his natural approach, is to encourage people to see clearly how *any* desire at all leads them to suffering. Meditation brings the elimination of wrong views. More and more we see the uselessness of striving for personal gain or happiness in the constantly changing world outside ourselves and realize the peace of mind that comes from non-striving. This natural unfolding of the path, of morality, clear view, and unselfishness is Buddhadasa's way of approaching Dharma. It is clear, simple, and unmystical, leading to the joy of wisdom, the end of suffering.

Buddhadasa speaks excellent English and has had numerous western disciples study with him. He moved from a very simple forest hut to a larger, more permanent cottage nearer the entrance to the monastery where he receives many visitors. He is open and easily accessible. Further talks of the Venerable Buddhadasa may be found in *Toward The Truth,* a book of his writings edited by Donald Swearer and published by Westminster Press.

Insight by the Nature Method

7

by Achaan Buddhadasa

In this talk we shall see how concentration may come about naturally on the one hand and as a result of organized practice on the other. The end result is identical in the two cases: The mind is concentrated and fit to be used for carrying out close introspection. One thing must be noticed, however: The intensity of concentration that comes about naturally is usually sufficient and appropriate for introspection and insight, whereas the concentration resulting from organized training is usually excessive, more than can be made use of. Furthermore, misguided satisfaction with that highly developed concentration may result. While the mind is fully concentrated it is likely to be experiencing such a satisfying kind of bliss and well-being that the meditator may become attached to it, or imagine it to be the fruit of the path resulting from the attainment of nirvana. Naturally occurring concentration, which is sufficient and suitable for use in introspection, is harmless, having none of the disadvantages inherent in concentration developed by means of intensive training.

In the scriptures there are numerous references to people attaining naturally all stages of enlightenment. This generally came about in the presence of the Buddha himself, but also happened later with other teachers. These people did not go into the forest and sit, assiduously practicing concentration on certain objects, in the way described in later manuals.

Clearly no organized effort was involved when full enlightenment was attained by the first five disciples of the Buddha upon hearing the discourse on non-self-hood, or by the one thousand hermits upon hearing the Fire Sermon. In these cases, keen penetrating insight came about quite naturally. These examples clearly show that natural concentration is liable to develop of its own accord while one is attempting to understand clearly some question, and that the resulting insight, as long as it is firmly established, can be quite intense and stable. It happens naturally, automatically, and in just the same way as when the mind becomes concentrated the moment we set about doing arithmetic. Likewise, in firing a gun, when we take aim, the mind automatically becomes concentrated and steady. This is how *naturally occurring concentration* comes about. We normally overlook it completely because it does not appear the least bit magical, miraculous, or awe-inspiring. But through the power of just this naturally occurring concentration, most of us could actually attain liberation. We could attain the fruit of liberation, nirvana, full enlightenment, just by means of natural concentration.

So don't overlook this *naturally occurring concentration*. It is something most of us either already have or can readily develop. We can use it, as did most of the people who in ancient times succeeded in becoming enlightened, while knowing nothing of modern concentration techniques.

Now let us have a look at the nature of the stages of inner awareness leading up to full insight into 'the world', that is, into the five aggregates. The first stage is joy, mental happiness, or spiritual well-being. Doing good in some way, even giving alms (considered the most basic form of merit-making), can be a source of joy. Higher up, morality, or completely blameless conduct of word and action, brings an even greater joy. Beyond this comes the joy of concentration. We discover that there is great delight associated with even the lowest stages of concentration.

As rapture is developed it has the power to induce tranquility.

Normally the mind is quite unrestrained, continually falling slave to all sorts of thoughts and feelings associated with enticing things outside. It is normally restless, not calm. But as spiritual joy becomes established, calm and steadiness are bound to increase in proportion. When steadiness has been perfected, the result is full concentration. The mind becomes tranquil, steady, flexible, manageable, light, and at ease. It is now ready to be used for any desired purpose, especially for the elimination of defilements.

121

The arising of this rapture and tranquility does not result in the mind's being rendered silent, hard, and rocklike. Nothing like that happens at all. The body feels normal, but the mind is especially calm and suitable for use in thinking and introspection. It is perfectly clear, perfectly cool, perfectly still and restrained. In other words it is fit for work, ready to know. This is the degree of concentration to be aimed for, not the very deep concentration where one sits rigidly like a stone image, quite devoid of awareness. Sitting in deep concentration like that, one is in no position to investigate anything. A deeply concentrated mind cannot practice introspection at all. It is in a state of unawareness and is of no use for insight. *Deep concentration is a major obstacle to insight practice.* To practice introspection one must first return to the shallower levels of concentration; then one can make use of the power the mind has acquired. Highly developed concentration is just a tool. Rather than deep concentration, we aim at a calm, steady mind, one so fit for work that when it is applied to insight practice it gains right understanding with regard to the entire world. Insight so developed is natural insight, the same sort as was gained by some individuals while sitting listening to the Buddha. It is conducive to thought and introspection of the right kind, the kind that brings understanding. And it involves neither ceremonial procedures nor miracles.

This doesn't mean, however, that insight will arise instantaneously. One can't be fully enlightened straight off. The first step in knowledge may come about at any time, but depends on both the intensity of the concentration and how it is applied. Through concentrated, clear seeing, what insight does arise is experienced as quite special, extraordinarily clear and profound. If the knowledge gained is right knowledge, it will correspond with the direct experience of reality, and as practice deepens it will progress, developing ultimately into right and true understanding of all phenomena. Even if insight develops in small measure, it may convert a person into a saint of sorts at the lowest stage; or, if it is not sufficient to do that, it will just make him a high-minded individual, an ordinary person of good qualities. If the environment is suitable and the proper qualities of mind have been adequately established, it is possible even today to become fully liberated. It all depends on the circumstances. But however far things go, as long as the mind has natural concentration, this factor called insight is bound to arise and to correspond more or less closely with reality. If we as meditators hear about, think about, and study the world, the mind and body, or five aggregates honestly in the hope of coming to understand their true nature, it follows that the knowledge we acquire while in a calm and concentrated state will not be misleading. It is bound to be always beneficial.

The expression 'insight into the true nature of things' refers to seeing transience, unsatisfactoriness, and non-self-hood, seeing that nothing is worth getting, nothing is worth being, seeing that no object whatsoever should be grasped at and clung to as being a self or as belonging to a self, as being good or bad, attractive or repulsive. Liking or disliking anything, even if it is only an idea or a memory, is clinging. To say that nothing is worth getting or being is the same as to say that nothing is worth clinging to. 'Getting' refers to setting one's heart on property, position, wealth, or any pleasing object. 'Being' refers to holding onto the awareness of one's self-image, identifying with one's status as husband, wife, rich man, poor man, winner, loser, or human being, or even the awareness of being oneself. If we really look deeply at it, even being oneself is no fun, is wearisome, because trying to be anything is a source of suffering. If one can completely give up clinging to the idea of being oneself, of any self image, then one will no longer suffer. This is what it is to see the worthlessness of being anything, and is the gist of the statement that being anything, no matter what, is bound to be suffering in a way appropriate to that particular state of being. When there exists 'oneself', there are bound to exist things which are other than that 'self' and belong to it. Thus one has one's children, one's wife, one's this, that, and the other. Then one has one's duty as husband or wife, master or servant, and so on. There is no state of being such that to maintain it will not involve struggle. The trouble and struggle necessary to maintain one's state of being are simply the result of blind infatuation with things, of clinging.

If we were to give up trying to get or to be anything, how could we continue to exist? This is bound to be a major source of scepticism for anyone who has not given much thought to the matter.

The words 'getting' and 'being' are based on mental defilements, on craving, on maintaining the idea of 'worth getting, worth being', activating the mind to 'get' and 'be' in real earnest. This is bound to lead to depression, anxiety, distress, and upset, or at least to a heavy burden on the mind. Knowing this truth, we must be constantly alert, keeping watch over the mind to see that it doesn't fall slave to 'getting' and 'being' through the influence of grasping and clinging. We should be smart enough to stay aloof from these unwholesome influences.

123

If, however, we are not yet in a position to withdraw completely from having and being, we must be mindful and wide awake, so that when we do get or become something, we do so without entanglement, without emotional upset.

The world and all things have the property of impermanence, of worthlessness, and of not belonging to anyone. Any individual who grasps and clings to anything will be hurt by it—in the very beginning when he first desires to get it or to be it, later while in the process of getting it and being it, and then again after he has got it or been it. All the time, before, during, and after, when anyone grasps and clings, he will be bound by this clinging as a chain and receive his full measure of suffering, as what he clings to passes away. It is even the same with goodness, which everyone values highly. If anyone becomes involved with goodness the wrong way and clings to it too much, he will derive just as much suffering from goodness as he would from evil. In becoming involved with goodness, we have to bear this in mind, and be careful to perform even good acts without clinging.

A sceptic may ask: "If nothing at all is worth getting or being, does it follow that nobody ought to do any work or build up wealth, position, and property?" Anyone who comprehends this subject can see that a person equipped with right knowledge and understanding is actually in a far better position to carry out all tasks that need to be done in the world than one subject to strong desires, who is foolish and lacking in understanding. *We can certainly work and act in the world, but in becoming involved in things we must do so mindfully; our actions must not be motivated by craving.* We can then allow whatever the results of our work are to flow out of this in a natural, unobsessive way. The Buddha and all his enlightened disciples were completely free of desire, yet succeeded in doing many things far more useful than any of us are capable of doing. If we look at accounts of how the Buddha spent his day, we find that he slept only four hours and spent all the rest of the time working. We spend more than four hours a day just amusing ourselves.

If the defilements responsible for the desire to be and get things was completely eliminated, what was the force that motivated the Buddha and all the enlightened disciples? They were motivated by discrimination or wisdom coupled with good will (metta). Even actions based on natural bodily wants, such as receiving and eating alms food, were motivated by discrimination. They were free of defilements, free of all desire to keep on living in order to be this or to get that; but they did have the ability to discriminate between what was worthwhile and what was not as the motivating force that sent their bodies out to find food. If they found food, well and good; if not, never mind. When they were suffering with fever, they knew how to treat it, and did so as well as possible on the basis of this knowledge. But if the fever was overpowering, they also recalled that to die is natural and that the body is ultimately not in control. Whether they lived or died was of no significance to them; the two were of equal value in their eyes. They were desireless.

If one is to be completely free of suffering, this is the very best attitude to have. There need be no idea of self as master of the body; discriminating wisdom alone enables the body to carry on by its natural power. It is this discriminating wisdom which allows the natural unfolding of body and mental processes to occur and be seen clearly without grasping or desire. The example of the Buddha shows that the power of pure discrimination and pure good will alone is sufficient to keep a being who is free of desires alive in the world, and, what is more, doing far more good for others than people still subject to craving. Defiled people are likely to do only what benefits themselves since they act out of selfishness. By contrast, the deeds of enlightened beings are entirely selfless and so are perfectly pure.

When the ordinary worldly man hears that nothing is worth getting or being, he is not convinced, he doesn't believe it. But anyone who understands the real meaning of this statement becomes emboldened and cheered by it. His mind becomes master of things and independent of them. He becomes capable of performing any task sure in the knowledge that he will not become enslaved by it. The reason a person is usually incapable of doing his job perfectly, faultlessly, is that he is always far too concerned with getting something and being something, always motivated entirely by his own desires. As a result he is not master of himself, and cannot be consistently good, honest, and fair. In every case of failure and ruin, the root cause is slavery to desire.

To come to know the true nature of things is the true objective of every Buddhist. It is the means by which we can liberate ourselves. Regardless of whether we are hoping for worldly benefits, wealth, position, and fame—or for benefits in the next world, such as heaven—or for the supramundane benefit of nirvana, the fruit of liberation—the only way to achieve it is by means of this right knowledge and insight. We thrive on insight. In the texts it is said that we become purified through insight and by no other means. Our path to freedom lies in having the insight, the clear vision, that in all things there neither is, nor has ever been anything at all of value. We have things and are things only in terms of worldly, relative truth. Commonly we say we are this or that just because in any society it is expedient to identify with names and occupations. But we must not believe that we really are this or that; as is assumed on the level of relative truth. To do so is to behave like crickets, which, when their faces become covered with dirt, become disoriented and muddled and bite each other until they die. We humans, when our faces become covered with dirt, when we are subject to all sorts of delusions and desires, become so bewildered and disoriented that we act contrary to how we would if we could see under ordinary circumstances—even killing, for example. So let us not go blindly clinging to relative truths that are essential for communication in a society but nothing more. We have to be aware what this body-and-mind really is, what its true nature is. In particular we have to be aware of its impermanence, unsatisfactoriness, and non-self-hood, and make sure we always remain non-attached to it.

As for the wealth, position, and so on which we feel we can't do without, let us regard these too as relative truths so that we can break free from the custom of saying, "This belongs to so-and-so. That belongs to such-and-such." The law watches over ownership rights for us; there is no need for us to cling to the idea of 'mine'. We ought to possess things purely and simply for the sake of convenience and ease, and not so that they can be master over our minds. When we have this clear knowledge, things will become our servants and slaves and we shall use rather than be used by them. If our thoughts go the way of craving and attachment, so that we become conscious of having so-and-so, and being so-and-so, clinging firmly to these ideas, things will use us. We will spend our lives striving to gain and fearful of losing possessions, fame, wealth, or whatever, and we will become servants and slaves, under their

125

control. The tables can quite easily be turned in this way, so we have to be careful. We have to arrange things in such a way that we are sure of staying independent, and on top of things. If we don't, we will surely find ourselves in a most unenviable position when what we were attached to passes away, as all things must.

When we have really come to perceive clearly that nothing is worth getting or being, wholesome detachment with the world develops in proportion to the intensity of our insight. This is a sign that clinging has become less firm and is starting to give way. It is a sign that we have been slaves for so long that the idea of trying to escape has at last occurred to us. This disenchantment and disillusionment occurs when one becomes fed up with one's own stupidity in grasping and clinging to things. As soon as disenchantment has set in, there is bound to come about a natural, automatic process of disentanglement, as if a rope with which one had been tightly bound were being untied; a rinsing out, as when the dye that had been firmly fixed in a piece of cloth is washed out by soaking it in the appropriate substances. This process whereby clinging gives way to a breaking free from, or a dissolving out from the world, or from the objects of that clinging, was called by the Buddha 'emancipation'. This stage is most important. Though not the final stage, it is a most important step toward complete liberation. When one has broken free to this extent, complete liberation from suffering is assured.

Once freed from attachment to forms and feelings and ideas, one need never again be a slave to the world. One becomes pure and uncontaminated where previously one was defiled by grasping, anger, and ignorance. To break free from slavery to the delightful tastes of the world without grasping is to achieve our pure and natural condition. This real purity, once it has been attained, will give rise to a genuine calm and coolness free from all turbulence, strife, and torment. This state of freedom from oppression and turbulence was called by the Buddha simply 'peace.' It is stillness, coolness in all situations, one way of experiencing a kind of nirvana in this very life.

Nirvana has been translated as 'absence of any instrument of torture'. Taken another way, it means 'extinction without remainder'. So the word *nirvana* has two very important meanings: firstly, absence of any source of torment and burning, freedom from all forms of bondage and constraint; and secondly, extinction, with no fuel for the further arising of suffering. The combination of these meanings indicates a condition of complete freedom. There are several other useful meanings for *nirvana*. It can be taken to mean the extinction of suffering, or the complete elimination of defilements, or the state, coolness, realm, or condition that is the cessation of all suffering, all defilements, and all karmic activity.

Though the word *nirvana* is used by numerous different sects, the sense in which they use it is often not at all the same. For instance, one group takes it to mean simply calm and coolness, because they identify nirvana with deep concentration. Other groups even consider total absorption in sensuality as nirvana.

The Buddha defined *nirvana* as simply that condition of freedom from bondage, torment, and suffering which results from seeing the true nature of the worldly condition and all things, and so being able to give up all clinging. It is essential, then, that we recognize the very great value of insight into the true nature of things, and endeavor to cultivate this insight by one means or another. Using one method, we simply encourage insight to come about of its own accord, naturally, by developing day and night the joy that results from mental purity, until the qualities we have described gradually come about. The other method consists of developing mental power by following an organized system of concentration and insight practice. This latter technique may be appropriate for people with a certain kind of disposition, and some may make rapid progress with it if conditions are right. But we can practice the development of insight by the natural method in all circumstances and at all times—just by making our own way of daily living so pure and honest that there arise in succession spiritual joy, calm, insight into the true nature of things, disenchantment, withdrawal, escape, purification from defilements, and then the peace of nirvana, coolness. In this way we come to get a taste of freedom from suffering steadily, naturally, day by day, month by month, year by year, gradually approaching closer and closer to total freedom, to inner perfection, to nirvana.

Summing up the path of natural concentration and insight, we can see how it enables a person to attain nirvana and liberation by verifying all day and every day the truth of the statement that nothing is worth getting or being. Anyone who wishes to experience this liberation must strive to purify himself and to develop exemplary personal qualities. From this purity he will find in himself a spiritual joy in both work and leisure. This very joy induces clarity and freshness, mental calm and stillness, and serves, naturally and automatically, to give the mind the ability to think and introspect. With this introspection arises the insight that truly nothing is worth getting or being and the mind loses all desire for the things it once used to grasp at and cling to. It is able to break free from the things it used to regard as 'me' and 'mine', and all blind craving for things ceases. Suffering, which no longer has anywhere to lodge, dwindles away, and the job of eliminating suffering is done. This is the reward, and it can be gained by any one of us in a natural way. This inner peace beyond grasping, beyond identifying any experience or object as 'me' or 'mine', is the culmination of the path of purification, the true liberation of the Buddha.

In order to complete our discussion of insight training we must also here take note of the organized systems of insight training which were not taught by the Buddha but were developed by later teachers. This kind of practice is suitable for people at a fairly undeveloped stage, who still cannot perceive the unsatisfactoriness of worldly existence with their own eyes, naturally. This doesn't mean, however, that the results obtained by these systems have any special qualities not obtainable by the natural method; because when we examine the scriptures closely, we find the natural method is the only one mentioned. Some people found it difficult to understand the natural method or believed that natural insight could be developed only by someone who had become so remarkably virtuous or had such a suitable disposition that for him to come to a full understanding of things was just child's play. What was a person to do who lacked transcendent virtues and the appropriate disposition? For such people, teachers laid down ordered systems of practice, concise courses which start from scratch and have to be followed through thoroughly and systematically.

These systems of practice for developing insight are now known by the technical term *Vipassana*. Vipassana or insight is contrasted with study or intellectual learning; the two being considered nowadays complementary aspects of training. Vipassana is study done within; it is strictly mental training, having nothing to do with textbooks. Neither intellectual study nor Vipassana is mentioned directly in the scriptures, both appearing only in later books; but Vipassana is nevertheless a genuine Buddhist practice, designed for people intent on eliminating suffering. It is based directly on sustained, concentrated introspection. In order to explain Vipassana to people, teachers in former ages considered it in terms of the following questions:

What is the basis, the foundation of Vipassana?

What are the characteristics by which we may know that this is Vipassana?

Just what is the activity called Vipassana?

What should be the ultimate result of Vipassana?

Asked what is the basis, the foundation of Vipassana, we answer: morality and concentration. *Vipassana* means 'clear insight', and refers to the unobscured vision that may arise when a person's mind is full of joy and devoid of any defilement. Joy develops when there is moral purity; morality is a prerequisite. This is stated in the Buddhist scriptures, where the practice is described as proceeding in a series of stages called the seven purifications,[1] and culminating in nirvana. Teachers regard the attainment of moral purity as the first of the seven purifications.

When it has been perfected, that is, when tranquility of bodily activities and speech has been achieved, the result is bound to be mental tranquility, conducive in its turn to the further stages of purification: freedom from misunderstanding, freedom from doubt, knowledge as to what is the path to be followed and what is not, knowledge and vision of the progress along the path, and finally full intuitive insight. These last five stages constitute Vipassana proper. Purification of conduct and mind are merely the entrace into the path of Vipassana.

Currently, insight by organized training is being taught by many Buddhist teachers. The practices consist of first concentration exercises such as mindfulness of breathing followed by Vipassana or insight practices, or in some systems formal meditation which begins with insight training from the first. In pursuing organized training, the meditator will usually go to a special retreat center or into isolation for a period of time. During his retreat his life will consist of nothing but the intensive practice of meditation, trying to develop enough concentration and mindfulness to balance the mind and come to experience the supramundane, the liberation of nirvana. Whether a meditator practices in an intensive isolation setting or by the natural method, eventually he must come to an automatic integration of Vipassana and mindfulness in his daily life. Truly the wise man has no past and future; he sees that freedom lies in understanding that there is nothing to be lost nor gained, nothing to get and nothing to be. May this understanding be the cause for the true happiness and liberation of all beings.

[1] *See "Achaan Naeb."*

ACHAAN NAEB

CHAPTER
EIGHT

Achaan Naeb was born into the family of a Thai governor in a province bordering Burma. At age thirty-five she began the study of Buddhist psychology and insight meditation under Achaan Pathunta U Vilasa. Twelve years later she began teaching, establishing centers for study and meditation at many temples, and finally under royal patronage established a Buddhist Research and Mental Welfare Association at Wat Sraket in Bangkok. Although in her late seventies, she still teaches and her disciples continue her work spreading insight practice.

Wat Sraket is an island of quiet, cool chambers and halls in the center of modern Bangkok. A visit to Achaan Naeb is a chance to hear clear and direct Dharma.

She may first instruct the visitors to sit comfortably and then ask them not to move. Shortly, of course, one automatically begins to change position. "Wait, hold it. Why are you moving? Don't move yet." The teachings of Achaan Naeb point directly to the most obvious source of suffering, our own bodies. If we simply stay still and try not to move, eventually the pain increases so we must change posture. Almost all of our actions throughout the day follow the same pattern. After waking, we arise and go to the bathroom to ease the bladder pain. Then we eat to ease the discomfort of hunger. Then we sit down to ease the pain of standing. Then we read or talk or watch TV to distract us from the pain of our turbulent mind. Then we move again to ease another discomfort. Each movement, each action is not to bring happiness but to ease the inevitable suffering that comes from being born with a body. Achaan Naeb's method has the simple approach of looking at the cause and effect of suffering in our daily lives and actions. Clear perception of this process is the direct entry to the end of suffering and the happiness of the Buddha.

Achaan Naeb makes a number of other important Dharma points. First, she emphasizes that one must have right conceptual understanding before practice. She states that establishing the middle path is not easy. Without right understanding and awareness, wisdom will not develop. This right understanding is knowing how to be correctly aware of mind and matter. It is also knowing how defilements arise from craving and being able to distinguish between the clear knowing of present objects, which is correct practice, and the development of tranquility, which is incorrect practice.

The distinction between insight practice and concentration practice is stressed. Any attachment to tranquility or to a particular regimen in practice is seen to block wisdom. Insight comes only from the direct observation of the nature of mind and matter in the present moment. *No strong effort nor special concentration is necessary.* Instead we are urged to know mind and matter directly as they appear in all postures. We will see clearly how pain and unsatisfactoriness drive us through our daily acions. We will also see how mind and matter are separate, empty phenomena which change constantly.

It is only through the direct knowing of mind and matter in insight practice that wisdom will arise, says Achaan Naeb. She emphasizes the uniqueness of the Buddha's teaching and focuses on the four applications of mindfulness as the one way to all insight. She stresses that no special effort need be made, only to practice by simply observing the present moment, especially mind, matter, and why we move as we do.

Achaan Naeb encourages us to listen with understanding so that we may acquire wisdom. She says: "To listen with understanding means that we are listening without any preconceived ideas or opinions. If we listen with a closed mind, our preconceived ideas and opinions will inevitably conceal the truth, and that being the case we shall fail to attain wisdom. These should be put aside, and we should listen with an open mind and not think about what 'our' teacher has taught before. Moreover, we should not think about the speaker; who he is, whether or not he is our teacher, nor hold any prejudiced opinion against him. We must listen with an open mind and try to find out if what is being spoken is reasonable, if what is being spoken leads us to the truth."

133

A number of centers in Thailand (and Burma as well) teach according to this tradition, and Westerners are welcome to visit and practice to experience for themselves the growth of wisdom and liberation.

The Development of Insight

8

by Achaan Naeb

There are in Buddhism two methods of mental development. One is the development of insight (Vipassana), and the other is the development of tranquility (Samatha). The latter aims only at concentration, whereby the individual is constantly conscious of one object, and this concentration is directed along a single channel of one-pointedness until a serene tranquility is reached. This kind of mental development does not bring about an understanding of reality, nor of its cause and effect. It brings only tranquility. The development of insight, on the other hand, calls for an understanding of the 'truth of existence'; or, to put it another way, an understanding of form or matter and mind or mental states. This understanding is the aim of the development of insight.

134   To begin with, I shall explain what concentration in the development of tranquility is composed of, because the development of concentration according to this method cannot be used at the same time as the development of insight, or vice versa. Please do not misunderstand this point, for one can begin with the development of tranquility, and after having achieved concentration, one may then proceed to the development of insight. But the mixing of these two cannot achieve the desired results of insight.

Tranquility meditation is cultivated by concentrating the mind and holding it one-pointedly on a particular object. The traditional objects through which concentration can be achieved, according to the development of tranquility, are forty in number: the ten colors and elements, ten impurities, ten recollections, four sublime abodes, four boundless meditations, one reflection upon the loathsomeness of food, and the analysis of the four primary qualities—namely, solidity, cohesion, heat, and vibration. Any one of these may be taken as the meditation subject for the development of tranquility.

Concentration upon any one of the forty foregoing objects cannot lead to insight, because insight meditation must have the changing of mental states and matter as its object of meditation. Although concentration can lead to the development of great powers of mind and extraordinary happiness, this great happiness is temporary and still very different from the application of mindfulness which leads to nirvana. Only insight practice brings a permanent end to sorrow.

Before speaking further about the development of insight, I think that we should first understand what insight is, its function and its usefulness. In brief, insight is wisdom which enables one to see that mental states and matter are impermanent or transitory, unsatisfactory or suffering, and impersonal or non-self. What we regard as 'self' or 'ego' or 'soul' are miscomprehensions arising from a lack of knowledge of absolute truth. In reality, 'self' is but a very rapid continuity of birth and decay of mental states and matter.

Having thus learned that insight is this kind of wisdom, what then is its function? Insight has as its function the destruction of all hidden defilements, craving, and wrong views. With regard to its usefulness, insight will enlighten us to the true nature of mental states and matter. But what is this true nature? It is the understanding that mental states and matter are not lasting, that they are full of suffering and that they are not a personality or soul or self. In other words, development of insight does not create these three characteristics of existence—impermanence, suffering, and impersonality—nor does this kind of development deceive you into perceiving these characteristics. No! These three characteristics of existence are there in nature. Whether or not anyone sees or understands them, they are always present. The reason that we do not see or understand these characteristics is that we use the wrong methods in trying to perceive and analyze them. It is only through cultivating the right methods of development of insight that we can see existence as it really is.

135

Such is the sole purpose of the development of insight. There is nothing else which can be attributed to this kind of mental development. I have read about people who, having made no study of the development of insight, claim to see heavens and hells while closing their eyes. Others claim they can heal illnesses and that childless parents can have children by development of insight. Still others profess that by means of the development of insight they can see lottery numbers, tell the future of others' lives, or that they can float in the air, walk on water, penetrate the earth, render themselves transparent, or become clairvoyant or clairaudient. All of these performances are not the achievement of the development of insight and have no bearing upon it. These peculiar feats may only be the effects of concentration. The sole function of insight is to destroy the defilements, qualities of mind such as craving, wrong view, and ignorance, which form the basis of the rebirth cycle (samsara). This is the growth of wisdom.

Wisdom has three sources, namely:

1. Wisdom which results from pondering the teachings heard from others.
2. Wisdom which results from one's own considerations and reflections, pondering and thinking about the truth of existence, which, during periods of reflection, can temporarily destroy the defilements.
3. Wisdom which results through personal *experience* that enables one to see the truth of the three characteristics: im-

permanence, suffering, and impersonality. This experiential aspect is insight wisdom. It is the tool by which the defilements can be destroyed completely and permanently.

After we are well versed in the wisdom of teachings, this in turn can give birth to consideration. This right understanding of the teachings leads then to right awareness and the results of right awareness lead to the birth of insight wisdom. This insight wisdom is dependent upon the other two aspects of wisdom.

No worldly wisdom compares. Only these three kinds of wisdom serve to destroy progressively the conditions of rebirth. They are cultivated until the three characteristics of existence become clear. This perception is the main aim of the development of insight. This was the purpose of the Buddha's propagating his teachings, to enable all beings to appreciate and realize the Dharma, the truths of nature.

Next it should be understood just what prevents us from realizing the three characteristics of existence. Factors obscuring impermanence, suffering, and impersonality, the three characteristics known by wisdom, were explained by the Buddha. That which masks impermanence is continuity, which refers to rapid change in all formations; that is, mental states and matter are constantly and very rapidly arising and falling away. This process happens so quickly that we are unable to perceive the arising and falling away of mental states and matter; thus it seems to us that mental states and matter are permanent. This is how continuity hides impermanence. In order to illustrate this, let us take seeing a movie as an example. Although continuous movement appears on the screen, it is not the projection of only one picture but actually hundreds of them. The rapidity of the change from one type of matter to another gives us the impression that there is only one matter instead of separate matters. Similarly, as we cannot see the many individual pictures making up a movie, we cannot see that in reality there are many kinds of mental states and matter. Moreover, mental states and matter arise and fall away far more rapidly than the individual pictures which go into the making of a movie. This is why it is extremely difficult for us to perceive the changes. When we cannot perceive this truth, the delusion which claims impermanence as being permanent arises.

What is it that obscures suffering? The Buddha said that it was the lack of consideration upon the bodily positions. Not paying attention to the body, we do not realize that mental states and matter are painful, and that suffering is oppressing us at all times.

When we do not realize this truth, then wrong view occurs, and we see our life, mental states, and matter as good and bringing happiness. Following this, the craving for happiness arises, leading to greater suffering.

What is it that obscures impersonality? Before answering, let us talk a little about this characteristic. Impersonality is the heart of Buddhism and it is a doctrine different from other philosophies and religions. In other religions, there must be one fundamental thing to act as the foundation, or a supreme leader, or else a permanent or sacred thing which is held on to or depended upon. But in Buddhism, we find that everything is impersonal; there is no soul or self; there is no 'Powerful One'. Thus all existence has the characteristic of impersonality. Now, what is it that prevents us from realizing impersonality? The Buddha said that it is the massing together of compounded perceptions of mental states and matter. This gives us the opinion that mental states and matter are one whole solid mass or entity which is permanent. We then add the notions that mind and matter are wholesome and important; that the five aggregates (form, feelings, perceptions, mind objects, and consciousness) are good. Although we may have heard that the five aggregates arise and fall away very rapidly, we are not able to see the separation of each mental state or each of the five aggregates and thereby realize its true characteristics. This inability to separate them is the reason why we do not realize impersonality. This lack of realization creates the illusion of solidity, or personality, that is to say, the belief that there is a permanent 'I' or 'self'. When this happens, the illusion of personality becomes the mental factor causing desire. Desire, in turn, will cause one to think that both mental states and matter are lasting and can bring happiness. It is necessary to correct this misperception to understand the three characteristics of existence and become liberated.

There are many varieties of mental states and matter. We, as ordinary people, are not able to analyze them and shall never be able to do so unless we (1) develop insight, (2) understand the principles which govern this kind of development, and (3) acquire right purpose. Only with right purpose will we be able to overcome the obstacles to enlightenment. Otherwise we will succumb to the influence of cravings and whimsical fancies (or wrong judgments), which lead to the perpetual cycle of birth and death.

Right purpose is understanding that the importance of insight is to destroy the painful cycle of birth, old age, ill health, and death, and all the lesser sufferings which occur in daily life. If we want to

137

practice because we think that we will gain merit, or because we wish to create some supranormal happenings, or to achieve something extraordinary, we do not have the correct understanding of the basic principles.

Up to now I have been talking about the effects of the development of insight and as yet have not dealt with the practice itself. During the actual development of insight we must continually be aware of mental states and matter so that we may perceive their characteristics. Only after we have thoroughly understood mental states and matter can we deepen the development of awareness of them. Such mental development must follow the sequence outlined in the Buddha's discourse, *Application of Mindfulness*. In this text are found four classifications of objects for development of insight, namely, the physical body, feelings, consciousness, and Dharma. These can be boiled down to mental states and matter.

After we have understood the basic theory of insight meditation, we must begin to actually develop insight by being aware of the four fundamental positions of the body and the attendant mental states. Please keep in mind that the purpose in being aware of the position of the body is to see the inherent suffering and misery clearly. In other words, the requirement is to be conscious constantly of every position and movement of the body. If we are not so aware, we will never realize the true extent and nature of suffering. We must exercise awareness on each movement of the body as it is taking place, as when we move to sit down, to lie down, to stand, or to walk; we must be aware of every such movement.

While we are sitting, standing, lying, or walking, we shall be mindful of this position as matter. The walking position is the movement of the body and not the feet touching the floor. It is the same with the sitting position. We must be careful that we are mindful of the whole sitting position and not just the portion of the body which is touching the object we are sitting on. The matter which is touched and the sitting position are different. Sometimes the practitioner intends to be mindful of the sitting position but, instead, is mindful of the touching. He therefore is unaware of the sitting position. If the practitioner is mindful of the touching, then he must be mindful when he is touching. If he is mindful of the sitting position, he has to be mindful right at the time when he is sitting. The touching and sitting positions have different characteristics and they are different matter and have different doorways of recognition. They are different in all aspects. Whenever we want to see any matter we have to be mindful of the correct object.

We must also be aware of all the kinds of mental states and physical actions in a particular position, as to whether we are doing something or thinking about things. Suppose we take the sitting position as an example. We should be conscious and aware of the sitting position, and we must realize that the sitting position is matter and the awareness of that position is a mental state. We must separate the matter from the mental state. While we are looking at a mental state or at matter, we also have to realize which type of mental state or which type of matter it is. By understanding that there are different positions, we will then know that each experience of matter is different. If we do not know that matter is 'sitting matter' at a given moment, or if we know only that it is just matter, we are not practicing the correct method. Because if we merely know that it is only matter, and fail to perceive the separation or change of matter, we will mistakenly think that there is only one continuous matter, and that that 'one' continuous matter sits, stands, walks, etc. When we see only unchanging matter, then wrong view, belief in an unchanging self, arises. Therefore, while practicing insight, we have to be aware at all times of precisely what type of matter or what type of mental state we are looking upon. As soon as we begin to consider any one form of existence, we will be able to determine, little by little, whether it is a mental state or matter.

The situation is the same as when we began learning how to write. At first we had to learn what the letter was, whether it was *a* or *b*. We had to study and remember the shape of each letter. If we didn't remember the shape of each letter, then we could not read. Some children have no difficulty in saying the ABCs, but if you ask them to point out any one letter, they are unable to do so because they did not learn the shape of each letter. In the same way, if the practitioner of development of insight does not realize the characteristic of, for example, the sitting position, but just says or thinks to himself, *sitting, sitting*, he is not practicing correctly. Practicing insight without understanding the different types of mental states and matter is like trying to read the ABCs without having learned the shape of each letter, or looking at a row of letters without being able to read. For this reason, we have to try to be aware of the position of matter and each type of mental state in order to know the particular characteristic of each and how it differs from the others, since each has its own characteristic. We will then be able to see the constant change of these states. If we cultivate wisdom in this way, we shall realize the true characteristics of mental states and matter.

The Buddha said that, we must practice insight to see clearly that which is. To do so we have to first destroy attachment and aversion for the object. Therefore, while being mindful of mental states and matter, we have to be carefully watchful and mentally alert. Developing desireless awareness is the right understanding of the applications of mindfulness. It is similar to watching the characters acting in a play. As for the character who has not yet appeared, we do not desire to see him. Similarly we do not desire to follow or hold the characters who are going off stage. We keep our attention upon the character who is acting. Our only interest is in seeing the characters performing the play and not the directing of it. We are composed of aggregates (matter and mind or feelings, perceptions, mind elements, and consciousness) which are like a movie picture that continues throughout the day and night, even while we are sleeping, sitting, or breathing. It continues acting with every breath, in and out, until we die, and then begins to act another role, continuing on endlessly. This is known as samsara.

It is not necessary to search elsewhere to learn about mental states and matter. During the practice we must have a neutral feeling toward whatever arises, like the attitude toward the role which a character is playing, or appearing in, at every moment. We have to be aware as an onlooker with a neutral feeling. So, if our mind is wandering about, and we do not like it wandering about, this attitude is not correct. The correct way is to be aware of the act of wandering itself. We should also realize that we are aware of the mental state which is wandering about. We must realize that the wandering mind is a mental state, or we will mistakenly think it is 'I' wandering about and thus the idea of personality will remain instead of being eliminated.

As we analyze in this fashion, while being aware of the wandering mind, we should check to see that there is no desire to have the wandering mind disappear.

Meditating upon the wandering mind, thinking that the purpose of insight practice is to make it disappear, is entirely incorrect; insight cannot be attained at all this way. Why? Because one is wrongly trying to control nature, deluded that there is a self which can control the mind or force the wandering mind to disappear. Now, if through great effort it would disappear, as we would like it to, wisdom would not result, but instead merely cause wrong views and cravings for certain peaceful states of mind to spring up. We would feel happy as soon as the wandering mind disappeared and believe that our meditation was very effective, thus reinforcing the illusion of a self, a doer. After the wandering mind disappears, the concentrated or tranquil mind takes its place. At this point we feel we can control the world, and we lose the opportunity to realize that mental states and matter are impersonal and are ultimately not in one's power or control.

No one can govern or command mental states and matter to behave in a certain manner. If a person wrongly thinks that he can control mental states and matter, such thinking will only bring misunderstanding. In fact, even though one does not meditate, nor want the wandering mind to disappear, it will disappear anyhow, because anything which arises must fall away. All kinds of mental states and matter have the three characteristics. When we do not look wisely upon them, then misunderstanding occurs and the defilements of like, dislike, or self arise. When the defilements exist, they hinder insight. When the mind is wandering and the practitioner does not want this to happen, the feeling of dislike will result. When he has the feeling of dislike, he tries to concentrate strongly so as to have a 'concentrated mind' and stop the 'wandering mind'. In other words, his mind aims at peacefulness or pleasure. He finds himself stuck, attached to tranquility. The practitioner who meditates correctly should not be creating attachments and aversions.

One reason why the practitioner is often unable to develop the application of mindfulness is that he does not have correct understanding of how to be mindful. For instance, while he is mindful of a position, pain must sooner or later occur in that position. When pain occurs, he should be aware of the painful feeling without trying to suppress it. It is the same as in the case of awareness of the wandering mind. If we concentrate on the pain to suppress the pain, this kind of mindfulness is the object of craving, rather than just observing the object. This means that the proper mental factor for the middle path of mental balance is missing because our consciousness is turned toward our feelings of like and dislike. When we want pain to disappear, it is attachment, and when we dislike it if pain has not yet disappeared, it is aversion. Should the pain disappear as we desired, there follows further attachment. Such practice is not the correct application of mindfulness, and the awareness is not seeing clearly the 'present' object because we wish it to be different in the future. If it is not the 'present' object which we are aware of, then the practice is off the middle path. We can see that establishing the balance of the middle path is not easy. For this reason, it is of extreme importance to have right understanding first. We must see that insight does not depend only on effort or on strong concentration. Nor does it depend upon our wish to know or to realize, but rather, *it depends upon right awareness*. If we do not achieve keen awareness, although we try to use much effort and concentration, wisdom still will not result.

As an example let us take this lecture. While you are listening, those of you who have never practiced mindfulness at all will get only a certain amount of understanding from it. Those who have practiced mindfulness might attain some understanding of the matter of insight; and if you are very keen, you might have deep insight wisdom arise while you are listening. For if you have the right understanding and awareness, you can meditate anywhere on the 'present reality' (that which exists independent of our desires) which is occurring at any moment. When we are aware of present reality with right understanding and awareness, we can reach at any moment the first stage of enlightenment. The same situation happened during the Buddha's lifetime. Often when he finished expounding his teaching, a great number of people would reach the various stages of enlightenment. So insight depends upon right understanding and not on effort nor strong concentration.

Now let us go back and review what has been mentioned before. Why are we aware of our positions? So that we can realize the nature of suffering or pain. If we are not aware of a position, then can that position show us the truth of suffering? Furthermore, if we do not understand how to be aware properly, we cannot realize pain. When changing position, if we are not aware that the old position was painful, the new position may cover up the truth of pain. Therefore, we should be alert and wisely find the reason why we changed our position. If we discover the reason before changing, then the new position will not cover up the truth of pain. When we are aware of the position at all times, we find that pain will occur after a certain period of time, and it is only then that we wish to change position. When there is pain in a position we do not like that position; and when we do not like a position because it is no longer comfortable, any desire for that position will disappear. When the desire for a position disappears, then aversion may replace our initial attachment for that position. The emotion of aversion arises with painful feeling.

As for changing position, although we once liked the old position, desire for it disappeared, and instead dislike arose. When dislike enters the mind, desire will attach itself to a new position because it is comfortable. Thus we can see that in all kinds of positions there are attachment and aversion. However, the practitioner usually does not recognize this. To be aware of a position, the practitioner should understand that before changing a position he must find out at all times why he must make that change. If we do not know the cause or reason for our changing, then we cannot and will not recognize pain as pain. At times I have asked a practitioner if he knows why he has to change the bodily positions. One of the replies was that he sat too long and that he just 'wants' to change. Such reasoning as this, of course, is not correct. This reason does not in the least show the true nature of pain to him. Therefore, I must further ask him why he has to change after sitting a long time. There must be some other cause or reason. It is not that after sitting for a long time one just 'wants' to change; one must find a more precise reason as to what it is that forces one to 'want' to change a position. If he is questioned in this manner, he will see that he was forced to change by the influence of suffering or pain. It is pain forcing him to change position at all times.

143

Now, let me ask a counter-question. Can a human being assume one position and not move or change it at all? The answer, of course, is 'no'. Even if we do not want to change, are we not forced to change regardless of our wishes? Previously we said that we sat because we wanted to sit, we stood because we wanted to stand; but now can we say that we sit or change a position because we want to? As we see, then, we change position due to pain or suffering, because we are uncomfortable. That is why, to develop insight, the practitioner must find the reason each time he changes position. When he is lying down before falling asleep and he turns or changes position, he must find the reason; he must know that each time he changes it is because of pain or suffering. If the cause is realized in this manner at all times, and we are aware of the present object, we shall recognize the basic characteristics of existence.

Now, when we realize that we are forced to change positions because of pain, we should question further to find out if there are other reasons. If the answer is that we change because we want to be comfortable, this is incorrect. It is incorrect because it is a distortion of happiness. The correct answer is that we change in order to 'cure' the pain. We do not change to acquire happiness. The wrong answer comes from misunderstanding, and if we do not have the right comprehension when we change positions, defilements can and will spring up.

Changing positions to 'cure' pain indicates that we have to remedy the situation at all times. We should not misjudge and think that the reason is to attain happiness, since the curing of pain all the time is the same as having to take medicines constantly. It is like nursing a continuous sickness. Thus, we should not look upon nursing sickness and curing pain as being happiness at all.

Pain in the old position is easy to realize, but the pain in a new position is difficult to realize. With wisdom one can fathom the pain in the new position. If there is no wisdom, craving will surely arise. That is why we must have a way to find suffering or pain in the new position. And what is that way? To realize why we change position. When we realize that we change positions because of painful feeling, we must further recognize the fact that actually there is pain in all positions. Sitting becomes painful, standing becomes painful, so we change; all positions become painful and it is necessary to change positions repeatedly. We lie down for a while, but then pain will occur. At first we think that lying down is happiness and we want to lie down, but after experiencing the lying position for a while, we notice that it also is painful. Let us, therefore, realize that the truth of suffering is found in all positions. In this way the illusion, which claims it to be happiness, will certainly disappear. As soon as we think that any position is happy, illusions arise and we will be unable to eliminate them.

As I said earlier, it is easy to realize suffering in an old position, because the painful feeling is obvious, but it is difficult to realize suffering in a new position. We have to recognize the different kinds of sufferings and the necessity to change or to 'cure' suffering all the time; and realizing that all formations, mind and matter, are inherently painful, is wisdom.

When we are practicing insight, we should not cling to any particular state. To understand this we can again work with the postures. If we ask someone who is meditating which position he likes best, he may say that he likes the sitting or standing or walking position best. We will have to question him further as to why he meditates more in one position than another. His answer may be that he just likes it. So again we must question him as to why. His answer may be that he likes one position more than another because in that position his mind is more able to concentrate and it does not wander so much. Some people may say that when they sit, the mind wanders a great deal and, therefore, they have to walk because they 'want' the mind to concentrate and be centered on one point. All of these motives are created by the influence of desire. Walking because the mind will then be able to concentrate is wrong, and if we have an attitude like this, we have wrong understanding and think that walking is good or useful; we will think that walking will bring us happiness and what we desire, because we believe that the concentrated mind has the ability to bring wisdom. If we walk for these reasons, it is not correct. We cannot walk with desire and have wisdom at the same time. If we hold onto concentration while walking, desire will arise and cover the truth of the walking position; by misconstruing the walking position as good and useful, we shall want to be in this position. 145

If there is any question as to why we cannot concentrate the mind first and then practice insight later, I would only say that if the concentration has an insight object (mind and matter), then it is all right. But if, on the other hand, the concentration occurs because of your desire or because you create an object, then you will be unable to practice insight with that object. A constructed object cannot be an insight object. We cannot find the truth in a constructed object because direct experience is covered up. Insight wisdom must realize the truth in all daily activities which are 'realities' and not consider any special object which has been produced and which differs from daily activities.

Sometimes, when someone cultivates the development of insight, he will know that he is supposed to recognize the three characteristics. He may then think that mental states and matter are impermanent or suffering or impersonal, and he will repeat this within his mind, without direct awareness of their present existence. But to recognize mental states and matter as being impermanent results from awareness in the practice. If we do not know how this understanding comes about, we think about the characteristics of mental states and matter instead of being aware of their present existence. This means that we think of the idea only, and we believe that in order to practice insight meditation we only have to think in this manner until insight wisdom occurs. This, however, is a wrong understanding, because to know through thinking instead of experiencing is not the way to gain insight. We must cultivate the right causes so that the right results will occur. Then we will see for ourselves how suffering, impermanence, and impersonality are related. We will see that anything which is impermanent is ultimately unsatisfactory and impersonal, out of control.

A most important point in the practice of the application of mindfulness is to be mindful of the present existence rather than wishing for anything in the future. This prevents the arising of defilements in all positions. If we sit in order that our mind may become peaceful, or stand so that our mind may become quiet, we are not developing insight, and desire will not be destroyed. The desire for peacefulness is attachment. No matter what position we are mindful of, we must be careful to know, at each moment, whether defilements exist or not. This clear knowing of mental states and matter is correct practice. Do not force yourself to sit for a long period of time, nor stand for a certain length of time. If we practice like this, it is incorrect. We must not force ourselves. If we do, all our practices are done in connection with the illusion of 'self' and this illusion will follow in all positions. Attempting to control actions in this manner cannot bring insight wisdom. In order to have insight wisdom there must be no control or time schedules (such as holding a bodily position for a prescribed period of time or appointing a time to do certain activities). Simply be aware of the appropriate cause which compels you to change positions.

If we truly consider, we will realize that we have to change positions continuously, and it is not happiness at all. When we realize this truth by having considered all our positions, we then destroy the delusions which obscure suffering. After these delusions are destroyed, the wrong view, which mistakes suffering for happiness, is also destroyed and wisdom arises. To realize this is to have right understanding. Suffering is the first of the four noble truths, and whoever realizes suffering is said to have recognized the truth of existence. To destroy the hindrance which prevents realization of suffering is one of the ways of realizing the truth.

Furthermore, we should acquaint ourselves with an additional reason for being aware of all positions. This is to understand the truth of impersonality. When we are not aware of, say, the sitting or lying positions, we do not know *what* is sitting or *what* is lying down. If we do not know what is sitting or what is lying down, it must be 'I' who sits or lies. Accordingly, when suffering occurs in any position we will suppose that 'we' are suffering. This is because we still believe it is 'I' who has the suffering. If we still feel that 'we' have suffering or that suffering has 'us', we have not as yet eliminated the 'I' concept. Who is suffering? Is matter suffering, or mental states suffering? If examining mental states and matter has not yet shown us the true characteristics of things, we still cling to the illusion of 'self'. That being the case, when we are mindful of the positions we should be careful to observe whether there is anything other than matter or mental states and whether these are permanent or 'self'. This is a very important point to remember, otherwise we will not be able to eliminate the illusion of 'self' or the 'I'.

Mindfulness of all matter and mental states is the basic practice along with special attention to bodily positions. It is also necessary to be continually mindful of all seeing, hearing, smelling, tasting, and touching. In doing so, when we acknowledge an object through the eyes, we must be aware that it is the mental state which sees. When we acknowledge an object through the ears, we must be aware that it is the mental state which hears. It is not necessary to be mindful of the sound, but rather to be mindful of hearing. If a teacher does not have right understanding, he or she may tell the practitioner that it does not matter whether one is mindful of the sound or of the hearing. Therefore, the teacher may advise the student to be mindful of the sound if the sound is more prominent or clearer. If we practice mindfulness in this manner, it is incorrect practice.

Being mindful of color or sound cannot lead to insight because, if we are more mindful of sound or color, we shall have more concentration instead of insight. This, as I stated before, is not the correct practice because craving, wrong view, and conceit continue to assert a belief in 'I'. It is the hearing which makes us think that 'we' hear, sense, etc. That is why it is not necessary to be mindful of the sound since craving and wrong view do not mistake the sound as being 'I' when hearing arises. Wherever craving, conceit, and wrong view exist, that is the place where we will have to eliminate them by mindfulness. Accordingly, we must be mindful of hearing when we hear. We must also know that hearing is a mental state, otherwise we mistake the hearing as 'I' hear. We must be mindful of hearing so that we may eliminate the illusion of 'I' or 'self' from the hearing. Hence it is of extreme importance to realize that when we hear or see, it is simply the mental state or process which hears or sees. Similarly, when the mind is wandering, we must be mindful of the mental state which is wandering about. Do not be mindful because you want to stop the wandering of the mind, or crave a peaceful mind. Do not let such notions sneak into the practice. We have to set our minds to observe the mental states which are wandering about, but with balance. Again, the situation should be the same as when one is watching a play or movie (the actor being the wandering mind). When we are

147

observing the wandering mind we do not try to stop it. The wandering mind itself can also show the truth of the three characteristics of existence. It is not as though the wandering mind does not have these characteristics for us to see, nor are the three characteristics only in the peaceful mind. In fact, we can realize the three characteristics in the wandering mind much more easily than in the peaceful mind. This is because we can easily see how the wandering mind is out of control, not 'I', and also is painful.

148

Continuing practice, we must consider each object at the doorways of perception. We have become aware of the mental states in perception. Now we should also be mindful of matter. When we smell something, we should be mindful of the smell and realize it is matter. When we acknowledge taste or when the taste touches the tongue, we should be mindful of taste and how it is matter. In addition, we must realize that it is not according to our desire that taste arises. For example, when we take salt, even though we may not like the salty taste, we cannot change it because its basic nature is salty. Therefore, if we see how the salty taste appears naturally, and not according to our wish, then craving does not exist at the time. This is why keeping in the present moment is the most important instrument to prevent the arising of attachment and aversion. *The meaning of present moment is: existence which occurs at a given time independently of our desire.* We must be mindful of each object and perceive its true nature. If any object occurs through our desire, then defilements also arise. We must realize that any object which we perceive with desire cannot reveal the truth, as it is a constructed object. How can we realize the true nature of an object which has been constructed? The only object which can reveal the truth must be the 'present object', which occurs by itself and independently of our wishes.

We must understand what the present object is. Sometimes we may think that what we are mindful of is the present object, but in reality this may not be the case. Considering the present object, which occurs in just a split second, is like catching a fish in water. We think that we can catch a particular fish because we see it swimming in one place, so we stretch out our hand to catch it. But we fail to catch it because it slips off in another direction. It is the same in being mindful of the present object, since attachment and aversion are always pushing the present existence aside.

Whenever we are mindful of any object which occurs by itself, then the object is the present object; but most of the time we are not mindful of the present object or existence. Let us take an example. While we are mindful of the sitting position which is, let us say, the present object, our mind moves to the idea of peacefulness. Our aim being peace or comfort, we are not at such a time mindful of the truth of the object of sitting at all. We do not want to find the truth in the sitting position; instead we are mindful of the object for attaining peace of mind which has not yet occurred.

We must observe clearly in the present moment all our activities, matter and mind states. We will then see how they are without 'self' and are suffering. Not having the present existence as our present object, we will be wasting our time during the practice. But if we realize suddenly that our mind has slipped away from the present object, we then can mindfully set the mind on the present object once more. If we understand these characteristics of mental states we will then be able to have mindfulness on the correct object for longer periods of time and have more opportunities to realize the truth.

Let us see how to apply this while eating. We should be mindful and consider the reason why we take food. It is indicated in the Buddhist texts that we take food not because we want it, not because it is good, but rather because it is necessary to sustain the body. The Buddha also told of a further reason why we want the body to live, which is to have sufficient strength to develop the path which leads to the ending of all suffering or sorrow. It is necessary to have such consideration, otherwise we will not be able to prevent defilements from arising. We must understand that we do not take food because it tastes good, but in order to cure pain and satisfy hunger. When we take food to satisfy hunger, even though the food is not good, it will satisfy the hunger. Suppose we take food for the sake of its flavor. If it is not good, then aversion will occur. On the other hand, if it is good, then greed will occur. This would mean that we are taking the food to encourage defilements. When food is good, greed or attachment will occur. When it is not good, dissatisfaction will occur. To eat without consideration is to create more cycles of desire, of birth and death, which is the endless continuation of suffering. Therefore, when we are applying the application of mindfulness as we are going to take food, we must understand the reason at each mouthful; so that when we are eating, it will be solely for the purpose of being free from suffering. While we are taking food, if attachment and aversion do not arise at that time, then insight can occur.

When we take a bath, we must also understand this act as an action curing suffering. In our daily duties we should see the reasons for our actions. We should not put on clothing for the sake of beauty, thus we do not select this or that color, but instead use clothing to protect the body against the coldness and to keep the insects, such as mosquitoes and flies, from biting us. So it means that whatever our actions may be, they are for the realization of nirvana and the deliverance from suffering. When we have this kind of thorough understanding, the attachment to the changing mental states and matter will become weaker and weaker. But remember, we must realize what mental state it is and what matter it is, and we must have this awareness or knowledge at all times. All kinds of existence are nothing more than mental phenomena and matter; no body, no soul, no woman, no man, is there who sits. There is no one who stands, walks, or sleeps; no one is there who smells, sees, or hears, etc. There is nobody who understands or knows these things.

STAGES OF PURIFICATION

After we have realized the empty nature of mental states and matter, then we attain the first degree of insight wisdom, which is called *mind-and-matter-determination-knowledge*. It is the level of insight which enables us to directly perceive the separate mental state and the separate matter in all phenomena. We must understand that the mental states and matter known from the *mind-and-matter-determination-knowledge* are not the same as the mental states and matter we know by learning or from listening. Anyone who has not experienced this determination-knowledge cannot distinguish the difference between the knowledge arising from 'theory' and that of 'realization'. So, whatever he perceives, it is still with the illusion of 'I' or the 'self' which hears or sees; he is under a delusion in spite of his theoretical knowledge of what is the mind or what is matter. For instance, if I ask whether the sitting position is mind or matter, he can answer that it is matter. But when he is actually sitting, does he realize that the sitting position is matter, and can he clearly separate the matter from the mental states involved? This is the difference between the practice and the theory. In fact, to attain *mind-and-matter-determination-knowledge* is not easy, even though it is the first degree of knowledge found in the development of insight. It requires strong mindfulness and concentration to be able to distinguish these clearly in every moment.

We must now proceed to develop the practice more deeply, which means we must be mindful of mental states and matter to a greater degree. At first, we had no concern for the fact that mental states and matter were factors relating to one another. We were just mindful, and only knew what was the mental state and what was matter. But now, the more we are aware of mental states and matter, the more we will see from what causes they arise. For 151 instance, when hearing arises, we realize that sound is a factor of hearing. When there is sight, we realize that color is a factor of seeing. In this manner we will also see what kind of mental state occurs as a result of sound and color. As for the different bodily positions or the movements of the body, we must continue to be aware at all times and we will see that matter which is moving has the mind as its factor or cause. It is motivated by consciousness. It is the consciousness which directs the body to stand, sit, walk, or change positions, so that the different positions occur. All of these positions of matter occur because they have mind as their cause, and when such a kind of mental state occurs, it has matter as its factor or cause. Thus mental states and matter will be seen to arise or occur from factors. This kind of insight knowledge will occur after we have reached *mind-and-matter-determination-knowledge*. When we are mindful in this manner the causal relationship between mind and matter will be disclosed. Before this time, though, we knew existence as mind and matter, we did not know how mind and matter occurred or from what cause. When we do not know this we might think that their existence occurs from a god causing it to occur, as described by other religious systems. But when we reach the degree of the *mind-and-matter-condition-acquiring-knowledge* we will know that mind and matter do not occur by the creation of anyone at all. Instead they are conditioned by causes and factors, they are in a cause-and-effect relationship with each other. Mind and matter are seen as independent factors. This is seen in the same way as we know that the sound of a bell ringing occurs from two things—the stick and the bell. If the stick does not strike the bell, then there is no sound. Nobody can create this bell sound, and there is no one who knows where the sound is or where the sound goes to; but as soon as there are the two above factors the sound will occur. If we thoroughly experience this in relation to mind and matter, then the question and mystery of how mind and matter occur and what causes them to occur will disappear.

In this degree of insight knowledge, although we now know the causes of mind and matter, we have not as yet fully realized their separation, not yet experienced the rapid sequence of mental states and matter and realized their falling away. Mental states and matter fall away exceedingly quickly and insight has not been keen enough, as yet, to see this. Therefore we must continue our awareness of mental states and matter, on and on, until we realize their falling away. For instance, when we are changing from the sitting position to another position, we will realize the falling away of the sitting position; or when we stand and when we stop standing, we will realize the falling away of the standing position, and we will realize the arising of a new position next. When we realize this, we will know that the standing position is not permanent. At first we will experience our positions and feelings in this light. When we realize the falling away of one position, we will notice immediately the arising of another new position. However, we realize the falling away of one position only when that position stops. We have still to realize the present arising and falling away of matter within that position. So far, when we realize the falling away of the sitting position, we see it only when the sitting position has changed to another posture. We have next to realize the falling away of matter in the sitting position while we are still sitting. This means that as the insight gets deeper we can experience the falling away of the matter while remaining in the sitting position. This occurs by noting the separation of the rapid sequence of the mental states and matter which we will experience while we are still sitting. As practice continues, our experiencing of this rapid sequence will become decisive and certain. Having this degree of insight knowledge, we will know that even in the past or future all phenomena will be impermanent in the same way. When we have this knowledge, we will have no doubt as to the nature of the future. When we experience and realize the arising and falling away of various existences, then we have attained the degree of insight called *mastering-knowledge*, and it is this knowledge which sees decisively that mental states and matter are not permanent. It can be said that this degree of insight knowledge realizes the three characteristics of existence, because it experiences the impermanence of mental states and matter, their moment-to-moment arising and falling away. But what it yet has to experience is the clear demarcation of the rapid sequence of the mental states and matter. The knowledge of this depth is still not strong or keen enough to uproot the most fundamental misunderstandings or wrong views buried deep within our consciousness.

152

If we continue our awareness, insight wisdom will grow keener and keener, and our awareness will become finer and more subtle. The more mindful we become, the more continuously will we acknowledge the present existence, irrespective of the object. Now the awareness of one present existence will become clearly disclosed and the sharp demarcation of the arising and the falling away of each state of mind and matter will be realized. When we experience this demarcation of the arising and falling away of mental states we will gain a degree of insight knowledge which is called the *arising-and-falling-away-knowledge*. This degree of insight knowledge also contains all the realizations of the first three knowledges in it. Now one experiences the first degree of knowledge, the insight wisdom which perceives all existence as simply mental states and matter; the second degree of knowledge or the insight wisdom which experiences the causal arising of mental states and matter; and the third degree of knowledge, the insight wisdom which first experiences the characteristics of the arising and falling away of mental states and matter, but not yet their clear demarcation.

The true path of Vipassana has now begun with the experience of the *arising-and-falling-away-knowledge*. This degree of knowledge is very important and it is this knowledge which first experiences the demarcations of the rapid sequence of mental states and matter. With increasing mindfulness, the *arising-and-falling-away-knowledge* becomes much more keen. This knowledge discloses momentary birth and death, it sees clearly the demarcation spaces of the rapid sequence of mental states and matter as they arise and pass away. To have insight of this degree is to possess a very keen wisdom. This kind of wisdom will uproot and destroy the illusion that mind and matter are permanent, it will show that they cannot be a source of lasting happiness and that they are empty of a 'self' or 'I'. This wisdom will remove many of the misunderstandings which have been established in our consciousness. However, this insight knowledge is still temporary, and it cannot as yet completely uproot all wrong views. It will begin to eliminate defilements, particularly the misunderstandings that mistake experience as true 'self'. This level of insight knowledge is very strong, so strong in fact that the teacher will not have to reassure the practitioner that he has realized the truth; his own insight knowledge will be able to judge accurately and with certainty. At this point, great joy and lightness will arise in the mind. The clarity of perception is such as has never before been experienced. This is the first taste of true liberation in the mind.

Realizing this clear demarcation of the arising and falling away of mental states and matter through direct experience is not the same as understanding or seeing it through listening or study. Regardless of how well you are listening or how much right understanding you may have through study, you still have not experienced the truth of existence. The truth of existence cannot be attained through contemplation or study. If we think or contemplate, we have only conceptual knowledge, and what we know concerns only the past or the future, and that which is true in the present will be ignored. When knowing through thought only, we just connect the past with the future through comparison, from thoughts which are not directly experiencing the present reality. Therefore these thoughts are not able to eliminate any of the latent defilements. They can be eliminated only through the insight wisdom which arises from the right causes and the right practices, from a mind which has been cleared of all self-misconceptions. Then doubt, uncertainty, or any kind of suspicion in these matters disappears. For example, on the question of how mind and matter arise, all doubt is eliminated. We see clearly the factors and causes for ourselves, and experience the truth, stage by stage, until all misgivings disappear.

The attainment of the wisdom and insight of *arising-and-falling-away-knowledge* is already a very high stage of practice. The meditator will have gained a radical new perspective on his perception of each moment of experience.

If the practitioner becomes attached to the *arising-and-falling-away-knowledge*, or if he has practiced concentration before and developed it strongly, then the defilements of insight may occur during this period. The phrase *defilements of insight* means that the practitioner has attained to this degree of insight knowledge, and then experiences subtle defilements. These defilements of insight, which are a very subtle form of attachment, are ten in number. They may be caused by attachment to the power of concentration, and however they occur, they will hinder the progress of the meditation leading to the higher degrees of insight. For example, the mind may become filled with happiness and rapture. Subtle attachment arises and the feelings and inclination for deepening insight will thus diminish and disappear. Thus we see how the defilements of insight are hindrances to insight progress. When the practitioner's wisdom is not keen enough to know and let go of such defilements, which are often exceedingly seductive, he is not

154

able to proceed further. Therefore we must have a precise understanding of this point which will permit wisdom to tell us which is the right and which the wrong path. Otherwise the wrong results will occur but we will not know what is wrong with our practice. It is difficult because the feelings can become so subtle, pleasing, and happy that they might mislead us to think that we have become enlightened, and that we have realized nirvana. Without right understanding or reasoning, we will not know at all whether the attainments in the insight practice are right or wrong.

155

Right understanding arises when we see that the path to higher insight requires that we let go of any attachment to the various mental states that arise. Rapture, bliss, concentration, even mindfulness can become objects of our subtle clinging. When we see that insight will continue to develop only by clear detached mindfulness, the defilements of insight pass. Now, as the wisdom of the *arising-and-falling-away-knowledge* is cleared from the defilements of insight, we can perceive the arising and falling away of mind and matter in a keen, sharp way with no interfering desires.

There arises then the stage of insight called *purity-by-knowledge-and-vision-of-the-path*. This insight sees that the path to nirvana requires letting go of even the most subtle attachment to any state of mind or matter.

Now, the levels of higher insight knowledge begin to develop progressively from this point. Awareness becomes sharper into the ongoing process. The more that awareness of the *arising-and-falling-away-knowledge* reveals the truth, the more wisdom develops. As this occurs, the next level of insight, the insight into the *dissolution-of-phenomena* arises. The more the practitioner's attention is directed toward the present object, the more he will experience the falling away of mind and matter. This dissolution of all he sees is frightening. Yet as he stays with the present object, it is only the falling away of mind and matter which holds his attention. The experiencing of this knowledge is called *dissolution-knowledge*, which means that all things are experienced as dangerous, frightful, unsubstantial, and not pleasant; thus he feels wearied and gradually becomes further detached from any clinging to mind and matter. The feeling of detachment which arises is called *aversion-knowledge*, and the desire to hold on to any states of mind and matter becomes weaker and weaker as the results of the insight practice.

Eventually the practitioner reaches the stage of highest clarity and detachment, *knowledge-of-equanimity-toward-all-formations*. It is from this stage, with a mind totally free of attachment, seeing clearly all experience with the arising of no defilements, that the practitioner may experience nirvana and the permanent uprooting of wrong view and other defilements.

This is a very sketchy description of the higher stages on the path of insight. I would like to conclude this description by re-emphasizing the importance of reaching the level of *arising-and-falling-away-knowledge*. This is a very important stage. If you practice and can attain this knowledge, then the higher knowledges, from this stage onward, will proceed accordingly until you eventually understand the nature of mind and matter in their fullest aspect and experience the cessation of the process, nirvana.

Now, I would like to discuss one more matter. You may have heard it said many times before that in order to attain nirvana it is not necessary to practice something special or follow certain procedures; that there is no rule, nor any set method, for whatever we do is right since there are many ways and, in the end, each way will lead us to nirvana. Such belief is absolutely not true according to evidence and reason. According to all evidence, all Buddhists know that the Buddha himself had acknowledged and confirmed that there is only one way which leads to nirvana. That way is the four applications of mindfulness. Only the Buddha showed us this way. If people were to practice meditation according to their own methods, then each person would create his own doctrine, because each person would say that in the end he would attain nirvana. Can this kind of misunderstanding be reasonable or at all possible? If so, then the Buddha was not a truthful person. If anyone or everyone can reach nirvana without the application of mindfulness, then it was not necessary for the Buddha to teach this practice. We know that during the Buddha's lifetime there were many religious sects and meditation practices. Even supranormal powers were practiced at that time; for example, flying in the air, walking on water, passing through mountains. All of these supranormal powers occurred quite frequently. However, the true way to nirvana had not yet been taught. Therefore, if anyone still has the mistaken notion that there are many ways, then let him think more deeply on this matter. Do not forget that we pay homage to the Buddha because he has shown us the method of mental development for the attainment of nirvana; namely the application of mindfulness, that which all other teachers in the world could not teach. That is why Buddhists deem the Buddha as the greatest individual in the world and pay homage to his virtues of wisdom, purity, and compassion. If we do not cultivate the development of insight according to the application of mindfulness, we cannot truly understand Buddhism. Even at the present time, there are few people who have the right understanding of the application of mindfulness. Actually, although this system is fully reasonable, it is not easy to have the right understanding immediately or quickly. We should study deeply and try to understand by reason, then we must prove its validity through practice. We must at all times test Buddhism through practice and see the truth for ourselves.

157

Let me conclude with some further directions for Vipassana practice:

1. Develop a thorough understanding of the way in which all existence is composed of only mental states and matter when beginning Vipassana.
2. The matter and mental states that concern you are those that occur in your own body. So, you must be aware of these moment to moment in the *present* to see their nature clearly.
3. Either mind states or matter should be the continual object of meditation, always those of the present moment. If feelings arise, examine these. If you lose track, don't worry but simply start afresh on your examination of matter and mental states.
4. During practice the meditator must take care that desire to see certain things or desire to develop certain insight is not aroused. You should simply watch your matter and mind states.
5. Don't try to examine both matter and mind states at the same time, but examine each separately, always in the present moment.
6. Stick to the four major postures of standing, sitting, walking, and reclining, and avoid minor movements.
7. If it is necessary to change position, make sure to know the reason or cause for the movement before changing.
8. Use your ordinary postures and positions and examine the matter and mind states in each of your ordinary positions.
9. Try to be natural and do not overexaggerate slow walking and moving to try to speed up insight. This desire will block insight.
10. When practicing, don't do anything which is unnecessary,
    —don't speak more than is required,
    —don't change postures until necessary,
    —don't eat until necessary.

11. Before you do anything, you must understand the necessary reason for the action and see how you are forced by suffering to do it.
12. Let go of the feeling that meditation is something special. It is not a time to acquire anything, but simply to examine the causes for our actions and the nature of our mind and body.
13. Do not try to attain any special mind states such as bliss or peacefulness through meditation.
14. The Vipassana meditator must be like a spectator at a play. Don't try to direct the activity, simply watch mindfully the constant flow of matter and mental states as they come into consciousness. This balanced stance will lead to wisdom.

ACHAAN MAHA BOOWA

Achaan Maha Boowa is a well-known abbot and teacher in the forest ascetic tradition of northeast Thailand. After studying basic Dharma for several years he mastered Pali, language of the scriptures, before setting out for meditation training. Achaan Maha Boowa spent many years practicing meditation as a forest monk, and received his instruction in large part from a famous Lao-speaking master, Achaan Mun. Achaan Mun is one of the most renowned of the Thai-Lao forest teachers of this century, known for his mastery of concentration and insight practices, for his great powers, and for the fierceness of his teaching style. It is told that Achaan Maha Boowa as a student had, after long practice, mastered some of the Buddhist concentration meditations, and spent his time sitting in much bliss before he went to see Achaan Mun. This mastery alone is quite an attainment. Achaan Mun on meeting him gave a very stern lecture on the difference between bliss and the wisdom of enlightenment and sent him off to the forest to practice more. For many years following this chiding, Achaan Maha Boowa was unable to enter into high and blissful concentration states. But when he again finally mastered them, it was with great wisdom and insight.

Achaan Maha Boowa emphasizes the development of strong and steady concentration in practice as the forerunner of the arising of wisdom. In this particular talk he also tells how it is possible to use wisdom, through study or investigation into the body and mind, to aid in the development of concentration and calm. This concentration then leads to even deeper wisdom. Although Maha Boowa discusses the three traditional parts of the spiritual path—virtue, concentration, and wisdom—he explains that these do not necessarily develop in any particular order. Instead, practice should not be "developing concentration stage by stage" but working with virtue, concentration, and wisdom concurrently to deal with defilements as they arise.

For starting practice, Achaan Maha Boowa encourages the use of word repetition or mantra to develop initial calm, either alone or in conjunction with visualizations. Then, once calm is established we are instructed to use this concentration to investigate the nature and parts of the body. We are later directed to investigate the nature of the mind and to see how ignorance and misunderstanding has led to a false view of self and to great suffering in these rounds of rebirth. Achaan Maha Boowa details some of the ways concentration can be developed, especially in regard to images and visions that arise in practice. He also distinguishes between what seem to be internally and externally caused phenomena that appear in meditation and how to use these. It is important, he notes, that "these do not occur in every case" and that "whatever type of concentration developed, wisdom is always the thing that is important." I have hesitated to include too much detail about the various images and phenomena that sometimes arise with developing concentration for fear that beginning meditators will latch on to these as important or necessarily desirable experiences. It can be a trap to expect the appearance of such phenomena or to consider them as a sign of progress, to try and make them happen in one's meditation. If one chooses to work with them to develop absorption in one's practice this is best done under the guidance of a teacher.[1] Do not be excited by descriptions of what seem to be strange or unusual experiences from a concentrated mind. They are not valuable. Only wisdom is important.

Maha Boowa frequently uses the term *heart*. This is not *heart* in the sense of certain emotional qualities such as compassion. For this article *heart* refers to mind. It is traditional in Buddhism to refer to the heart as the seat of the mind. It is the intention of the original translator, Bhikkhu Pannavado, to use the colloquial language just as Maha Boowa teaches. This is to preserve the Forest Dharma quality of this teaching, and though some terms may not correspond to direct scriptural interpretations, they are used as a guide to develop meditation in a most practical sense.

Achaan Maha Boowa's forest monastery, Wat Ba Ban Tat, is on approximately 100 acres of land in Udorn Province, northeast Thailand. The number of monks and cottages is small, no more than twenty. Discipline is very strict, and Achaan Maha Boowa teaches somewhat in the style of his own fierce teacher. More than a dozen Westerners have studied with him, some for many years now, as he usually expects a commitment of several years from new students. Much of the learning at Wat Ba Ban Tat, as in the other Thai-Lao forest monasteries, is through the disciplined, strict, and extremely simple way of life. One simple meal a day, small cottages, well water for bathing, alms round at sun-up, long periods of silence, and some isolation all contribute to a life that requires little

163

[1] *An even more detailed description of the development of absorption, signs, and their uses is found in several chapters of* The Path of Purification (Vissudhimagga), *a famous Buddhist meditation manual and commentary, published in a new edition by Shambhala Publications.*

worldly thought. The forest monastery then, as well as being a facility for intensive meditation, is also a very special educational environment. In its simple communal setting one can slow down, simplify, and observe the process of mind, of living, and so develop wisdom. Maha Boowa comes to Bangkok occasionally to teach, and there are a number of his talks published in English available through Wat Bavorniwas in Bangkok.

Wisdom Develops Samadhi

9

by Achaan Maha Boowa

MORALITY²

Morality is that which sets a limit to the 'outgoing exuberance'³ in a person's activities of body and speech. The responsibility for these activities and their results rests with the heart.⁴

For one who practices morality correctly, it is also for the purpose of living in a 'cool' way with a happy and easy heart. And if one associates with other people who themselves maintain morality, it is essential that one should oneself be a good person. Those

---

² Morality *is a translation of* sila. Sila *has a wider connotation in its higher and more subtle levels, for it includes all bodily actions and speech, which are assessed as right or wrong, depending on whether they make one's heart less or more passionate.*

³ Outgoing exuberance *is a translation of the Thai word* kanong, *which is more usually translated as 'high spirited', 'exuberant'. But the usage of the word in the context of this article is unusual, and means the display of self by way of body, speech, or thought, and involving the conceited opinion of self which such a display is designed to proclaim, both to oneself and others.*

⁴ Heart *is used throughout as the translation of the Thai word* chai. *It is*

who have low or vulgar minds are, however, not likely to understand the necessity for morality because they do not want to become good people, nor to get involved in the world of good people. They would rather try to break up the happiness of others and to instigate trouble and danger in the world whenever they get a chance to do so.

Natural moral behavior does not have to be asked for as precepts from a monk or dictated from someone in an official capacity before it is established. For if a person respects and likes those characteristics within himself which are right, good, and graceful, he will behave in this way personally as well as in association with others. Naturally avoiding actions which are contrary to such good behavior indicates that he has moral behavior within his character.

One should not think that moral behavior is exclusively a human faculty, for even animals can have aspects of it. One need only observe the animals which people look after in their own homes to see how in some degree the hearts and the behavior of animals are permeated with the nature of Dharma.

One who always has moral behavior as the basis of his character, besides being good natured and having the confidence of and being popular with the people of his village or district, will also be good natured within himself every day of this life and of the next life also.

Moral behavior is therefore a quality which is always necessary in the world.

CONCENTRATION

All types of meditation[5] are for controlling the 'outgoing exuber-

often translated as 'mind', but this is rather misleading since the mind is nowadays closely associated with the thinking apparatus, the brain and the head, whereas the chai is more emotional, and is not the physical body, a part of it, or even a function of it—though it does, of course, associate with it and there is a strong mutual influence between the two.

[5] Meditation is kammatthana Dharma. The word kammatthana is made up of karma, or action, and thana, or a place, a base. Thus it is a place or basis of action. The forty kammatthana are the objects and methods of meditation as given further on in this chapter. But the word kammatthana is

ance' of the heart. The heart which is not controlled by meditation is liable to the arising of 'outgoing exuberance' throughout life. From infancy to old age it is so, with the rich and the poor, with the clever and the stupid, with those in high and low position in life, with the blind, deaf, paralyzed, maimed, deformed, and so on endlessly.

In Buddhism such people are considered to be still at the age of a 'heart with outgoing exuberance'. Their hearts have no greatness, they find no contentment, they are ill fated as regards happiness of heart, and when they die they lose in all ways—like a tree which may have many branches, flowers, and fruit, but as its main root is damaged, will die and lose its greatness and everything else.

The baneful effect of the 'outgoing exuberance' of a heart which does not have Dharma as its guardian is that it never finds true happiness, and even if happiness does arise due to searching for it and finding it, it will be happiness of the type in which one is like an actor playing a part, which increases the 'outgoing exurberance', making the heart go increasingly in the wrong direction and not the type of happiness which is truly satisfying.

Concentration, which means calm or stability of heart, is that which opposes the 'outgoing exuberance'. The heart, on the other hand, does not want to take its 'medicine' and the medicine is the meditation.

Taking the medicine means training one's heart in Dharma and not allowing it to go its own way, for the heart always likes to have 'outgoing exuberance' as a companion. In other words, taking the medicine means that the heart brings Dharma into itself as its guardian.

The Dharma which is the guardian of the heart is called the meditation.

The Buddha taught forty types of meditation which variously accord with the different temperaments of people.[6]

Here we will confine ourselves to the consideration of a few of these methods which are in general use and which are found to give satisfactory results. They include:

1. Contemplation of the thirty-two parts of the body, including: hair of the head, hair of the body, nails, teeth, skin.

also used in a broader sense to refer to the way of applying the teaching of the Buddha in a practical manner as distinct from reading, theorizing, or learning about it.

[6] *See "Sunlun Sayadaw."*

2. Contemplation of the 'Buddha', the 'Dharma', and the 'Sangha'.

3. Awareness of breathing in and out.

Whichever method is used it should suit one's character, for characters differ, and to teach that everyone should use only one type of meditation may well prove to be a hindrance to some people, thus preventing their attaining beneficial results from their practice.

When one finds the type of meditation that suits one's character,[7] one should set one's mind to begin doing the practice with a preparatory repetition of a word such as in the body meditation, 'head hair'. One should then repeat the word mentally, not out loud, and at the same time one should keep one's attention fixed upon hair of the head. If, however, one finds that thinking on its own is not able to capture the heart, one may repeat the preparatory repetition in the manner of a chant so that the sound captivates the heart and it becomes calm and quiet. One should continue repeating the preparatory repetition until the heart has become calm and then one can stop. But whichever preparatory repetition is used, one should retain conscious awareness of that meditation. Thus in the foregoing example of 'head hair', one should retain conscious awareness of the hair on one's head.

If one uses one of the preparatory repetitions 'Buddho', 'Dhammo', or 'Sangho', one should set up knowledge of it just in the heart alone. These are like the other types of meditation, for here one should repeat 'Buddho' (or 'Dhammo' or 'Sangho') so that it is in continuous contact with the heart and remains there until the one who repeats the 'Buddho' of the preparatory repetition and the 'one who knows'[8] who is in the heart, are found to be identical.

The development of awareness of breathing uses the breath as the objective support of the heart and consists in knowing and

167

[7] It may be asked how one is to know which type of meditation suits one's character. Unless a reliable teacher specifies a particular type, one can only know by the method of trial and error. One may say that the type of practice which one finds intriguing, which holds one's attention, or which 'gets under one's skin' in one way or another is suitable. Also, one should generally feel cool, bright, and calm after a period of correct practice.

[8] The 'one who knows' is in fact a mode of the citta (heart). For example, suppose that one has told a lie to someone; one's actions, speech, and thoughts may all be in accordance with the lie, but somewhere inside there is the 'one who knows', and it is always aware that this is a lie. It must however

mindfulness of in- and out-breathing. In becoming aware of breathing, one should at first fix attention on the feeling of the breath at the nose or the palate (roof of mouth),[9] as it suits one, because this is where the breath initially makes contact, and one may use this as a marker point for holding one's attention. Having done this until one has become skilled, and the in- and out-breathing becomes finer and finer, one will progressively come to know and understand the nature of the contact of in- and out-breathing, until it seems that the breathing is located either in the middle of the chest or the solar plexus.[10] After this, one must just fix one's attention on breathing at that place and one must no longer be concerned about fixing attention on the breathing at the tip of the nose or the palate, nor about following it in and out with awareness.

In fixing attention on the breath, one may also repeat 'Buddho' in time with the breath as a preparatory repetition to supervise the in- and out-breathing, in order to assist the 'one who knows' and make the 'one who knows' clear with regard to the breath. Then the breath will appear more and more clearly to the heart.

Once one becomes skilled with the breath, every time one attends to the breathing process one should fix attention at the point in the middle of the chest or the solar plexus.

In particular, it is important to have mindfulness established. One must establish mindfulness to control the heart so that one feels the breath at every moment while it is entering or leaving, whether short or long, until one knows clearly that the breathing is becoming progressively finer with every breath—until finally it becomes apparent that the finest and most subtle breath and the heart have converged and become one.[11] At this stage, one should fix attention on the breath exclusively within the heart, and there is no need to worry about the preparatory repetition, for in becom-

be borne in mind that except in rare cases, the 'one who knows' is still under the influence of ignorance (avijja), so that although it knows, there are many things that it knows wrongly.

[9] *This method of practice is not done with one's mouth open, so the breath as physical air does not pass over the palate. Nevertheless, many people have a strong feeling response at this point, as though the breath were passing back and forth.*

[10] *The breath is seen (or felt) in the middle of the chest or the solar plexus, much as it is felt at the tip of the nose in the earlier stages of the practice. On being questioned, the author said that the middle of the chest and the solar*

ing aware of the breath as entering and leaving, and as short or long, the preparatory repetition is only for the purpose of making the heart become subtle.

When one has attained the most subtle level of breathing, he will be bright, cool, calm, happy, and just knowing the heart—and there will be no connection with any disturbing influence. Even if finally at that time the breath disappears, there will be no anxiety because one will have let go of the burden and one will just have knowledge of the heart alone. In other words, it will be non-dual. This is development of absorption.[12]

169

This is the result that comes from developing the practice of mindfulness of breathing. But it should also be understood that whenever meditation is practiced, and whoever practices it, this is the result that should be attained.

Concerning the preparatory development and word repetition, by using one of these forms of meditation for controlling the heart with mindfulness, one will gradually be able to curb the 'outgoing exuberance' of the heart. Calm and happiness will then arise and develop, and there will be only one thing influencing the heart, which will be a knowing of the heart alone without any distur-bance or distraction, for there will be nothing which can irritate or disturb the heart to make it fall away from this state. This is the nature of happiness of heart, the heart being free from all vain imaginings and thought creations.

It is also possible that during practice of a given type of medita-tion, the characteristics of that form of meditation may appear to some people. For example, hair of the head, or hair of the body, or nails, teeth, skin, flesh, sinews, or bones, may appear and be seen clearly with the heart, as though one were looking at it with one's eyes. If this happens, one should pay attention to it and see it clearly until it becomes fixed in one's heart.

When the above object has been intimately fixed in one's heart, one must appreciate it in the right way by attending to the un-

plexus were one place, located at the bottom end of the breast bone. But he also said that if one understood them to be two separate places, either of which could be the location for awareness of breathing, one would not be wrong. Note also here the correspondence to the development of the heart center in the practice of Achaan Dhammadaro and U Ba Khin.

[11] In other words, it seems as if the heart is the breathing, and as if the breathing is the heart.

[12] See Glossary.

pleasant and loathsome aspects of it, for this is the nature of all the parts of the body, both internally and externally. One may further take such objects and contemplate them as rotting and decayed, as being burnt, as being eaten by vultures, crows, and dogs, and see them breaking down into their basic elements—earth, water, fire, air.

Doing the practice in this way will be of great value for the purpose of reducing and eliminating delusion in regard to the nature of the body, this delusion being what gives rise to sexual craving—which is one aspect of the 'outgoing exuberance' of the heart. One's heart will then become progressively more calm and subtle, and wisdom will grow.

A person who does not see the parts of the body should understand that all preparatory meditation is for the purpose of leading the heart to a state of both calm and happiness, so one should not feel doubtful about any of these methods. They will all lead the heart to a state of calm, and later on to see danger[13] with wisdom. One must be determined in whichever meditation one is practicing, and repeat whichever preparatory repetition suits one, without becoming disheartened or feeling like giving up.

It should be realized that whichever method of meditation is practiced, it leads to the same goal as all the other methods, and it should also be realized that all these methods of Dharma will lead the heart to peace and happiness—in other words, to nirvana— which is the final goal of all types of meditation development. Therefore one must do one's own meditation practice and not be concerned about other types of meditation, otherwise one will be in a state of doubt and uncertainty, and unable to decide which of them is the right way. This would be a constant obstacle to one's heart, preventing one from carrying out one's original resolve.

Instead, one must determine that one will be really mindful in the practice, and one must not arrange to practice virtue, concentration, and wisdom in any special order, nor let them go away from the heart, because the defilements of passion, hate, delusion, and the rest, dwell in the heart and nobody has arranged them in order. When one thinks in wrong and faulty ways, it arouses the defilements in one's heart. One does not decide or arrange that this one will come earlier and that one later, for whatever type it is, so

[13] Danger *means the danger of the body which may die at any time from any one of many causes, and also the danger of the defilements which lead one to suffering and to bad or terrible realms and births.*

170

it arises, and they all make one hot-hearted or passionate in the same way. The defilements are always bound to be of this nature, and it is of no consequence in which order they arise, for all of them are able to make one hot and passionate.

Therefore, in curing the defilements one must not wait to develop virtue first, then concentration second, and wisdom third—which may be called 'developing concentration stage by stage'—for this keeps one always in the past and future, and by this one would never be able to attain calm and happiness.

171

WISDOM DEVELOPS CONCENTRATION

The true purpose of meditation practice is to bring about calm in the heart. If one cannot attain calm by lulling the heart with a preparatory method, one must use the way of subduing it by intimidation. In other words, wisdom is used to search out and examine those things to which the heart is attached and, depending on how skillful one's wisdom is, to search for a way to goad the disobedient heart with what wisdom reveals, until it surrenders to wisdom and the heart accepts the truth about the things to which it is attached. Then the heart cannot be distracted and restless and must drop into a state of calm. This happens in the same way as a work animal whose 'outgoing exuberance' must be trained by constant goading so that it surrenders to the will of its master.

The following analogy may help to illustrate this method. In a place where there are few trees and each one is standing on its own, if a man wanted to cut one down he could do so and make it fall where he wanted. He could then take it and use it as he wished with no difficulty.

But if he wanted to cut a tree down in a forest where its branches were entangled with other trees and creepers, he would find it difficult to fell the tree and to make it fall just where he wished. So the woodcutter would have to use his wisdom and examine carefully to find out what was entangled with the tree, and then by cutting away all the entanglements he could fell it where he wanted and use it however he wished without difficulty.

All of us have characters which are comparable with these two trees. Some people do not have much in their environment to burden them and to act as a drag on their minds. When they use only a preparatory meditation such as repeating 'Buddho', 'Dhammo', or

'Sangho', the heart is able to become calm and cool and drop into a state of concentration. This becomes the basis for the development of wisdom and enables them to go ahead with ease—in this case, 'concentration develops wisdom'.

But there are other people who have many things in their environment to burden and oppress their hearts, and their natures are such that they like thinking a lot. If they train themselves by using a preparatory meditation as described in the foregoing section, they are not able to cause the heart to drop into the calm of concentration. They must therefore carefully use wisdom to examine the reasons for this, in order to sever the root cause of their distraction by means of wisdom.

When wisdom has been nagging at those things to which the heart is firmly attached, what the heart knows about them cannot be superior to that which wisdom reveals, so the heart will then drop into a state of calm and attain concentration. People of this type must therefore train the heart to attain concentration by using wisdom; in this case 'wisdom develops concentration'.

When concentration steadily develops due to the use of wisdom, the concentration then becomes the basis for further wisdom at a higher level. This latter stage then conforms with the basic principle, 'concentration develops wisdom'.

A person who wants to train his heart to become skillful and to know what is behind the deluding tricks of the defilements, must not be attached to study and learning in Buddhism to such an extent that it gives rise to the defilements. But also he must not abandon study and learning, for to do this goes beyond the teaching of the Buddha.

In other words, when one is practicing meditation for the purpose of developing concentration, one must not let the heart grasp at what it has learned by study, for it will be led into thoughts of the past and future. One must instead make the heart keep to the present, which means that one's only concern must be just that aspect of Dharma which one is developing.

When there is some question or point of doubt in connection with one's heart which one is unable to resolve, one may then check it by study and learning after one has finished meditation practice. But it is wrong to check one's practice all the time with what one has learned by study, for this will be mere intellectual knowledge and not knowledge which comes from development in meditation.

Wisdom which brings calm can come from appropriate study of

the Buddist scriptures. It can also come from contemplation of the true nature of the parts of the body. Seeing their impermanence and unsatisfactoriness will lead the heart to calm. Also, wisdom can come from the investigation and examining of our attachments, our worries, our fears. This wisdom and further contemplation of the mind and body, the aggregates of the elements, will then lead to greater detachment and eventual calm and concentration. So, if the heart attains calm with an object of calm such as a preparatory repetition that one is developing, one should continue with that method. But if it attains calm only by the use of wisdom, using various expedient methods to overcome difficulties, then one should skillfully use wisdom to help in the attainment of calm. The results which come from training in both these ways ('concentration develops wisdom' and 'wisdom develops concentration'), are the development of deep calm and wisdom, which will have a hidden radiance coming from the heart.

173

DEVELOPING CONCENTRATION

Concentration or samadhi is by name and nature 'calmness'. There are three kinds of samadhi. One is momentary concentration, in which the heart becomes unwaveringly fixed and calm for a short time, after which it withdraws. The second is access concentration, which is similar but of greater duration. The third type is full, absorptive concentration which is subtle, firm, and unwavering, and in which one can remain concentrated for a long time. One may remain concentrated in this state or withdraw from it as one wishes.

Access concentration is important to discuss further, for it is crucial to the development of deeper concentration and wisdom. In access concentration, when the heart has dropped into a calm state it does not remain in that state, but partially withdraws to follow and get to know various things which have come into contact with the heart.

In access concentration, sometimes in front of one there appears an image (nimitta[14]) of oneself lying down dead with body decayed

[14] Nimitta *is an appearance that may take place in terms of seeing, hearing, smelling, tasting, touching, or mental impressions, and which arises based upon the heart and not upon the relevant sense organ. Examples of nimittas*

and swollen, or it may be the dead body of someone else. Sometimes it is a skeleton, or bones scattered about, or maybe one sees it as a corpse being carried past.

When such a sign appears, a clever person will take it as his learning sign. This will steadily lead to concentration becoming firm and to wisdom becoming penetrating and strong. But this person must have a strong ability to maintain a detached, rational attitude to be successful in gaining value from such a sign. He can then develop mindfulness and wisdom when faced with it.

Working with a learning sign is the most suitable basis for development of deeper concentration and a fixed sign. The learning sign is the basic one that 'uprises' or comes into being. When this breaks up into its components, it becomes the fixed sign. For example, the vision of one's physical body may be the learning sign, but when this breaks open and displays all the parts and organs it becomes the fixed sign. One must develop the learning sign into a fixed sign and then absorb the impression of this fixed sign into one's heart. This brings the noble truth to light in our heart.[15]

When one has become skilled at concentration, one may let the heart go out and follow the sign and find out what is taking place. It will then be of great value to understand the events of the past and future.

One must make the heart bold and fearless when the various kinds of signs arise from access concentration, and at the outset see them in terms of the three characteristics of impermanence, suffering, and non-self as soon as they appear.[16] Then they will not cause any trouble.

Sometimes external signs may pass by, although one may not always know whether they are external or whether they arise from oneself. But when one has become skilled with internal signs

are the seeing or hearing of visions, lights, objects, sounds, and experiences like ghosts.

[15] *Absorbing the impression of the fixed sign into one's heart means that one opens one's heart to it. If this sign is one such as the image of a dead body or body parts, then this is taking the noble truth of suffering into the heart.*

[16] *This means that one should keep to the middle way, avoiding the extremes of desire for a pleasant sign and aversion from an unpleasant one. Also, that one should not become attached to a pleasant sign and then be sorry when it changes or goes. By seeing impermanence, suffering, and non-self in all signs, one remains detached and safe.*

174

which arise from oneself, one will be able to know which are external signs. External signs are associated with many different occurrences of people, animals, ghosts, etc. When such incidents occur, they may last for a long or short time depending on various internal and external conditions. When such signs die away and the heart withdraws, it may have spent several hours in the state relating to them.

For however long the heart remains concentrated in this way, when it withdraws one will find that it has not increased one's strength of concentration, nor made it more firm and durable, nor will it have helped to develop and strengthen one's wisdom. It is like going to sleep and dreaming; when one wakes, one's mind and body will not have gained in strength.

But when one withdraws from the type of concentration in which one became concentrated and then remained in that one state, one will find that the strength of one's concentration has increased and it has become more firm and durable. It is like someone who sleeps soundly without dreaming; when he wakes his body and mind feel strong.

It should, however, be understood that the kind of concentration in which these signs appear does not occur in every case, and where it does not occur, no matter how long the heart remains in a concentrated state, hardly any signs appear. These are the types of people of whom one may say 'wisdom develops concentration'. With these people, even when the heart has dropped down into a calm and concentrated state, signs do not arise however long they remain in this state, because wisdom is associated with and gets involved with the concentration. Wisdom means one is constantly examining and investigating the states of mind while concentration is present, and this effectively prevents any signs arising.

Whatever type of concentration is developed, wisdom is always the thing that is important. When one has withdrawn from concentration, one must contemplate the elements and the aggregates with wisdom, because wisdom and concentration are a 'Dharma pair' which go together and cannot be separated. So if concentration does not progress sufficiently, one must use wisdom to assist it.

Basically, though it is concentration of all types that aids and supports the development of wisdom, the extent to which it does this depends on the strength of one's concentration. In other words, concentration which is gross, middling, or subtle aids and supports wisdom which is gross, middling, or subtle respectively, and it is up to a wise person to turn his concentration to use by developing wisdom.

But generally speaking, whatever type of concentration is attained, one who practices meditation is likely to become attached to it, because when the heart drops into a concentrated state and rests there, a state of calm and happiness is present. It can be said that in being attached to calm the heart has no problems while it remains concentrated, and it can remain at rest for as long as one wishes, depending on the level of one's ability to concentrate.

An important thing is that when the heart has withdrawn, it still longs for its state of deep repose. Although one has enough calm to meditate using wisdom—and one's calm is sufficient to use very effectively—one still tries to stay in a state of deep calm, without being at all interested in the development of wisdom. This is becoming addicted to concentration and being unable to withdraw from it in order to go further.

WISDOM

The right and smooth way for one who practices meditation, once the heart has become sufficiently calm to see the way, is to begin by training it to investigate the parts of the body with wisdom, either singly or in many parts, opening up and looking into one's own body.

Things which do not fulfill any of one's hopes are about and within this body. Delusion with regard to beings and formations[17] is delusion with regard to this body. Attachment to beings and formations is attachment to this body. Separation from beings and formations is separation from this body. The infatuations of love and hate are infatuation with this body. Not wanting death is anxiety about this body—and when one is dead, the weeping and mourning of relatives and friends is because of this body. The distress and suffering from the day of one's birth to the time of

[17] Formations (sankhara) *means those factors, functions, and relationships which are grouped together to form a body, a person, an animal, or other entities and things. For example, the parts which are put together to form a motor car may be called its sankharas. The underlying idea is that there is no entity which can be found to correspond to 'motor car' as such, for it is all sankharas.*

one's death is because of this body. All day and night, animals and people run this way and that in swarms, searching for food and places to live because of the nature of this body.

The great cause in this world is the wheel that whirls people and animals around without ever letting them open their eyes properly to the nature of their state; it is like a fire burning them all the time. The body is the cause of it all. Beings are inundated by defilements until they are quite unable to extricate themselves from this situation, because of this body. In brief, the whole story of this world is the story of what alone concerns this body.

177

When the heart views the body in the foregoing way, with wisdom, it will become wearied both of one's own body and the bodies of other people and animals. This will reduce one's pleasurable excitement in regard to the body, and will thus withdraw fixed attachment to the body by abandoning it. At the same time, one will know the body and all its parts as they truly are, and one will no longer be deluded by love or hate for the body of anyone.

The heart, in using the spyglass of wisdom to go sightseeing in the 'city of the body', can see one's own 'body city' and then that of other people and animals quite clearly, until one comes to see in greater detail that all the roads, streets, and alleyways are divided into three aspects (which are the three characteristics: impermanence, suffering, and non-self) and into four aspects (which are the four elements: earth, water, air, and fire). This is so throughout every part of the whole body. Even the lavatory and the kitchen are to be found with this 'body city'.

One who is able to see the body clearly in this way may be classed as one who knows the world and understands all realms of existence. To see clearly within the 'city of the body' throughout all the three world spheres by means of 'seeing in a true way everything within the body' and coming to the end of all doubts with regard to the body, is called the *Dharma of form*.[18]

We now go on to a discussion of deep insight that arises out of concentration in connection with the Dharma of mind.[19] The

---

[18] Form Dharma (rupa) *means 'the way', the facts or the teaching as it applies to matter. Although* rupa *literally means 'form', in practice it nearly always refers to the physical body.*

[19] Mind Dharma (nama) *in a similar manner, means 'the way', the facts or the teaching as it applies to mind.* Nama *literally means 'name', but it is normally understood as referring to the mental constituents of the five aggregates—i.e., feeling, perceptions, formations, and consciousness.*

Dharma of mind includes vedana, sanna, sankhara, and vinnana—four of the five aggregates. These are mind which is more subtle than the aggregate of form. One cannot look into them with one's eyes, but one can come to know them by way of the heart. More precisely these aggregates are defined in this way:

178

Vedana means those things (feelings) which are experienced by the heart that are sometimes pleasant, sometimes painful, and sometimes neutral.

Sanna means perception and includes memory and recollection.

Sankhara means mental formations, volitions, mental relations to objects besides the quality of feeling and perception.

Vinnana means consciousness or knowing of forms, sounds, smells, tastes, or things which touch us, and of mental objects, just at that moment when these things come into contact with the eye, ear, nose, tongue, body, or heart respectively.

These four mental Dharmas are the activities of the heart, they come from the heart, they may be known in the heart, and if the heart is still not careful they are also its deceivers, and so they are also the things which can hide or obscure the truth.

Investigation of these four mental Dharmas must be done with wisdom, and entirely in terms of the three characteristics, because into whatever mode they change, these aggregates always have the three characteristics present within them. But when investigating these aggregates one may do so singly or use any one of the three characteristics as one prefers, or one may investigate all of them together because each of the aggregates and characteristics are aspects of Dharma which are linked and related. Thus if one investigates only one of the aggregates or characteristics it will lead one to understand and to see deeply and fully into all the other aggregates and characteristics, the same as if one were to investigate them all together at the same time, because all of them have the noble truths as their boundary, their territory, and as that which accommodates them. For whenever one looks into the three characteristics and the aggregates, one finds the four noble truths. It is like eating food, which goes into one stomach, then permeates all parts of the body, the total territory that accommodates it.

One who practices must set up mindfulness and wisdom so as to get close and intimate with the Dharma of mind—which are these four aggregates. These aggregates are changing all the time, for they appear, remain for a time, then die away and cease; being impermanent they are also suffering and without a self, impersonal. This is the manner in which they display and proclaim their true nature, but they never have time to stop and look at it. They never have time to become calm, not even one moment. Internally, externally, everywhere throughout every realm, they proclaim with one voice that they are impermanent, and are thus unsatisfactory and non-self, and that they reject the longings of beings—which means that they have no owner. They proclaim that they are always independent and free, and that whoever out of delusion becomes attached to them only meets with suffering, depression, and sorrow which fill his thoughts and heart until in the end his tears of misery are like an over-flooded river; it will continue to be thus throughout time while beings remain deluded and entangled. Yet it is not easy to point out that the aggregates are the well of tears for those who are steeped in delusion.

179

Investigating all the aggregates and the aspects of our universe, or Dharmas in nature, with right wisdom so as to know them clearly, minimizes one's tears and diminishes the process of becoming and birth. It can even cut them away from the heart entirely, so that one may experience perfect happiness.

Dharmas of nature, such as the aggregates, are poisonous to one who is still sunk in delusion, but one who truly knows all the aggregates and Dharmas in nature as they are cannot be harmed by them and may still obtain value from them in appropriate ways. It is like a place where there are thorny bushes growing: They may be dangerous to anyone who does not know where they are and who gets entangled in them. But someone who knows all about them can use them to make a fence or a boundary for a building site, thus obtaining value from them in appropriate ways. Therefore, one who practices must act skillfully in relation to the aggregates and Dharmas in nature.

All these things arise and die away based on the heart, and one must follow and know always what is happening to them. One must take this up as an important task to be done in all postures, without being careless or forgetful.

As practice deepens, the person who is doing the practice will be completely absorbed in his research into the true nature of the aggregates and Dharmas in nature which are proclaiming the truth of themselves. He will hardly have time for lying down and sleeping because of the power of diligence in his nature which searches, without resting or stopping, into the aggregates and Dharmas in nature by way of wisdom.

Then from the aggregates and Dharmas in nature he will obtain the truth, and it will be made clear to his heart by wisdom that all the Dharmas everywhere throughout the three world spheres are of such a nature and normality that none of them seem to be the defilements and craving (kilesa and tanha) in any way whatsoever, which is in contrast to the deluded understanding of most people.

The following simile may help to explain this. Supposing some things are stolen by a thief; those things become tainted by association with the thief. But the authorities carefully investigate the case until they have sufficient witnesses and evidence and are satisfied that the stolen goods which have been recovered can be returned to their original owner or kept in a safe place so that no blame shall be attached to them. The authorities are then no longer concerned with the stolen goods, but only with the punishment of the thief. They must then obtain evidence against the thief and arrest him and bring him to trial in accordance with the law. When the truth of his guilt is established by reliable witnesses and evidence, the blame is put on the accused in accordance with the law, and any others who are not to blame are allowed to go free, as they were before the incident.

The behavior of the heart with ignorance, and all the Dharmas in nature, are like this simile, for the aggegates and Dharmas in nature throughout all the three world spheres are not at fault and are entirely free from any defilements or evil ways, but they are associated with them because the heart, which is entirely under the power of ignorance of the true nature of things, does not itself know the answer to the question: "What is ignorance?"

Ignorance and the heart are blended together as one, and it is the heart which is completely deluded that goes about forming loves and hates which it buries in the elements and aggregates —that is, in forms, sounds, smells, tastes, and bodily feelings, and in the eye, ear, nose, tongue, body, and heart. It also buries love and hate in form, feeling, perception, mental formations, and consciousness throughout the whole universe. It is the Dharmas in nature which are seized, and it is love and hate which come from the whole of this deluded heart that grasp and seize them.

Because of the power of seizing and grasping, this 'ignorant heart' wanders through birth, old age, sickness, and death, going round and round in this way through each and every life, regardless of whether it is higher or lower, good or evil, through all the three realms of becoming.

The different kinds of birth that being may take in these realms of becoming are countless, yet the heart with ignorance is able to grasp at birth in any of these realms in accordance with the supporting conditions of this heart and depending on how weak or strong and good or evil they may be. This heart must then go and be born in those circumstances that present a complete environment to which the heart (with these supporting conditions) is related.

Thus the heart gradually changes into ways which are false to its true nature, due only to the power of ignorance, and it begins to stain and color everything in the universe in a false manner, thus altering the natural state. In other words, the original basic elements change and become animals and people, and birth, old age, sickness, and death, in accordance with the usual delusion or ignorance of beings.

When one understands clearly with wisdom, that the five aggregates and the Dharmas in nature are not the main story, nor the ones who started the story, but are only involved in the story because ignorance, authority, and power makes the story, compelling all phenomena to be of this nature, then wisdom searches for the source of it all, which is the 'heart that knows', the 'well' out of which all 'stories' arise endlessly, and wisdom loses no confidence in this 'knowledge' which is in the heart. Wisdom has penetrated to the fact that the 'one who knows' (refer to footnote 8) is still full of ignorance, and that the 'one who knows' often knows wrongly.

Now, when the mindfulness and wisdom which have been developed by long training are fully proficient, they will be able to surround and penetrate straight through to the 'great center'. Although the 'one who knows' (that is, the heart that knows) is full of ignorance and does not hesitate to fight against wisdom, this ignorance can no longer stand against the 'Diamond Sword'. With unshakable mindfulness and wisdom, ignorance falls away from the heart which has been its supreme throne for aeons.

As soon as ignorance has been destroyed and has dropped away from the heart due to the superior power of 'path knowledge',[20] which is the right weapon for use at this time, the whole of the truth which has been suppressed and covered by ignorance for countless ages is then disclosed and revealed as the 'goods which had been stolen',[21] or as the entire and complete truth. Dharma which was never before known, then finally appears as knowledge

[20] Path knowledge is *the clear knowing of the noble eightfold path, and the way in which it is practically applicable within oneself.*

[21] *This passage means that under the influence of ignorance, the heart has usurped the aggregates and Dharmas in nature and thinks of them as being its*

and true insight into all Dharmas—which are revealed without the least thing remaining hidden or obscured.

When ignorance, the lord who rules the round of death, has been destroyed by the weapon of wisdom, nirvana will be revealed to the one who thus acts truly, knows truly, and sees truly—it cannot be otherwise.

All the Dharmas in nature, from the five aggregates or the internal and external senses[22] up to the whole of the universe, are the Dharma which is revealed as it truly is. There is, then, nothing that can arise as an enemy to one's heart in the future—except for the vicissitudes of the five aggregates which must be looked after until they reach their natural end—there is nothing else.

So the whole story is that of ignorance which is just 'false knowing' which goes around molesting and obstructing natural conditions so that they are changed from their true natural state. Just by the cessation of ignorance, the world—which means the natural state of things everywhere—becomes normal and there is nothing left to blame or criticize. It is as if a famous brigand were killed by the police, after which the citizens of the town could live happily and need no longer go about watchfully in fear.

The heart then knows, sees, and follows the truth of all the Dharmas in nature, and this knowledge is balanced and no longer inclines to one-sided views or opinions.

From the day that ignorance is dispersed from the heart, it will be entirely free in its thinking, meditating, knowing, and seeing into the Dharmas in nature which are associated with the heart. The eye, ear, nose, etc., and form, sound, smell, etc., then become free in their own natural sphere respectively, without being oppressed and forced, nor promoted and encouraged by the heart as usually happens. Because the heart is now in a state of Dharma and impartiality, it is impartial toward everything so that it will no longer have any enemies or foes. This means that the heart and all Dharmas in the universe are mutually in a state of complete peace and calm by virtue of the perfect truth.

The work of the heart and of insight into the Dharmas of mind

property. When ignorance is destroyed, it is seen that these are 'goods which have been stolen', not the property of the heart at all, but neutral, natural phenomena.

[22] Spheres of sensation are ayatana. They include the internal ayatanas— eye, ear, nose, tongue, body, and heart—and the external ayatanas—the spheres of sight, hearing, smell, taste, touch, and mind.

which are associated with the citta ends at this point.

I want to beg the pardon of all who practice for the purpose of getting rid of the defilements using the Dharma of the Buddha, and who find this exposition different from those that you have been used to. But one should see that the Dharma in all the old Buddhist texts also points directly at the defilements and the Dharma which is within oneself, for one must not think that the defilements and Dharma are hidden elsewhere, external, apart from oneself.

183

One who has Dharma which leads inward firmly in his heart will be able to free himself, because the Buddhist Dharma is taught for each of us, to be used and experienced in each of our hearts. One should never think that the Dharma teaching of the Buddha is a thing of the past or future and that it concerns only those who are dead and those who are yet to be born. One should realize that the Buddha did not teach people who were already dead, nor those who were still to be born. He taught people who lived at that time and who were still alive in the same way as all of us are still alive, for it is the nature of Buddhism to exist in the present and to be always a thing of today.

May you all be happy without exception, and may blessings come to all of you who read or hear this.

TAUNGPULU SAYADAW

CHAPTER
TEN

I know little about Taungpulu Tawya Kaba Aye Sayadaw except that he has been teaching in Burma for a number of years now. His main monastery is in the Meiktila District. This talk on practice was given to me by a friend, a fellow monk and meditation student I met in Rangoon.

The inclusion of the methodical practice of meditation based on the parts of the body is presented here to broaden the scope of current Buddhist meditation teachings. Traditionally, the number of concentration meditations in the Theravada scriptures includes forty subjects. Mindfulness on the parts of the body is one of them. Development proceeds by memorization and visualization as described. This practice is also used as a balance for those meditators who have a particularly strong attachment to bodily form. On following this practice, attachment to one's body, lust for others, and identification with the body as 'I' and 'mine' fall away. In beginning my own practice, while meditating on breathing, I had appear spontaneously visions of parts of the body, especially bones and skeletons. At that point my Lao teacher instructed that I fix these images in my mind as a way to sharpen my faculty of concentration and one-pointedness, and to balance the other spontaneous visions of dancing female forms. Eventually this practice led into a series of meditations on death and dead bodies, those at the monastery burning grounds, as well as visions of my own and those of close friends. Such meditation, directly coming to terms with the feelings involved in one's own death, is a powerful way to put ego and melodrama into perspective. When we attain freedom from the fear of death by acknowledging it fully, dropping the *attachment* to being, we can really be free.

Meditation on parts of the body and on death is most commonly taught among monks in the forest ascetic traditions of Theravada Buddhism. Taungpulu stresses that Buddhism is taught only as the means for attaining enlightenment. This enlightenment comes when we see the true nature of our being: impermanent, unsatisfactory, and made of simply impersonal constituents. Meditation on the parts of the body will break our illusion of the solidity and desirableness of our existence. This perception of our true nature will lead to liberation and enlightenment.

The Methodical Practice of Mindfulness Based on the Thirty-Two Constituent Parts of the Body

10

by Taungpulu Sayadaw

HONOUR TO HIM, THE EXALTED ONE, THE BUDDHA SUPREME

Buddhism is a perfect system of mental culture or meditation. The mind is the most essential factor in Buddhism, and must therefore be well trained; for only the cultured mind can develop wisdom which will enable one to see light and truth.

The whole teaching of Buddhism is based on the four noble truths. They are: (1) the truth of unsatisfactoriness or suffering, (2) the truth of the cause of suffering, (3) the truth of cessation of suffering, and (4) the truth of the path leading to the cessation of suffering. These truths teach that the existence of every sentient being, the five aggregates of mind and body, are the source of all kinds of misery and all forms of suffering. This existence is the inevitable and necessary effect of attachment or craving.

Existence is also the result of ignorance of the truth. By desire, continual existence is produced. Cessation of existence or suffering is effected only by the destruction of craving. The practice of the noble eightfold path, which consists of (1) right view, (2) right thought, (3) right speech, (4) right action, (5) right living, (6) right endeavor, (7) right mindfulness, and (8) right concentration, leads to the extinction of human craving or passion. This destruction of passion leads to the four stages of emancipation, which in turn leads to nirvana. Without this emancipation, nirvana cannot be realized or attained.

The fundamental doctrine of the Buddha regards birth as the result of ignorance and craving which arises from the error of belief in a self or ego entity to protect and satisfy. This leads to continued misery and suffering. The Buddha therefore enjoins all his followers to attain enlightenment through continual practice of mindfulness.

The goal of Buddhism is bodhi, enlightenment, or the awakening to reality. This means coming to realize nirvana, the cessation of all kinds of suffering. Buddhism is simply a means for attaining this enlightenment. In other words, the whole practice of Buddhism may be regarded as a process of attaining right understanding of reality.

Right understanding develops from mindfulness. It is only through practice of mindfulness or vigilant awareness and meditation on mind and matter that one can see things as they really are. This mindfulness must be based on our own experience, our own minds and bodies. Analytical reflection upon the constituent parts of the body reveals the fact that we are devoid of any permanent soul or self. The awareness of the fact puts an end to the erroneous views about self, individuality, or personality which are based upon illusory conceptions, and this enables us to escape from the world of suffering in samsara.

Fundamentally, Buddhism teaches that man must rely on himself in working out his own deliverance. Man can liberate himself from suffering and the woeful consequences of perpetual existence of birth and death only by the perfect realization of the very nature of suffering, its origin, its cessation, and the way leading to cessation. There is no one who can save a man but himself. It is he himself who must tread the path of understanding leading to nirvana.

Mental training or practice is essential for understanding, and this development must be carried out in a methodical way for absolute purification of the mind. It is the practice of mindfulness by which purification and right knowledge is gained.

We can apply mindfulness to body, feelings, consciousness, and states of mind. The method of mental training, of strengthening awareness allows these to be seen more clearly in their true nature. Awareness of these fourfold foundations of mindfulness is the ingredient which is the primary factor in the practice of the noble eightfold path: Right mindfulness amounts to practicing all the factors of the noble path together. The practice of the four foundations of mindfulness is the only right way for one's attainment of peace and realization of nirvana. "This is the only way to nirvana," the Buddha said. "It is the only way that leads to the attainment of purity, to the overcoming of sorrow and lamentation, to the end of pain and grief, to the entering upon the right path and the realization of liberation."

How can one best practice this mindfulness? If one analyzes his own being into its constituent parts, either by dividing it into the aggregates of body, feeling, perception, mental formations, and consciousness, or by other more minute divisions, one will finally realize the truth that there is no self or soul anywhere to be found. What he took to be a self or soul was only an idea holding together the constituent parts of his being. It is this tenacious illusion which stands in the way of seeing reality.

The following passage appears in a discourse by the Buddha.

> Oh! Rohitatha. I do not preach that the cessation of the world of suffering can be done without attainment or nirvana. Within this fathom-long body, with its thoughts and emotions, I declare is found the world, the origin of the world, the cessation of the world and the path leading to the cessation of the world.

For the rapid gaining of right concentration, the Buddha has taught mindfulness of body as a basic meditation. Therefore the constant contemplation and visualization of the constituent parts of the body is an ideal meditation subject for the purpose of practice leading to liberation.

If we are mindful of the body, no special effort is required for the practice of the other three aspects of mindfulness, namely mindfulness of feeling, of mind, and of mind objects. Mindfulness of the body is the main meditation and it automatically facilitates the exercise of the three other aspects of mindfulness. In fact, as practice deepens it will be seen that the fourfold foundations of mindfulness do not arise independently of each other; they must arise together. 189

Here then is the methodical practice of mindfulness based on the thirty-two constituent parts of the body. The benefits derived from this noble practice of mindfulness of one's body are described in relevant extracts from the Buddha's *Gradual Sayings*. The thirty-two constituent parts composed of twenty solids and twelve liquids are divided into six groups, each group to be contemplated on for at least five days. The six groups are as follows:

1. Hair of the head, hair of the body, nails, teeth, and skin.
2. Flesh, sinews, bones, marrow, and kidneys.
3. Heart, liver, membranes (diaphragm), spleen, and lungs.
4. Bowels, intestines, mesentary, feces, and brain.
5. Bile, phlegm, pus, blood, sweat, and solid fat.
6. Tears, liquid fat, saliva, mucus, synovic fluid (oil of the joints), and urine.

To follow the 165-day course, meditators should proceed with the constant recitation and visualization of each of the six groups above, first forward five days apiece and then backward five days apiece. After this first sixty days, they should repeat both forward and backward five days apiece. Then the meditator should add together first one, then two, then three, up to the full six groups, for his recitations and mindful visualizations, each time taking five days for the addition of a new group forward and five days for recitation backward. In the end, after approximately six months, the meditator will reach a point of mindfulness of the full thirty-two parts of the body.

The effect of repeated practice will be that the constituent parts become more and more clearly envisioned, the repulsive and destructive nature of the body becomes more and more reflected upon, and the distracted mind becomes more and more undistracted and gradually concentrated.

Verbal recitation is also to be carried out during the course of visualization. For proper development, the practice must be a repeated verbal recitation and visualization. This is essential and it is also in accordance with the saying of the Buddha which runs thus:

190

> *The verbal recitation is a condition for the mental recitation and the mental recitation is for the penetration of the characteristics of the foulness of the constituent parts of the body.*

It is important to note that the meditation of mindfulness of the constituent parts of the body, starting with hair of the head and ending with the urine is the most eminent one among all meditations that relate to the fourfold foundations of mindfulness.

The meditation of mindfulness of the body is unlike any other. It is brought to light and propagated only in the times when Buddhas arise.

The practice of this single, simple meditation assures the attainment of enlightened wisdom. The Buddha has declared this practice as unique and has made it a compulsory meditation to both monks and laity.

In one of his discourses to his disciples, the Buddha has recommended thus:

> *Monks, when One Unique Law is practiced and repeatedly done so, it leads from a sense of great terror, to great benefit, to great cessation of bondage, to great mindfulness and awareness, to acquisition of the knowledge of wisdom, to a happy life here and now, to realization of the fruits of clear vision and deliverance. What is the Unique Law? It is mindfulness of the body and thus, Monks, those who taste mindfulness of the body experience the taste of deathlessness, liberation. Monks, those who do not taste mindfulness of the body do not experience the taste of deathlessness. Thus, Monks, those who have perfected the practice of mindfulness of the body have experienced the taste of deathlessness. They are not ignoble or mean, nor are they reckless or unsteady. Those others who have neglected the practice of mindfulness of the body have missed the taste of deathlessness; they are ignoble or mean, and also they are reckless or unsteady.*

The meditator should go on practicing in the way described continually. The benefits are great and those who have attained nirvana by virtue of meditation on the parts of the body are so many they are uncountable in numbers.

Through repeated recitation, the constituent parts become more and more familiar, the mind becomes highly concentrated, and being thus prevented from going astray, the constituent parts of the body become evident in their true nature.

191

The discourse on the foundations of mindfulness is delivered as the highest course of practice in insight meditation and the practice of mindfulness of the constituent parts of the body leads not only to insight but is also the highest course of practice in the concentration for the calmness of the mind.

The final message of the Buddha was one of mindfulness: "And now, O disciples, I remind you; all conditioned things are transitory; be mindful."

Let us therefore put into real practice the method of mindfulness of the body parts while walking, standing, sitting, lying down, in order to work out our own deliverance with mindfulness and diligence in accordance with the last words of the Buddha.

On contemplation on the thirty-two constituent parts of this one fathom-long body, it will be realized that there is nothing real or substantial in this body. The meditator will see that there is nothing worth protecting, no desire that is satisfying, no lasting self that is to be found in this impersonal collection we call body and mind. Indeed, it will be seen as loathsomeness personified, absolutely unclean and undesirable. This will lead to clear understanding of emptiness and suffering and to an increasingly clear, non-attached, and pure mind.

May all those who are connected with this meritorious practice be happy and liberated.

MOHNYIN SAYADAW

CHAPTER
ELEVEN

This is a free translation of a talk given in Burmese by the Venerable Mohnyin Sayadaw in the 1960s. There are a number of disciples of Mohnyin teaching throughout Burma and there is a center in Rangoon, the Mohnyin Monastery of Boundary Road. Mohnyin's teachings come not only from mastery of insight meditation, but also from his scholarship as a teacher of the Abhidharma, the exposition of Buddhist psychology.

There is probably more emphasis and use made of the Abhidharma teachings in Burma than in any other Buddhist country. Mohnyin's approach to Dharma, through first the study of Abhidharma concepts and then their application to practice, has many followers in Burma. The *Abhidharma*, the last third of the Theravada scriptures, contains volumes of detail and explanations of mental processes and the subtleties of Dharma, probing the finest split-second characteristics of mind and matter. One may enter the monasteries of Burma and find monks working on immensely complicated cybernetics-like flow charts of the processes of mind. These studies based on the *Abhidharma* can lead one to a clear intellectual understanding of non-self, and the accompanying principles of constant change and its relationship to suffering. Later as one practices the meditations, this understanding is deepened by the clarity of direct experience.

Mohnyin Sayadaw stresses that meditators become familiar with the most basic concepts of the *Abhidharma* before undertaking practice. This prior knowledge will help them direct attention to the true nature of all phenomena in a precise and clear way. The most essential concepts one should understand before meditation are descriptions of those ultimate realities that make up our seemingly solid and continuous world. The elements as we perceive them—consciousness, the sense organs and their objects, and the corporeal groups of matter— appear to us as a solid world because of their rapid change. It is by examining the arising and dissolution of these groups and elements and consciousness in the body and the mind that the meditator develops true insight knowledge. As this deepens, he sees all perceivable events as fleeting and unsubstantial, no place to cling or look for happiness. No longer fooled by their nature, no longer clinging, he experiences true liberation.

Cognitive Insight Exercises

11

by Mohnyin Sayadaw

May all meet with success.

The following exposition is in two parts. The first is teachings on the basic concepts of the universe as viewed by the Abhidharma, the second is a description of the way of practice of insight meditation based on these concepts. The practice especially focuses on insight arising from examination of movement and change of posture. This leads to further stages of insight and wisdom that are both the subject and the result of practice.

QUESTIONS ON BASIC CONCEPTS FOR THE YOGI TO UNDERSTAND

Question: Explain the nature of physical and mental phenomena.
Answer: All physical phenomena are destructible, impersonal, and non-substantial. All mental phenomena are impersonal and non-substantial.

More precisely, twenty-eight kinds of physical phenomena exist in the bodies of all beings. There also exist numerous mental phenomena, which include consciousness, mental factors, and nirvana. It is important for our insight practice to focus on and see the nature of the material qualities of all physical phenomena. This can be done by breaking down all physical entities into their eightfold parts.[1] These are:

The four basic elements:
    The element of solidity or hardness.
    The element of cohesion or the fluid.
    The element of kinetic energy or heat and cold.
    The element of motion.
Plus
    Color.
    Smell.
    Taste.
    Nutrient qualities.

Q: Is this what the yogi must study to find ultimate truth?
A: All created things have the characteristics of ultimate truth. Therefore ultimate truths exist in all physical and mental phenomena and can be seen when we examine their functions and properties. These truths are hard to see because of our concepts, because of the illusion we have of solidity or permanence in the physical and mental world.

Q: How can we get beyond our concept of solidity and coherence of matter?

[1] *These are the properties of all physical matter as we directly experience it, before names and concepts. For example, a 'floor' is known either through the eyes as patches of color, or by touch as cold, hard, unmoving. All our perceptions are of these elements from which we create concepts and names.*

195

A: One way is to examine conventional objects to discover their true nature as being made up of parts. For example, when water is poured into milk, the 'groups' of milk fill up spaces between the 'groups' of water. This is true for all other inanimate objects—they give an illusion of coherence and solidity but ultimately they are made up of elements, groups which in various combinations make up the whole universe. Purity of knowledge results when the yogi understands this through direct experience in the meditation.

196

Q: How does the question of ultimate truth apply to animate objects?
A: Animate objects like inanimate objects must be viewed by the yogi so as to reveal their underlying nature. All creatures, whatever their form, conceal their true nature through the appearance of solidity and coherence. In order to discard this illusion and the illusion of self the yogi should see animate objects as being made up of mental and physical 'groups', 'parts', 'elements', with no self nor being behind them. Following this principle, you should try to see all objects you meet as merely elements to which we attach the idea of names, calling them *man, woman, animal,* and so forth. These distinctions exist only on the conventional level but are not the ultimate truth. Thus, analytical knowledge developed in Vipassana sees all beings not as permanent souls or personalities.

Seeing beyond the concepts and ideas, the yogi will see that all animate objects are but heaps of corporeal groups,[2] or elements. This knowledge will then lead to clear insight into the nature and relationship of form and mind, and finally to equanimity in regard to the coming and going of all these objects, to profound inner peace. The yogi will see even exercises of charity, morality, loving-kindness as relative, not to be taken at face value, and will not cling even to these.

Q: How does the Buddhist concept of elements fit in with modern physics?
A: By discarding the concept of solidity, scientists have analyzed all matter into more than 100 elements. Ultimately even these elements and atoms when examined become waves of energy in largely empty space. The particles/waves are always dynamic so that modern physics points to the basic impermanent and souless nature of all matter.

---

[2] *Corporeal groups are the smallest particles of matter from which all seemingly solid physical objects are made. These particles are constantly changing.*

Q: What are the ultimate realities according to Buddhist psychology?
A: The yogi should understand there are four kinds of ultimate reality:[3]
1. Material form.
2. Mental factors/formation.
3. Consciousness.
4. Nirvana.

These stand beyond any ideas and concepts and may be experienced and examined directly by the yogi. He will see too that the first three have as a characteristic constant change.

Q: How can we understand consciousness?
A: There are six kinds of consciousness:
1. Eye consciousness.
2. Ear consciousness.
3. Nose consciousness.
4. Tongue consciousness.
5. Body consciousness.
6. Mind consciousness.

These have the characteristic of 'bending toward' or 'knowing' the objects of consciousness. Now we may expand our understanding to our 'whole world' as the Buddha taught it, which is:

CONSCIOUSNESS	SENSE BASE	OBJECT
eye consciousness	eye	visible objects
ear consciousness	ear	sounds
nose consciousness	nose	odors
tongue consciousness	tongue	tastes
body consciousness	body	sensations/ tangible objects
mind consciousness	mind-element	mind objects

These eighteen make up our world. The yogi can see that eye consciousness arises in conjunction with, and is dependent on, the eye and a visible object, that ear consciousness arises in conjunction with and is dependent on the ear and sound, and so forth.

[3] *These ultimate realities out of which the whole of Buddhist psychology is built also correspond to the five aggregates. Consciousness is the aggregate of consciousness. Mental factors include the aggregates of perception, feeling, and mental formations, while material form corresponds to the aggregate of form. Only nirvana is outside of this changing flow of aggregates.*

Each moment brings the arising and ceasing of one of these six consciousnesses in conjunction with a sense organ and an object. By developing penetrating awareness the yogi will see that there is no permanent 'I' or 'self', only a succession of the arising and ceasing of these eighteen senses, bases, and consciousnesses. The yogi should contemplate until he is free from the belief in a soul or permanent personality. He should examine the true nature of mind and body until he understands the relationship of the two.

198

Q: How can we be free from doubt about what produces form and objects, and what produces mental phenomena?
A: The freedom from doubt as to the origin of form and mental phenomena comes from right contemplation. Karma (actions of body, speech, and mind), consciousness, temperature, and nutrition are the producers of all animate objects.[4] Likewise, the six sense bases and the sense objects are the producers of mental phenomena. All karmic action has results that come from the wholesome or unwholesome nature of particular actions. This karmic process is at the heart of the never-ending cycle of the world coming into being. The yogi who wishes to understand must completely examine his own mental and material phenomena until he can see clearly how this process works in his own mind. Then, he will no longer have doubts about the nature of the Dharma, the Buddha, and his teachings. He will see the origin and end of samsara or the rounds of death and rebirth and understand the nature of the dependent origination of all mind and matter.

To explain further, dependent origination is the cyclic nature of the conditionality of all physical and mental phenomena, the understanding of which, together with non-self, forms the basis for the realization of the teaching of the Buddha. It shows how the various physical and mental phenomena of existence conventionally called *ego, personality, man, woman, animal*, etc., are not a mere play of blind chance, but the outcome of causes and conditions. It explains that the arising of rebirth and suffering is dependent upon conditions and also how, through the removal of these conditions, all suffering must disappear. The twelve links of the process of dependent origination are:

1. IGNORANCE, lack of wisdom, which is the root of all evils. This is the condition for the arising of karma formations.

---

[4] *These are traditionally known as the nutriments of life and are the causes or conditions for the arising of all animate objects.*

2. KARMA FORMATIONS, which depend on ignorance.
3. CONSCIOUSNESS, which depends on karma formations.
4. MENTAL AND PHYSICAL EXISTENCE, which depends on consciousness.
5. SIX SENSE ORGANS, which depend on mental and physical existence.
6. SENSE IMPRESSIONS, which depend on six sense organs.
7. FEELINGS, which depend on sense impressions.
8. CRAVING, which depends on feelings.
9. CLINGING, which depends on craving.
10. PROCESS OF EXISTENCE, which depends on clinging.
11. REBIRTH, which depends on the process of existence.
12. DECAY AND DEATH, which depend on rebirth.

Links 1, 2, 8, 9, and 10 are the five karmic causes of rebirths; and links 3, 4, 5, 6, and 7 are the five karma-results in the round of rebirths.

This is a brief but complete list of the rebirth chain of cause and effect, of the physical and mental phenomena based on which rebirth occurs.[5] If a yogi contemplates and finally understands these causes of mind and matter he will attain the purity of escape from doubt.

THE PRACTICE OF PURIFICATION

To attain the knowledge relating to the paths of sainthood, a yogi must acquire the following kinds of insight: insight in the determination of all phenomena of existence as impermanent, suffering, and impersonal; insight into the arising and vanishing of all phenomena; insight into the dissolution of all phenomena and the resulting insight into the terror, misery, and cause for aversion of all conditioned existence; and finally insight into the desire for deliverance and high equanimity regarding all formations of mind and matter. This is the perfect balance of mind necessary to attain nirvana.

Of these, in practicing for the development of insight relating to the three characteristics (impermanence, suffering, and the impersonal nature of existence), the yogi should perform insight exercises by observing the process of change in regards to all his body

[5] For further explanation of how this works, see "Mogok Sayadaw."

movement and postures. Here he can clearly see the nature of change within him. This gives rise to understanding beyond concepts, to the ultimate truth that existence is a mere process of continually changing physical and mental phenomena within which no permanent ego or personality can be found. It is most appropriate to start with this level of understanding and to experience the three characteristics here before developing higher levels of insight.

In starting Vipassana, the yogi must microscopically examine his modes of moving and changes of posture, for here he can see the three characteristics very clearly. In moving his hand from one position to another, a yogi will first find his whole hand moves. In examining this process more closely (especially through the sensation) the yogi will see that each moment old 'groups' of energy-physical matter arise and vanish yielding place to new ones, and observing thus the yogi will come to understand impermanence. Moving his hand from one position to another *again and again* he contemplates the impermanence of form and sensation. In the ultimate sense the diffusion (the process of oscillation or vibration born of mental activity) gives the appearance of a hand moving. Watching this process using concentration and insight, the yogi develops understanding of impermanence through the fleeting, unsubstantive nature of his experience of all the physical and mental phenomena involved. When insight into impermanence is developed, the practitioner will also be able to realize the unsatisfactory, insecure, and self-less nature of all phenomena.

Though an ordinary person will say there is the same hand in all positions, in the ultimate sense, trillions of 'groups'—physical/energy configurations—arise and vanish in the process of oscillation as the hand is moved. It is like a bucket of sand. Let us say you pierce a hole at the bottom and allow the particles of sand to fall down in a stream. Although you find that a stream of sand drops from the bucket, in fact, particles of sand combine together and form a stream. Thus the concepts, our ideas—of shape, continuity, and compactness—conceal the real truth. If the yogi sees clearly he will come to know how causally conditioned mental and physical phenomena arise and vanish instantaneously, like sand grains in the stream of sand.

Bearing this in mind, the yogi should contemplate the experience of the dissolution of mental and physical phenomena contained in the body during all daily activity, rising from bed, washing his face, going to the bathroom, eating food, coming and going in all postures.

The Buddha spoke of contemplation of the body in the body. So a yogi who is able to determine the dissolution of the physical phenomena in moving the hand from one position to another can easily see the dissolution of the physical phenomena all over the body, while sitting. This is correct contemplation of the body in the body. Close your eyes and reflect on the dissolution of the corporeal groups, or physical/energy configurations, all over the body. Then turn your body to the right, to the left, and bend your body forward and backward. In all of these positions and at every moment you will notice that older physical phenomena arise and vanish, yielding place to newer ones. Repeat these exercises until you can experience this clearly. The yogi can also use breathing to develop his insight into the arising and vansihing of all phenomena. In contemplating the dissolutions of physical phenomena related to breathing, just as in the case of the hand movement, a yogi should examine the qualities of the physical phenomena in the middle part of the body. It is not necessary to watch the in-and-out breathing at the nasal aperture, as is done in exercises on breathing. Keep your mind on the middle part of your body; you will then perceive the movements of rising and falling of this part of the body—rising while breathing in and falling while breathing out. Contemplate the dissolution of the physical phenomena both in the case of breathing in and breathing out, and you will eventually realize directly the constant change which is the nature of all we can perceive.

It is through the examination of body and bodily sensations, especially those involved in various postures, that the yogi can best understand the ultimate Dharma.

In contemplating the body in the body and perceiving the arising and passing away of phenomena, the yogi can then understand the process of oscillation, physical movement born of mental activity. This is how he sees the cycle of dependent origination.

The yogi knows that if there arises the thought, "I shall stand," that thought produces the process of oscillation. This process of oscillation produces bodily expression. The raising upright of the whole body from below, owing to the diffusion of the process of oscillation, is called *standing*. If there arises the thought, "I shall march by the right leg," a yogi is able to discern the arising and vanishing of the physical phenomena during the process of oscillation and also during the advancing stages of lifting, pushing, and placing.

Having known thus, a yogi should contemplate as follows: "Even while I am standing, the mental and physical phenomena

arise and vanish rapidly at every moment, thus showing impermanence." It will be apparent in the mind of a yogi that it is the
basic nature of all causally conditioned physical and mental
phenomena to arise and vanish instantaneously. The yogi must
contemplate the impermanence according to this method continuously, for however many days or months it takes to understand
completely.

202   In deepening contemplation he can pay particular attention to
the dissolution of all experience. Thus, when a yogi starts walking
by the right leg, he determines the dissolution of the physical and
mental phenomena noting *dissolve, dissolve; disappear, disappear;
exists no more, exists no more;* or *impermanent, impermanent*. He
should adopt the same procedure when he walks by the left leg
also. It is very important that a yogi carry on these exercises for
enough days and months so he is able to perceive the passing away
or dissolution of the physical and mental phenomena while he is
walking either slowly or quickly. To carry on these exercises is to
live contemplating the body in the body internally.

It is equally important for the yogi to examine mental
phenomena as well as physical ones. If there arises the thought, "I
shall walk," a yogi should determine the arising and passing away
of the mental phenomena contained in the 'mental activity' of
thinking. He should also note the arising and passing away of the
physical phenomena contained in the leg at every point of his step.
He can now observe both the mental and physical phenomena as
they arise and pass away at each step.

A yogi while walking understands, "I am walking," and whatever the posture of his body may be, he understands that posture
and at the same time observes the dissolution of the mental
phenomena contained in the thought of 'walking', the dissolution
of the physical phenomena contained in the leg, and also the dissolution of the physical phenomena in experiencing the ground on
which the steps fall. Thus he dwells objectively examining his own
body. He is either mindful of arising in the body or of passing away
in the body; or of both arising and passing away in the body.

In beginning the walking exercise, a yogi has to stand before
moving. He will then observe the inherent qualities of the mental
and physical phenomena contained in his body, and conceive thus:
"Now, the 'I' which is now standing is nothing but a collection of
the physical and mental 'groups' contained in the body in its
standing posture due to the process of oscillation born of mental
activity."

Again, if there arises the thought, "I shall go by the right leg," that thought produces the process of oscillation; the diffusion of the process of oscillation produces expression in the following movement: lifting, pushing, placing. A yogi should contemplate the dissolution of the physical phenomena contained in the body at every posture, and also the simultaneous dissolution of the physical phenomena in the ground on which his right step falls. He should carry on such kinds of exercises for days, by moving slowly and quickly. This contemplation should be pursued in all postures—walking, standing, sitting, and lying—until the yogi penetrates to full understanding of the characteristics of existence.

It is essential that the yogi contemplate the arising and vanishing *in the present moment*, for only then can he see the characteristics clearly. It is often helpful for the yogi to begin his exercises with very slow movements so that the arising and vanishing of mental and physical phenomena are more easily observed.

One who contemplates the arising and vanishing of phenomena at every posture during the four modes of deportment will eventually realize that the mental and physical phenomena having arisen disappear immediately and the new formations of existence arise in place of the older ones, just as sesame seeds are disintegrated with cracking sounds when heated in a frying pan.

During the practice of Vipassana at the point where the yogi can clearly perceive the arising and vanishing of all phenomena, there arises in him the 'defilements of insight'. These are especially likely to arise in the yogi who has been practicing Vipassana combined with tranquility or concentration meditation. Some of the subtle defilements that arise are attachment to the rapture, tranquility, happiness, effulgence of light, energy, awareness, equanimity, and delight that arise in him.

These subtle attachments or defilements are overcome when the yogi realizes that none of them are the true path to the cessation of suffering, and that he must relinquish his attachment and simply continue contemplating clearly the process of all phenomena arising and vanishing.

Just to enable the yogi to grasp the idea as to how these phenomena of existence vanish so rapidly, he may watch the bubbles of water formed on the surface of a water pool during a heavy rain. He will then behold that the bubbles arise and disappear immediately. In the same way, the mental and physical phenomena pertaining to the five groups of existence also arise and disappear very rapidly. Again, in the allegory of the sand bucket, you will notice that although a stream of sand is seen coming out of a hole at the bottom of the bucket, the seemingly solid stream is made up of many particles of sand and that the momentary groups of these particles arise and vanish immediately, the older ones having vanished, yielding place to newer ones.

When a yogi has perceived the dissolution of the phenomena in every posture of the body, and also in all external matters, he will soon be able to perceive that the karma formations producing ever-new existences are insecure, frightful, oppressive, and miserable; and being disgusted with worldly life, he will gradually acquire deeper insight.

He will become clearer and clearer about the nature of the four noble truths and the suffering inherent in all phenomena. Both bodily and mental painful feelings and sensations are clearly suffering. The truth of suffering, or unsatisfactoriness, does not merely refer to painful feelings, but teaches that, on account of the all-abiding Law of Impermanency and Change, all the phenomena of existence are unsatisfactory, and bear in themselves the seed of suffering and misery.

Feeling aversion for all formations of existence, getting weary of them, and finding no more delight in them, the mind of a yogi does not cling to a single one of all these formations, and in him arises a desire for deliverance.

His contemplation is now centered on reflecting on the three characteristics of existence—impermanence, suffering, and impersonality—with the desire of finding deliverance from all forms of existence growing stronger in him.

Just as a reed or a bubble or a mirage is without substance, without contents, and empty, so corporeality, feeling, perception, mental formations, and consciousness are without substance and contents, empty, futile, impersonal. They are without master, or anyone who has power over them, they are neither child, nor woman, nor man, nor personality, nor anything belonging to personality, neither 'I' nor 'mine', nor do they belong to anybody else.

Eventually, while continuing to investigate the formations of existence, the yogi overcomes all fear, delight, and indifference and there arises in him a profound equanimity. He sees all causally conditioned, arising and vanishing, physical and mental phenomena are free from anything in the nature of soul-entity, 'I', 'mine', 'his', and 'one's own'.

They are anatta, or:

1. Free of any abiding personal entity or soul.

2. Void of pith or essence.
3. Ungovernable, uncontrollable.

Now, while continuing to contemplate the three characteristics of existence, the mind tends toward the tranquility of nirvana. The peace and equanimity of mind become the threefold gate to deliverance, the three ways to enter nirvana.

Three gates of deliverance are leading to escape from the world of conditioned phenomena. The mind knows all formations as changing and limited, and rushes forward to the 'conditionless element'.

The mind is stirred with regard to the inherent unsatisfactoriness of all formations of existence, and rushes forward to the 'desireless element'. The mind regards all things as empty, as foreign, and rushes forward to the 'void-element'.

So, in practicing the Vipassana meditation according to these instructions, a meditating disciple will find that by paying constant attention to the characteristics (the alterations, displacements, disturbances, modes of changing of body and mind), he is developing his mental faculties in such a way that the deep insight experienced by him will be free from both eternity and annihilation beliefs.[6] His insight will dispel the following illusions: (1) the idea of permanence, (2) the idea of worldly happiness, (3) the idea of ego or fixed personality, (4) the idea of pleasure in lust, (5) greed, (6) becoming,[7] (7) grasping, (8) the idea of compactness or solidity, (9) wrong view about karma formations, (10) the idea of stability, (11) the conditions of becoming, (12) delight, (13) clinging, (14) grasping and adherence to the idea of substance, (15) adherence to delusion regarding the ego and the world, (16) attachment, (17) thoughtlessness, and (18) getting entangled in any aspect of body or mind. These are the fruits of proper Vipassana practice. This truth will lead to escape from old age, sickness, death, and rebirth.

The yogi who wishes to undertake this practice should begin by reciting the three refuges in the Buddha, Dharma, and Sangha. He should undertake to keep the moral precepts and repeat the following loving-kindness blessing:

May I be happy, may I preserve my happiness and live

[6] *This refers to the wrong belief either in an external soul as one extreme or in the total annihilation of the mind-body process at death, the opposite extreme.*

[7] *This means the wish to continue becoming to be in the rounds of samsara.*

without enmity.

May all beings be prosperous and happy: May they be of joyful mind, all beings that have life, be they feeble or strong, be they minute or vast. Visible or invisible, near or afar, born or to be born, let all beings be joyful.

Let no one deceive another, let none be harsh in speech, let none by anger or hatred wish ill to his neighbor. Even as a mother, at the risk of her life, watches over and protects her only child, so with a boundless heart of compassion I cherish all living things, suffusing love over the entire world, above, and all around without limit; thus I cultivate an infinite goodwill toward the whole world.

Standing or walking, sitting or lying down, during all my waking hours I cherish the thought that this way of loving is the noblest in the world.

Thus shall I, by abandoning vain discussions and controversies, by walking righteously, be gifted with insight, subdue the longing for the pleasures of the senses, and never again know rebirth. May this also be the cause for all other sentient beings to be fulfilled in the conditions leading to their attainment of nirvana. May all sentient beings escape the dangers of old age, disease, and death. May all beings be liberated.

MOGOK SAYADAW

CHAPTER
TWELVE

Mogok Sayadaw follows in the footsteps of Ledi Sayadaw, a prolific and widely respected Dharma master who taught in Burma at the turn of the century. Ledi Sayadaw had increased understanding of the Law of Dependent Origination among Burmese Buddhists, and Mogok Sayadaw revived and emphasized its importance in his teaching. Mogok was a renowned scholar in monastic circles and spent more than thirty years as a teacher of Buddhist psychology and scriptures in upper Burma. One day it occurred to him that he was like a cowherd who in spite of tending the animals did not have the opportunity to use the milk given by them. He left his teaching position and traveled to Mingun where he undertook intensive practice of Vipassana. After some years passed, at the request of devoted Buddhist layfolk, he began the teaching of insight meditation in several towns. Although he shunned popularity and did not teach in the capital, his fame as an enlightened teacher was widespread. Since Mogok Sayadaw's death not many years ago, a number of his disciples have been carrying on the important teachings of insight meditation in his style.

In Rangoon there is a large center which teaches Vipassana according to the method of Mogok Sayadaw. It is run by the Venerable U Than Daing, compiler of this English version of Mogok's teaching. Most of the instruction is oriented toward laymen and periodic intensive meditation sessions are offered. Westerners are welcome.

Practice consists of three parts which will be explored in more detail in the following section. First, Mogok stresses the importance of intellectual understanding of Dharma before actual meditation practice. He teaches the distinction between concepts and ultimate reality, and how ultimate reality is composed of the elements and aggregates. Then he explains the cycle of dependent origination, showing how through cause and effect, craving and desires keep us trapped in the rounds of becoming and suffering.

Meditation is then developed based on this prior understanding. First yogis start with mindfulness of breathing to concentrate the mind. Then practice is changed to either meditation on consciousness (the knowing faculty of mind) or meditation on feeling. Each of these is explained as mindfulness of thirteen different aspects of consciousness or feeling.

Finally, as the meditation deepens, Mogok emphasizes how all perception becomes simply that of the arising and vanishing of the five aggregates, the process of body and mind. This constant change which must be directly experienced (and not simply noted as *change, change*) shows how unsatisfactory and empty of self our whole existence is. On penetrating the true nature of the aggregates as they arise and vanish, the yogi becomes ripe for the cessation of this process and the stopping of the wheel of dependent origination which is the highest bliss, nirvana.

The most outstanding point in Mogok Sayadaw's teaching is the use of the Law of Dependent Origination. He explains how this causal chain works and then directs us to experience this process in our own bodies and minds. The insight that develops leads to the freedom beyond this process, the truth of the Buddha.

Meditation on Mind and Feeling

12

as taught by Mogok Sayadaw

The purpose of Buddhist Dharma or teaching is to lead one to liberation, nirvana. This teaching describes a path with progressively higher stages. Virtue is the first stage on this path and the practice of it brings happiness and peace of mind. Concentration, the second stage, brings even higher happiness, for a mind purified by concentration can experience many degrees of heavenly states, lightness, and bliss. Concentration alone, though, still lacks the power to uproot permanently the defilements in our minds which entangle us in ignorance and rebirth. Only the wisdom of Vipassana, the next stage on the path, can permanently liberate us and lead us to the highest happiness, nirvana.

In coming to our own liberation we must develop an understanding of Vipassana, how it is practiced and what its purpose is. The Buddha said the yogi must use Vipassana to eliminate his wrong views about himself and the world. Vipassana is a way of seeing the world clearly. Our incorrect views have led us through continuous rounds of existence and suffering. Therefore we must undertake this practice like a man whose hair is on fire or whose chest is pierced by a spear. The opportunity to undertake Vipassana training is precious indeed.

When we develop wisdom through Vipassana it leads to stream entry, the experience of nirvana, which has the power to destroy for good our incorrect views of the world. Forever the Buddha stated that the benefits from the first attainment of nirvana were greater even than the attainment of becoming monarch of the whole universe because a stream enterer has completely liberated himself from the danger of falling into rebirth in any of the lower realms. At the very most he is said to have seven existences to live out before final enlightenment.

Yogis are therefore urged to endeavor to attain at least this first stage of enlightenment, the path and fruition of nirvana. In order to attain this stage, we can follow the practical method formulated and simplified by Mogok Sayadaw based on the contemplation on mind and the contemplation on feelings. As feelings and mind are co-arising, co-existing, and co-dissolving, contemplation on the one is the same as contemplation on the other.

In practical application this meditation will be found to be more comprehensible than meditation on body process. It cannot be denied that mind also arises in conjunction with in-breathing or out-breathing and other aspects of the body. However, meditation directly on the process of the mind is seen as the most straightforward and beneficial for yogis in our time.

Before he enters into any meditation, it is highly essential and necessary for the yogi to have conceptual knowledge of certain things. These are prerequisites of meditation.

He must know the difference between ultimate Dharma and conceptual Dharma. Ultimate Dharma is fourfold: consciousness, mental factors, matter, and nirvana. Vipassana meditation is based on contemplation of the ultimate Dharma, that which underlies the world of concepts.

To further understand, here is a breakdown of the categories of the ultimate Dharma, or ultimate reality, those aspects of our world which can be *directly* experienced without concepts:

CONSCIOUSNESS—There are eighty-nine kinds of consciousness, but, for the purpose of Vipassana meditation, Mogok Sayadaw has narrowed these down to thirteen kinds of consciousness which can be said to be all-embracing and inclusive.

MENTAL FACTORS—There are fifty-two mental factors. It is only necessary for yogis to be familiar with contact, feeling, perception, volition, attention, greed, hatred, ignorance, conceit, wrong view, envy, jealousy, and doubt.[1]

MATERIAL AGGREGATES—There are twenty-eight material aggregates, out of which the following are most important for yogis to note:

Element of hardness and softness.
Element of cohesion and fluidity.
Element of motion and vibration.
Element of heat and cold.

These are called the four primary elements.[2] There are also twenty-four derived elements.

NIRVANA—This is the fourth category of ultimate Dharma because it can be directly experienced by the mind.

---

[1] *Consciousness and mental factors together comprise all that we call mind.*

[2] *These four primary elements make up the whole of the physical universe.*

Now, at this point it may help to distinguish conceptual Dharma. Concepts are ideas about a situation as opposed to the ultimate Dharmas which can be directly experienced. Conceptual Dharma includes all concepts, notions, ideas, and names, such as *my son, woman's voice, horse-cart,* etc. Although concepts are used for the purpose of convenience and for conventional parlance, they are not the ultimate objects of our experience and as such cannot be used as objects of contemplation that is aimed at understanding reality.

213

There are many varieties of concepts, but only a few need be mentioned here. These include:

Concepts of names.

Concepts as ideas or relations such as son, daughter, mother, and father.

Concepts of collections or groups, families, races, etc.

Concepts of forms, e.g. pagoda, monastery, school.

Concepts of locality, e.g. Bombay, Ceylon.

Concepts of time, e.g. 600 B.C., yesterday, tomorrow.

Concepts of space, e.g. a hole in the roof, a cave, horizon.

Concepts of continuity, e.g. a long train of caravans, a flow of a river, a movie.

Concepts of imagination, e.g. horns of a rabbit, hair of a turtle.

Vipassana is concerned only with contemplation of ultimate Dharmas and not with concepts. When the yogi has understood this and become able to distinguish ultimate Dharma and conceptual Dharma, he is further required to be familiar with these most important fundamentals, the basic aspects of existence: (1) the five aggregates, (2) the sense bases, (3) the elements, and (4) the Law of Dependent Origination.

The five aggregates are a description of those Dharmas which comprise the whole body and mind. They include:

Aggregate of form (the body and all material elements).

Four basic elements.

Derived elements.

Aggregate of feeling (an aspect of mind).

Pleasurable feelings.

Unpleasurable feelings.

Indifferent feelings.

Aggregate of perception (an aspect of mind).

Perception of things animate or inanimate or of colors or sizes.

Aggregate of mental factors.

There are fifty-two kinds, including anger, mindfulness, greed, love, and calm.

Aggregate of consciousness.
 Eye consciousness.
 Ear consciousness.
 Nose consciousness.
 Tongue consciousness.
 Body consciousness.
 Mind consciousness.

214 The yogi must become familiar with all these elements of mind and body. He must also understand that for each of the six kinds of consciousness there is a corresponding organ of sense (eye, ear, etc.) and a corresponding field of sense objects (color, sound, smells, etc).[3]

It is important too for the yogi to know how consciousness arises. The Buddha said each of the six kinds of consciousness arises depending on two causes, the sense organ and the object. Thus in seeing, there is only the arising of eye consciousness depending upon the impact on eye organ of visible object. Other than these three co-existing elements there is nothing else, no see-er, no 'I', 'you', or 'he' who sees. It is only a process of the arising of eye consciousness. In hearing, tasting, etc. the process is the same. In every experience of perception there are only the workings of this empty process.

It must be noted too that after its arising, consciousness does not remain the same for two consecutive moments. One moment it arises, the next moment it perishes, to be replaced by a new consciousness.

It is advised that before undertaking the meditation practice, the yogi study mental realities, the aggregates, elements, and consciousness, and that these be thoroughly comprehended. Furthermore, the yogi should become conversant with the Law of Causation which shows how physical and mental phenomena arise.

THE LAW OF DEPENDENT ORIGINATION (PRESENT ASPECT)

Mogok Sayadaw expounded the Law of Dependent Origination especially for the benefit of new yogis. This can be called a shortcut to the contemplation or meditation work for the yogi because it

---

[3] *See "Mohnyin Sayadaw."*

teaches the present aspect of the working of the doctrine. In other words, it enables a yogi to understand the aggregates, their beginning, their causes, and dissolution occurring each moment.

Start with the eye and visible objects as a beginning. When the impingement of the two takes place, there arises eye consciousness. It is to be noted that there is only the arising of eye consciousness. There is no see-er, there is no 'I', no 'he' nor 'she' in the eye or in the visible object. There is neither 'I', nor 'he,' nor 'she' in the eye consciousness. Eye consciousness is only eye consciousness, no more or no less, and this eye consciousness should not be confused with a 'self', it must not be personified.

215

The combination of eye, visible object, and eye consciousness is the condition from which arises contact, and depending on contact there then arises feeling. In the feelings too there is no 'I', 'he', 'she', no 'self' to be found. The process of dependent origination continues. Because of feeling there arises craving and because of craving there arises attachment or clinging and based on this attachment there arises physical action, verbal action, and thought or mental action. These actions are the making of karma and this karmic energy is the condition for the arising of further rebirth.

Following rebirth there must arise aging, decay, sorrow, lamentation, pain, grief, and despair. Thus, there arises the whole mass of suffering.

As is understood with the eye, object and eye consciousness, similarly we should understand this process with the ear, nose, tongue, body, and mind senses and the corresponding consciousnesses so we can understand the movement of the cycle of dependent origination.

For the purpose of clarification and lucidity, it will be better explained in conventional parlance.

When 'A' sees a beautiful object, he desires to own it, he clings to it, and he makes an effort to obtain it. This is craving, he is overwhelmed by the desire to possess the beautiful object. Then he makes all sorts of effort, mental, verbal, and physical, based on this clinging or attachment. This leads to rebirth, for even the subtlest attachment propels us to be reborn. Rebirth inevitably involves aging, death, sorrow, lamentation, pain, grief, and despair. Thus the whole train of dependent origination evolves. This can be seen clearly in examining the arising and disappearing of the five aggregates, our own process of body and mind. As we see more clearly we understand that ultimately the very nature of these aggregates and the rounds of rebirth of body and mind are nothing but suffering itself.

It will be obvious to the thoughtful reader how many times in a day we continue this ceaseless process: the arising of craving and clinging resulting in action or thought. We see, we desire, and we are overwhelmed by craving and attachment. To satisfy this, we commit all kinds of actions—mental, verbal, and physical. In the same manner, if we like or enjoy something we hear, craving arises, and when we are overwhelmed by craving, it generates clinging, and to satisfy this we become involved in all kinds of activities by which we hope to prolong our pleasure. The same analogy applies to smelling, tasting, touching, and thinking. Consciously or unconsciously, we fall into these processes all the time.

The reader should turn his attention to the fact that dependent origination is nothing but his own line of actions. He may focus his attention on the aggregates, the body and mind, and see for himself how his own action is categorically within this causal law and in accordance with the Law of Dependent Origination.

If he thinks it is time to bring to a stop his line of actions which run in accordance with this cyclical process, there is a way to get out of the round of rebirths. But if he continues to carry on as usual, the cycle will go on and continue its relentless process leading to sorrow, lamentation, and despair and the whole mass of suffering.

Here is an illustration: A parent hears the call of his little son on his return from school. As soon as he hears it, he feels anxious to see his son, anxious to hug him and caress and kiss him. He may think and say that he does all this because it is his son and he loves him; there is no offense or sin against him because he does not transgress any moral law. It is true, however, even here, not through the action itself, but from the attachment that motivates it, that the inexorable process of dependent origination has evolved and continues its ceaseless cycle.

We can see even in this seemingly harmless example how the Law of Dependent Origination starts revolving on the hearing of the voice of the young son returning from school. As soon as the son's voice is heard there arises craving to see and caress him; because of craving there arises overwhelming desire which is the cause of caressing the son. This caressing is action based on attachment and this force becomes the cause for further rebirth. When karmic force arises, birth is bound to follow. Even Buddhas are not able to stop karmic force.

From dawn to dusk, the process goes on. When an attractive

object is seen there arises craving and because of this craving there arises clinging, because of clinging karmic force arises, and as such the whole cycle continues its ceaseless revolution.

In fact, whenever a beautiful visible object, pleasant sound, pleasant odor, pleasant taste, pleasant touch, or pleasant idea enters through its respective sense door, there will usually arise craving and a series of other factors. Such series of processes are nothing but rounds of passions which in turn give rise to rounds of karmic or volitional actions, from which again emanate rounds of resultant effects, thus making the cycle complete.

217

This whole process from contact to consciousness and clinging and rebirth, moment to moment, should be observed and contemplated as Vipassana meditation; otherwise the ceaseless process of the cycle of samsara will continue ad infinitum bringing in its wake the whole mass of sorrow and suffering. As we practice Vipassana we can see more and more clearly how any volitional action leads to rebirth consciousness. This then becomes the condition for the arising of consciousness, mind and body, and we see how these lead inevitably to the senses and contact. Contact at the six senses (including mind) is the condition for feeling, which, followed by craving and clinging, inevitably brings karmic action and rebirth. Dependent origination is nothing but the ceaseless process of our own aggregates, the perishing of the old ones giving place to new. It is a causal continuum of the arising and vanishing of all physical and mental phenomena.

It is said that the beginning of samsara is inconceivable. Shrouded in ignorance and bound up by craving, there is no beginning of beings who are undergoing rounds of rebirths from one existence to another. If all the bones of a single being's endless forms were preserved in heaps, they would reach the height of the great Mount Vepulla, whose ascent takes four days. When samsara is said to be unthinkably long, it amounts to saying that the cycle of dependent origination is beginningless and that suffering has continued equally ceaselessly.

It is said that the potential or force for rebirth (samsara) is ignorance. This should not be mistaken for any first cause or supreme being. The question then arises: What is ignorance? It is ignorance of the four noble truths:

1. Ignorance of suffering.
2. Ignorance of the cause of suffering.
3. Ignorance of the cessation of suffering (nirvana).
4. Ignorance of the path leading to the cessation of suffering.

To illustrate:

1. Lack of the knowledge that our own aggregates or components of body and mind are ultimately painful and unsatisfactory is called *ignorance of suffering.*
2. It is inherent in every one of us to possess and crave both mental happiness and material wealth. This craving is the root cause of suffering. Lack of the knowledge of this is called *ignorance of the cause of suffering.*
3. Lack of the knowledge of the cessation of all suffering, nirvana, is called *ignorance of the end of suffering.*
4. Lack of the knowledge that the eightfold noble path is the path leading to nirvana is called *ignorance of the path.*

All our mental, physical, and verbal activities arise out of this ignorance. Therefore, the Buddha said, not knowing the root cause of all sorrow and suffering, one does or commits all sorts of activities for the sake of oneself, one's family, one's country, etc., employing all means of contrivances regardless of their natures (wholesome or unwholesome, moral or immoral) to amass wealth, rank, or to try and obtain happiness in the world of samsara.

A man may say that he is leading a good life as he carries on legitimate trade, but from the point of view of dependent origination he is still not breaking the chain of rebirth; on the contrary, he is continuing the process. When asked "What offense has he done?" we answer that it cannot be said whether he has committed an offense or not but that he has connected the cyclic order of the chain of desire and becoming, continuing the process of karmic accumulations.

It is for the yogi to decide at this juncture whether it is worthwhile to long for rebirth in his or her next existence. When rebirth is begotten what are its implications? What will be the eventual prize? It is obvious that rebirth is inevitably followed by suffering, aging, and death. This is the circumgyration of dependent origination as shown in accordance with the Buddha's teaching.

It is highly recommended to yogis who are intent upon entering into Vipassana practice to be well conversant with the fundamentals of Buddha Dharma. Without sufficient knowledge of these essential prerequisites, practitioners can make no progress in Vipassana meditation. The horizon of the yogi who has not mastered these prerequisites will be limited within the framework of egoism. A yogi cannot pass beyond ego without knowing the teachings.

It must be reiterated here again that these prerequisites include the five aggregates, sense bases, elements, dependent origination, and the noble truths. One is not to enter into contemplation without mastering the knowledge of these things because it is upon these very aggregates and processes that the contemplation is to be done. The yogi must be able to distinguish the ultimate realities and concepts to eliminate the false view of a permanent 'I' or 'self'.

Those who take interest and take pains in learning this basic Dharma will have laid the foundation for proper practice. Only then is it advisable for them to proceed with the Vipassana meditation.

219

INSIGHT MEDITATION (VIPASSANA)

Insight meditation means the contemplation mindfully of impermanence, suffering, and non-self. This is explained in the Buddha's discourse on mindfulness. There are four aspects of mindfulness; they are like four stairways to a pagoda. The platform of the pagoda, which is wisdom, can be reached by any of these four stairways. These stairways are the four aspects of mindfulness: 1) contemplation on body, 2) contemplation on sensations or feelings, 3) contemplation on mind or consciousness, and 4) contemplation on ideas or mind objects. It is important to note that by taking up one in meditation, one does not exclude the remaining three aspects. One of these aspects may predominate in the awareness.

According to Mogok Sayadaw, the practice of insight meditation is developed in three stages. The first of these is mindfulness or awareness in concentration. The second is contemplation on the arising and perishing of the five aggregates. The last is the clear knowledge of the path leading to the cessation of all formations, of the arising and vanishing of body and mind. These can be elucidated as follows:

1. Fixing or concentrating the mind on any given object, such as in-breathing or out-breathing or noting of the movement of the body or mind, is called *mindfulness in concentration*.
2. Contemplation of form, feeling, mind, or mind object and their arising and instantly passing away is called *mindfulness of process meditation*.
3. The knowledge of the nature of all conditioned phenomena, seeing the arising and perishing of the aggregates as repugnant and disgusting is called *the path leading to the termina-*

tion or cessation of all arising and vanishing. Until and unless there is knowledge of arising and vanishing of aggregates, until all is seen as impermanent, suffering, and self-less, meditation never amounts to true Vipassana.

True Vipassana begins when the yogi can observe the arising and vanishing of body and mind without looking on it as 'self', 'me', or 'mine'. This clear mindfulness where he does not think it is 'I' who meditates or 'my' mind which is concentrated is proper meditation. All five aggregates are seen clearly as impermanent, as suffering, and as not-self.

Development of only the first one or two stages listed above will not lead to freedom from the wheel of rebirth. The Buddha said it is not because of concentration alone that nirvana is realized. Only Vipassana can bear the fruit of nirvana or liberation. Nevertheless it is important to remember the place of concentration in the initial development of the meditation.

Before actually developing the Vipassana meditation of stages two and three, the yogi is required to build some concentration. This is best done by sitting and fixing the mind on the tip of the nostril, being fully aware of the incoming or outgoing air. The yogi should sit cross-legged with body erect in an atmosphere of calm and quietude. This concentration exercise should be practiced for at least twenty-to-twenty-five minutes before undertaking the Vipassana meditation. With the mind calm and concentrated, the yogi is ready to develop the Vipassana meditation on consciousness and feeling as taught by Mogok Sayadaw.

Where do we start? We must start with the mind. The Buddha explained the importance of meditation on the mind. He said, "I know no other single Dharma so conducive to great profit and benefit as the mind which has been cultivated and developed." It can be implied and understood that the results of the uncultivated and undeveloped mind are the reverse.

The mind is the forerunner of all our actions and precedes all phenomena. Nothing can be done, whether physical or mental, without the cooperation or coordination of the mind. When we do either good or evil deeds, the mind plays the prominent part. No action is possible without our first thinking about it; thought occurs only in the mind. When our mind is controlled, our body remains controlled. When the mind is reckless and uncontrolled, the physical action has no restraint, giving free expression of defilements through our thoughts and emotions. The mind is thus the central factor which controls all our actions.

220

It is the mind in which the wrong view of egoism or 'I-ness' or personality dwells. The delusion of 'I' or 'self' is the driving force behind the deluded mind. It is important to note that it is this element of identification with personality or egoism which clouds the mind. So to put an end to suffering, selfishness, and wrong view, we must penetrate into the mind.

Mogok Sayadaw has formulated a very simple method of meditation on mind which is considered to be the most suitable for present-day yogis. This meditation is Vipassana based on mindfulness of consciousness or mindfulness of feelings.

221

Although these aspects are given prominence, the remaining aspects of Vipassana are not being ignored. It is just like syrup in which fresh juice of lime, sugar, salt, and water are all contained as ingredients. As we become aware of any of these qualities we find that when one is noted, awareness of those remaining is also included, though not as predominant and pronounced as is awareness of the initial object. The four foundations of mindfulness coexist, are concurrent and synchronous in their arising and vanishing.

Why has Mogok Sayadaw chosen to emphasize meditation on mind? The great master Maha Sariputtra said that although it is not easy to read another's mind it is quite easy to know what is occurring in one's own mind. When there occurs in your mind craving, you can easily see how that craving is occurring. If hatred, delusion, ill will, or jealousy occurs in your mind you can at once know that it is occurring, and if it disappears, you also know that it disappears.

Another reason to emphasize meditation on mind, particularly mindfulness of consciousness, is to eliminate the prevalence of a deep-rooted wrong view which regards consciousness as permanent or 'self' or 'soul', even among many Buddhists. Almost all Buddhists are under the wrong impression that a soul transmigrates or reincarnates from one existence to another. Some go further to say that it is the soul which departs the body on the death of a being. Some even believe that the soul does not depart the body as long as there is no vacancy in which to dwell but hangs around until there arises a suitable place to be reborn. This kind of wrong view is deeply rooted and handed down from generation to generation. Such beliefs as transmigration of the soul or reincarnation from one existence to another are incorrect. As has been mentioned above, such wrong views are harbored and maintained because of the belief that consciousness is enduring and permanent and lasting even when the body perishes. People do not yet possess the appropriate knowledge of dependent origination enabling them to understand that consciousness too is impermanent and is subject to an endless process of arising and perishing. It arises for a moment in space and time and cannot move a single inch from where it arises nor remain the same for two successive moments.

222   To dispel our deeply conditioned wrong view and correctly understand the mind, Mogok Sayadaw taught Vipassana meditation based on mindfulness of consciousness and mindfulness of feeling. Both are suitable ways of practice for yogis of this age.

DEVELOPMENT OF MEDITATION ON CONSCIOUSNESS[4]

Those who aspire to attain final enlightenment must begin by exterminating wrong views and ego-belief. For this purpose, Mogok Sayadaw formulated a very simple method of contemplation on consciousness, easily applicable and suitable for all people. The following thirteen kinds of consciousness are to be contemplated. Only one consciousness at a time is to be contemplated or observed, as and when it arises, for it must be remembered that only one consciousness can arise at a time. As soon as one consciousness passes away, another arises.

It is generally believed that there are many kinds of consciousness which occur in our being. Although there may appear to be thousands of kinds, they fall into the classification of only thirteen types. They are as follows:

Internal visiting consciousness:
1. Eye consciousness.
2. Ear consciousness.
3. Nose consciousness.
4. Tongue consciousness.
5. Body consciousness.
6. Desiring consciousness.
7. Aversive consciousness.
8. Deluded consciousness.

---

[4] Consciousness *refers here to that aspect of mind which 'knows an object', our 'knowing faculty'.*

9. Non-greedy consciousness.
10. Non-hateful consciousness.
11. Mind consciousness.
Host consciousness:
12. In-breathing consciousness.
13. Out-breathing consciousness.

The above thirteen kinds of consciousness can be said to be all-embracing covering all those which belong to the ordinary human being. It should be noted that whatever consciousness arises it is only as a result of the contact of object and sense door.[5] Only through the six sense doors can consciousness arise; it can never arise outside the six sense doors.

It should also be noted that consciousness and feeling are co-existing, simultaneous phenomena. Feeling and perception as well are mental factors that arise with each consciousness. As the five aggregates are co-arising, co-existing, and co-vanishing phenomena, it can be said that the contemplation of one aggregate develops insight into all the remaining aggregates.[6] For our purposes, as these thirteen types of consciousness are predominant and pronounced mental elements, they are the focus for our meditation based on awareness of consciousness.

Reference to the list of the thirteen kinds of consciousness is invited. There is desiring consciousness in wishing to eat, to smell, etc. Jealousy and ill will are classified as aversion consciousness while thought to do service or charity comes under non-greed consciousness.

When we open our eyes we see everything as colors and shapes before our eyes. This is the arising of the eye consciousness and the yogi must comprehend and be cognizant of this arising when it occurs. When he hears a sound, ear consciousness arises and this arising must be cognized and comprehended. Again, if he feels any irritation or itch, any pleasurable or unpleasurable feeling, there arises body consciousness. The yogi must comprehend and be cognizant of each new arising and vanishing of consciousness, one at a time.[7]

[5] Sense door *here refers to our six avenues of perception: eyes, ears, nose, tongue, body, and mind.*

[6] *Although dependent origination was described as a chain or progression earlier, it is to be observed that in each moment the five aggregates which make up this chain arise and vanish simultaneously.*

[7] *There are many arisings and passings away of mind each second. When*

In the course of practice, the comprehension or insight of the yogi becomes more pronounced, distractions disappear, and his mindfulness becomes centered only on the arising and vanishing. His awareness of the arising and vanishing of the consciousness then becomes more rapid. Generally at this point the yogi clearly sees with insight that whatever consciousness arises, it terminates in the next instant. He can clearly see that no consciousness can remain for two successive moments the same. The life span of consciousness is momentary. When one moment of consciousness is observed it will be found that that consciousness has already vanished because the life span of any aggregate is only momentary. By the time it is observed it has passed away. One consciousness arises after another which has already vanished. Therefore, when contemplating, the yogi discovers that the consciousness upon which he contemplates has already perished.[8] It vanishes immediately after it has arisen. Hence when the yogi meditates or observes consciousness he will find only change, the perishing or vanishing of each consciousness. If on initial observation the yogi finds that consciousness does not vanish or disappear, he cannot pass beyond the notion of permanence. He must endeavor, then, with more concentration and mindfulness, to perceive the nature of the arising and perishing of the aggregates.

When he becomes aware of the arising he will become more aware of the passing away of consciousness. This observation and cognition must be done without the notion of 'I', or in other words he must cognize that this phenomenon of arising and passing away of consciousness is only consciousness and apart from consciousness there is nothing unchanging which can be found and personified as 'I', 'me', or 'mine'.

It is urged that the yogi contemplate until he perceives less and less of 'I-ness' and more and more of consciousness. From the stage of 'more and more of consciousness' he must go further and try to perceive 'more and more of arising and passing away'.

clearly observed, each birth of mind can be seen to contain one object, a consciousness or knowing of this object, and various mental factors such as feeling, volition, etc. (which determine how the consciousness relates to the object). The object, consciousness, and mental factors is another description of the arising and passing away of the five aggregates.

[8] In fact, the yogi will see how his observation is the next moment of consciousness looking back and seeing how the previous moment's consciousness and object has completely vanished.

During his contemplation all sorts of ideas or distractions will intervene which he must also contemplate upon and perceive as 'arising and passing away' because in actual fact whatever consciousness arises must terminate. So the yogi must perceive and cognize that there is nothing in this body or mind which is unchanging, enduring, and permanent.

Impermanence can never be realized in the strict sense by merely knowing about change nor by reciting *change, change*. It is important for the yogi to observe and deeply experience the impermanence which the aggregates reveal all the time, and not to be deluded by the concept of change he creates by reciting the words *change* or *anicca*. The fleeting state of the arising and dissolution of the thought moments is so rapid that it is almost indescribable. It is not necessary for the yogi to know exactly how rapid it is. What is essential at this stage is to focus on the experience of the arising and perishing of the aggregates, especially each new consciousness that arises. Coming to the breathing or host consciousness, for example, the yogi must be observant and mindful of the in-breathing consciousness and out-breathing consciousness. He must be observant and mindful of the process of the arising as well as the passing away of these two types of consciousness, as well as with all the other eleven types of consciousness elucidated above.

It may be asked: "When and where should this meditation on consciousness be practiced? At the Vipassana centers or monasteries?" The answer is: It can be practiced at the place where consciousness arises. For the arising of consciousness while walking, meditation must be done while walking. For the arising of consciousness while eating or drinking, meditation must be done then and there accordingly. For consciousness arising while sitting in your office, the meditation must be done then and there too. In meditation, what is required by the yogi is observation of his own consciousness with watchful awareness and understanding. The closer the watchfulness and observation of the arising and perishing, the more beneficial will it be to the yogi for the early realization of insight. Should there be distraction, restlessness, and confusion, defilements will find an easy place to abide and be reborn in one's being. It is important that the yogi prevent defilements by observing the clear arising and perishing of whatever comes in.

For more clarification we must note again that as the yogi observes consciousness, the first moment he sees vanishes and is clearly impermanent. Immediately following is a consciousness which observes the previous consciousness. This is the Vipassana

225

or insight path consciousness. Hence, when observing consciousness there will be a series of sequences of events: impermanence, insight, impermanence, insight, etc.

It is important for practicing yogis to gain the initial insight in their Vipassana practice that the preceding impermanence and the following insight go on concurrently one after another without allowing defilement to creep in between. In other words, the consciousness that perished and disappeared is not to be missed. It must be properly noted and observed and understood that it has already perished and the next immediately following consciousness is called *insight* because it perceives with direct insight that the preceding consciousness has already perished and disappeared.

During the practicing period, the yogi will come across all sorts of mind states which appear as relevant or irrelevant, desirable or undesirable. They must also be contemplated upon as objects of meditation. Yogis should not in any way be disappointed or frustrated by these distractions for these are to be regarded simply as objects of meditation.

Of the six attributes of the Dharma, one is 'ehipassiko'. This means 'come and see'. Hence the Dharma is calling everyone to come and see and to examine their true nature, and see how it is incessantly undergoing the phenomenon of arising and perishing.

When there are only a few misses in the yogi's observation and watchfulness, it can be said that he has developed his insight to some extent. When he is able to follow the process of arising and perishing without allowing any defilement to come in between, it can be said that he has reached the stage where he can shatter the false view of self. At this point, the first stage of enlightenment is near.[9]

The Buddha said: "The true disciple dwells, contemplating mind all the time without a miss, fully knowing, comprehending with insight that it is transient, impermanent and unenduring and cannot remain for two successive moments the same. Thus the disciple imbued with the knowledge of impermanence and free from defilement can attain and realize nirvana in this very existence."

[9] *Thus we can see that the development of Vipassana is really the refinement of our ability to observe the rapid change of the mind-body process. As the speed or frequency of noting increases to many times a second, insight deepens.*

It is important for the yogi to be continuous in striving to see with knowledge and comprehension the arising and perishing of whatever consciousness appears in each moment. The attainment of the initial insight of the arising and perishing amounts to the attainment by which one sees the aggregates as they really and actually are. Clearly they are nothing but arising and vanishing and therefore most unsatisfactory, a place of no security.

A question may arise: What benefit does the yogi derive who attains the level of awareness that sees the arising and perishing of the aggregates? An example can be used to answer: On the arising of greed consciousness, if Vipassana is practiced, the yogi comprehends that as soon as the greed has arisen it has also perished and is nowhere to be found. Seeing only this arising and perishing leads to no identification with greed. Hence the process of dependent origination is cut asunder in the middle or, in other words, greed is killed. If there were no contemplation on greed it would inevitably be followed by clinging which would in turn be followed by karmic action. When karmic action arises it is bound to be followed by birth. When rebirth is obtained it amounts to obtaining suffering and the cycle of samsara continues ad infinitum.

It should be clear, then, that the practice of contemplation on arising and perishing amounts to putting a stop to the rounds of rebirth. This is the work of breaking the spokes in the wheel of samsara. It is the work of cutting the links and chains of dependent origination. It is also the work of exterminating ignorance through gaining insight into the mind. Contemplating on the arising and perishing of the five aggregates and seeing how they are intrinsically nothing but suffering can only be developed and comprehended by Vipassana practice. When this penetrative insight is gained, ignorance disappears and insight into the truth of existence is manifest.

According to dependent origination, when ignorance becomes wisdom, karmic action or volition has no force to link with consciousness. When the linking does not take place, volition will not build up or produce any result that may bring about a fresh rebirth, or in other words, the cycle of becoming is broken from the beginning, and liberation is attained.

MEDITATION ON FEELING

In addition to teaching meditation on consciousness, Mogok Sayadaw also described how to develop insight by contemplation of feeling. Meditation on feeling will lead a yogi to the same deep insight into the nature of the mind-body process as meditation on consciousness. It will lead to the breaking up of the chain of dependent origination, the cycle of rebirth and suffering.

Where do we observe feeling? Feeling arises whenever there is the conjunction of three phenomena: sensory organ, object, and consciousness. The impact of these three is contact. The proximate cause of feeling is contact. Therefore feeling is not to be purposely searched for. It arises whenever and wherever there is contact.

Feelings arising on eye base, ear base, nose base, and tongue base are always neutral. Feelings arising in the body are either pleasurable or painful. Feelings which arise in the mind can be either pleasurable, unpleasurable, o neutral.

It is important to note that feeling as described here is not used as 'sensation' (its other often-used meaning), but only refers to the pleasant, neutral, or unpleasant quality of a sense object.

Sometimes one may enjoy pleasurable sensation, especially when in favorable and pleasant surroundings. At other times one may experience pain and be dissatisfied with unfavorable surroundings, or the state of body or mind. Sometimes one may experience neutral feeling in relation to one's present experience.

Mogok Sayadaw formulated and laid down an easy method of classifying feeling to be observed in meditation, as follows:

Six external visitors:
    Neutral feeling arising on eye base.
    Neutral feeling arising on ear base.
    Neutral feeling arising on nose base.
    Neutral feeling arising on tongue base.
    Pleasant feeling arising on body base.
    Unpleasant feeling arising on body base.
Three internal visitors:
    Pleasant feeling on mind base.
    Unpleasant feeling on mind base.
    Neutral feeling on mind base.
Three host visitors:
    In-breathing and out-breathing with pleasant feeling, joy, pleasure, or the state of elation.

In-breathing and out-breathing with unpleasant feeling, displeasure, pain, or despair.

In-breathing and out-breathing with neutral feeling, neither pleasure nor displeasure.

First it is important for the yogi to distinguish individual feelings. He must try to single out unpleasant feeling if there arises unpleasant feeling, pleasant feeling if pleasant feeling, and neutral feeling if there arises neutral feeling. Feeling also must be separated out from an idea of 'I'. In the expression, 'I feel pain, I feel happy,' there is the incorrect association or identification of feeling with 'I'. Feeling and 'I' are separated when feeling is clearly cognized as feeling only and nothing else. Feeling must not be personified with 'I', 'my' feeling. It is the feeling that feels. It is simply a process. There is no 'I' that feels. This truth must be apprehended. Until and unless the yogi is thoroughly familiar with the fundamental knowledge taught in this talk, it will be difficult for him to be able to dissociate feeling with 'I'. As such, the contemplation or meditation will amount to: It is 'I' who feels the pain or suffering; it is 'I' who enjoys happiness or pleasure. In that case, the yogi, however much he endeavors, will not attain nirvana, the fruit of practice.

229

The next important point for the yogi is that he must contemplate on feeling where and when it arises. It has been a practice elsewhere to fix attention on the chest or on the head, but feeling appears anywhere in the body whenever there is contact, so it cannot be said that this sort of practice is right. It is like aiming an arrow at a wrong target. Nobody can fix feeling in any particular place. It will arise wherever there is sense object preceding. If a yogi believes that the feeling he meditates on in one moment is the same one as in another moment, he has a long way to go. It should be cognized and seen with insight that each feeling is transient, impermanent, and never remains the same for two consecutive moments. If the yogi fails to cognize and perceive with insight wisdom that feeling is impermanent, he is still off the track. It is generally and wrongly believed that feeling is one long continuous experience, but with mindfulness and concentration the yogi will see all feeling as arising and ceasing moment to moment.

The yogi should dwell meditating on the arising of feeling and perishing of feeling, and on both the arising and perishing of feeling. It is important for the yogi to remember that feeling is not to be sought after purposely. It is generally believed that when one gets pain, ache, or illness, it is called *feeling*, but feeling is more than that. It is prevalent all the time. One of the six feelings is arising either on the eye, ear, nose, tongue, body, or mind at each moment of consciousness.

There is not a single moment that is free from feeling, so the yogi should try to cognize and comprehend the arising and perishing process. The nature of all five of the aggregates will become clear as the aggregate of feeling is understood fully.

230 The arising and perishing is impermanent; the comprehension of this is true insight. When the yogi can practice to the point where there is no intruding defilement or distraction between his observation of impermanence and insight, the experience of nirvana is within reach.

In order to gain this higher wisdom, the yogi should dwell first on feeling itself, then go further and concentrate his mind on the arising and vanishing, until he eventually sees clearly that feeling dissolves and is experienced as only a process of arising and vanishing phenomena. This is important, for now whenever he contemplates on feeling in place of simply noting the feeling, it dissolves and he fully comprehends the process of arising and vanishing. This is treading on the path of insight.

The contemplation on arising and vanishing is not a new technique. It is an ancient path taken by innumerable Buddhas, Bodhisattvas, and enlightened ones of the past. It is the technique of stopping the cause in order to prevent the effect. What this means can be understood in terms of the process of dependent origination.

The doctrine of dependent origination shows that because of feeling there arises craving. So the cessation of feeling brings the cessation of craving, and cessation of craving is the path to nirvana, to freedom. This whole process comes about as a result of the confidence, effort, and wisdom of the yogi. He can see in his own mind that the cessation of feeling brings the non-arising of craving. Therefore, it brings the end of defilements, for desire does not arise on the cessation of feeling. This end of defilements allows the attainment of nirvana in this very life.

FURTHER PRACTICE

As can be seen from the explication so far, a yogi must first acquire conceptual knowledge of the elements, sense bases, aggregates, and the process of dependent origination. He must develop this knowledge by meditating first on the breath for concentration and then on either the consciousness (knowing faculty) or feelings. In developing mindfulness of consciousness or feelings he will begin to see how these are in a constant state of change, arising and passing away.

The meditation so far has been directed to perceiving the arising and perishing of consciousness and feeling. Now the yogi must become fully aware of the fact that all of the five aggregates are co-arising, co-existing, and co-dissolving.   231

At the onset when the arising of consciousness takes place, the aggregate of form has already taken part in the eye organ; simultaneously feeling has also played its part by way of registering the pleasurable, unpleasurable, or neutral, agreeable or disagreeable, likeable or unlikeable. Perception too does not remain idle because it takes note or perceives the form, color, length, tone, pitch, or velocity, etc. Volition also comes forward to do its function by way of directing the eye organ toward visible objects, ear organ toward the sound, nose organ toward the smell, tongue organ toward taste, body organ toward touch, mind organ toward thoughts, ideas, and past experiences. It can be seen clearly that in each and every phenomenon all five aggregates arise or appear simultaneously and play their respective parts. It is necessary to place a good deal of emphasis on the fact that all of them then terminate themselves simultaneously. Our whole body and mind is simply the five aggregates arising and perishing together simultaneously. Therefore, it can be seen that besides the five aggregates which arise and perish there is no permanent 'I', 'you', 'man', 'woman', or 'person' in this process.

As the meditation deepens, eventually the yogi will reach a stage in which he perceives only the phenomenon of arising and perishing and nothing else. All around him, in all directions and in all quarters, whatever he cognizes is this phenomenon only. He sees nothing of the content of feeling or consciousness. On arising of ear consciousness he perceives only the arising and perishing. Similarly when nose consciousness arises, he perceives not the content of nose consciousness but only the arising and perishing. While tongue consciousness, body consciousness, and mind consciousness arise, these are only perceived as arising and perishing.

In all mental or physical phenomena, what he perceives is transient, impermanent, and changeful. His perception and cognition either of form, feeling, or consciousness as impermanent and unenduring become so steadfast that there arises in him the clear realization of the three signs, he sees the truth of impermanence, suffering, and non-self. Thus, being imbued with this realization, he sees what the aggregates really are: repugnant, detestable, disgusting, and insecure because they are incessantly tormented by arising and perishing. He sees and realizes that all compounded things are impermanent. When he perceives more of impermanence he becomes more disgusted with the aggregates. The desire or lust for the present or the future aggregates becomes abated as he is mentally tormented with the truth of unsatisfactoriness, impermanence, and egolessness.

It is at this point that the yogi is preponderantly bent on the emancipation from suffering, extrication from the rounds of rebirth in samsara. He is now ripe for the experience of the cessation of this process, the highest bliss—nirvana.

The experience of nirvana and the wisdom arising from seeing the true nature of the aggregates eliminates wrong view, especially clinging to the idea of self. When wrong view is eliminated, craving and conceit also diminish and the cycle of dependent origination is broken.

According to the Dharma, the arising and perishing of all body and mind is the noble truth of suffering, the cognition thereof is nirvana. Extermination of clinging brings the cessation of suffering and the end of the process of birth, old age, and death. Therefore meditation or contemplation on arising and perishing of the aggregates covers the whole of the four noble truths. This insight is the true purpose of Vipassana. Vipassana meditation should be practiced as soon as possible. We should remember there is imminent danger of disease and death in this high-pressure age, and meditate accordingly. The practice of Vipassana is the only way to forestall any latent dangers in the next rebirth and to put an end to suffering in this very life.

U BA KHIN

CHAPTER
THIRTEEN

U Ba Khin, meditation master and layman, was one of the most extraordinary figures of our time. He took up meditation practice at about age forty while remaining in government service. He studied extensively under his guru Saya Thet Gyi, a well-known Burmese lay teacher. He mastered practices of a number of types of concentration meditation or absorption and developed a most powerful technique for the practice of Vipassana insight meditation. This technique involves sweeping the mind through the body, giving special attention to the ever-changing play of sensations that can be perceived.

U Ba Khin was known as an extremely powerful man and his lifestyle was an indication of this inner power. After the British left Burma he became accountant-general, a cabinet rank officer, and at the same time founded and taught at the International Meditation Center in Rangoon. In fact, for several years after his retirement from government service, U Ba Khin not only developed his center and extensively taught meditation Dharma, but was also the acting head of four departments of the Burmese government.

U Ba Khin's full involvement in the demands of a worldly life as a householder and prominent civil servant is apparent in the system and style of his instruction. He emphasized the practical in preference to the theoretical understanding of

Dharma by the direct and intensive method of practice. U Ba Khin's teachings are based primarily on his own experience and therefore the terminology he employed to describe what he understood may seem imprecise in the most technical Buddhist sense or in modern scientific precision. This is because he was not really interested in any theoretical framework of Dharma but merely tried to provide a sufficient translation of his own experience to serve as a basis for meditation instruction. He considered Buddhism something to do rather than talk about.

Visa restrictions for the past decade have limited Western visitors to the International Meditation Center, though at one time there were many who studied there. The center consists of halls and rooms for lodging visiting meditators and a central shrine meditation stupa where instruction and meditation guidance are given. Although U Ba Khin died several years ago, he has a number of teaching disciples. At the center, a laywoman, the Venerable Saiyama, leads instruction, and Westerners who come to Rangoon are still very well received and carefully taught as time allows. Instruction is intensive and, although U Ba Khin taught many of the different concentration meditations, mindfulness of breathing is now most often used in conjunction with his insight practice.

The specific practice consisted, after developing a certain amount of concentration, of passing the attention systematically through the body and becoming aware of the physical sensations within it. Observing these sensations, the meditator develops an increasing awareness of anicca, the characteristic of impermanence. When, in U Ba Khin's words, "anicca is activated," the process of purification of defilement occurs in the psycho-physical continuum that we label *human being*. The agent, or the mode, of this purification, U Ba Khin referred to as *nib-*

bana dhatu. The nature of this nibbana dhatu is difficult to describe, because it is not a theoretical aspect or even a conceptual one. It is, in fact, an experience. As one penetrates more and more deeply into the nature of reality by observing anicca closer and closer to the actual *state* of impermanence, there arises a different mode, a different 'element' (the literal meaning of dhatu) that on the most basic level of being comes into contact with defilement and uproots it. This is a rough conceptualization of a process that U Ba Khin well knew was inexplicable but capable of being experienced. His own descriptions of it are similarly metaphoric:

237

"With the awareness of the truth of anicca (impermanence) and/or suffering and/or non-self, he (the student) develops in him what we may call the sparkling illumination of nibbana dhatu, a power that dispels all impurities or poisons, the products of bad actions, which are the sources of his physical and mental ills. In the same way as fuel is burnt away by ignition, the negative forces (impurities or poisons) within are eliminated by the nibbana dhatu, which he generates with the true awareness of anicca in the course of his meditation. . . . A note of caution is necessary here. When one develops nibbana dhatu, the impact of this nibbana dhatu upon the impurities and poisons within his own system will create a sort of upheaval which must be endured. This upheaval tends to increase the sensitivity of the radiation, friction, and vibration of the atomic units within."

This will grow in intensity, so much so that one might feel as though his body were just electricity and a mass of suffering.

"What is essential in Buddhist meditation is the realization of the coming into being and the dissolution of the five aggregates. It is only when the nibbana dhatu is developed, following a true appreciation of anicca, that the impact of nibbana dhatu upon the impurities within

creates a sensation of burning which in any case should not persist."

Nibbana dhatu, then, can be understood as the force generated by the awareness of anicca, the actual meditational experience of impermanence. This is a purification process and this purification process leads the meditator to experience the nirvanic peace within himself. This is the heart of U Ba Khin's teaching.

There are a few fine examples of U Ba Khin teachers available to Western meditatiors. In India, U Goenka, a powerful teacher in the style of his guru U Ba Khin, has for five years been leading ten-day intensive meditation sessions and has instructed several thousand Westerners in insight meditation. In America, recently Robert Hover and Ruth Dennison have been traveling, giving intensive sessions at retreats set up by interested students. This practice, as with other intensive methods, can lead serious students to deep insight into the Dharma in short periods of time. Then, of course, the yogi must continue the process of integrating the truth of his insight into his daily life.

The Essentials of Buddha-Dharma in Practice

13

by U Ba Khin

Though one may conquer a thousand times a thousand men in battle, he who conquers himself is the greatest warrior.

—Dhammapada

Buddhism is not a religion according to its dictionary meaning because it has no center in God as is the case in all other religions. Strictly speaking, Buddhism is a system of philosophy coordinated with a code of morality, physical and mental. The goal in view is 'extinction of suffering and death'.

The four noble truths taught by the Buddha in his first sermon which set in motion the wheel of Dharma form the basis on which is founded this system of philosophy. In fact, the first three of the four noble truths expound the philosophy of the Buddha while the fourth (the eightfold noble path which is a code of morality-cum-philosophy) serves as a means for the end. This first sermon was given to the five ascetics, led by Kondanna, who were his early companions in search of truth. Kondanna was the first disciple of the Buddha to become fully enlightened.

239

Now we come to the four noble truths. They are:
1. Truth of suffering.
2. Truth of origin of suffering.
3. Truth of extinction of suffering.
4. Truth of path leading to the extinction of suffering.

To come to a complete understanding of the fundamental concepts in the philosophy of Buddha, emphasis is laid on the need for the realization of the truth of suffering. To bring home this point, Buddha tackled the problem from two different angles.

0   First, by a process of reasoning. He made his disciples see that life is a struggle, life is suffering; birth is suffering; old age is suffering; illness is suffering; death is suffering. However, the influence of sensuality is so strong in mankind that we are normally apt to forget ourselves, to forget what we have to pay therefore. Just think for a moment how life exists in the prenatal period; how from the moment of birth the child has to struggle for existence; what preparations he has to make to face life; and that, as a man, he has to struggle until he breathes his last. Life is indeed suffering. The more one is attached to self, the greater is the suffering. In fact what pains and sufferings a man has to undergo are suppressed in favor of momentary sensual pleasures which are but occasional spotlights in darkness. But for this delusion which keeps him away from the truth, he would surely work out his way for emancipation from the rounds of life, suffering, and death.

Second, the Buddha made it known to his disciples that the human body is composed of *kalapas* (sub-atomic units), each dying out simultaneously as it becomes. Each kalapa is a mass formed of the following nature-elements:

1. Extension (earth)
2. Cohesion (water).
3. Radiation (heat and cold).
4. Motion (air).
5. Color.
6. Smell.
7. Taste.
8. Nutritive essence.

Everything that exists in this universe, whether animate or inanimate, is composed of kalapas (sub-atomic units), each dying out simultaneously as it becomes. Each kalapa is a mass formed of the eight basic elements. The first four are material qualities which are predominant in a kalapa. The other four are merely subsidiaries which are dependent upon and arise out of the former. A kalapa is the most minute particle in the physical plane, still beyond the range of science of today. It is only when the eight nature elements are together that the entity of a kalapa is formed. In other words, the co-existence for a moment of these eight nature elements of behavior makes a mass, just for that moment. The size of a kalapa is tens of thousands of times smaller than a particle of dust. The lifespan of a kalapa is a moment, there being a trillion such moments in the wink of an eye. These kalapas are all in a state of perpetual change or flux. To a developed student in Vipassana meditation, they can be felt as a stream of energy. The human body is not a fixed entity as it seems to be but a continuum of an aggregate of matter with life force coexisting.

To make my work of explanation easy for the present-day generation, I might draw attention to the writings on "Atomic Contents" in the book *Inside the Atom* by Isaac Asimov. He writes about the chemical reactions going on continuously in all parts of the body of a living creature at all times. This should be sufficient to bring home the point of view that all things, different as they are, are made of tiny particles called *atoms*. These atoms have been proven by science to be in a state of arising and dissolution or change. We should accordingly accept the concept of Buddha that all compound things are subject to change, decay, or impermanence.

But in expounding the theory of impermanence, Buddha started with the behavior which makes matter, and the matter as known to a Buddha is even finer than the atom which science of today has discovered.

To a casual observer, a piece of iron is motionless. The scientist knows that it is composed of electrons all in a state of perpetual change or flux. If it is so with a piece of iron, what will be the case with a living organism, say a human being? The changes that are taking place inside the human body must be more violent. Does man feel the rocking vibrations within himself? Does the scientist who knows that all is in a state of change ever feel that his own body is but energy and vibration? What will be the repercussion on the mental attitude of the man who introspectively sees that his own body is mere energy and vibration? To quench thirst one may easily drink a glass of water from a village well. Suppose one's eyes were as powerful as microscopes—one would surely hesitate to drink the very same water, in which one would be seeing the magnified microbes. So also, when one comes to a realization of the perpetual change within himself (anicca or impermanence) he must necessarily come to the understanding of the truth of suffering due to the sharp sense of feeling of the radiation, vibration, and friction of the atomic units within. Indeed life is suffering, both within and without, to all appearances and in ultimate reality.

241

When I say "life is suffering," as the Buddha taught, please be so good as not to run away with the idea that, if it is so, life is miserable, not worth living, and that the Buddhist concept of suffering is a terror which will give no chance of a reasonably happy life. What is happiness? For all that science has achieved in the field of materialism, are the peoples of the world happy? They may find sensual pleasures off and on, but in their heart of hearts they are not happy for what has happened, for what is happening, and for what may happen next. Why? This is because while man has mastery over matter, he is still lacking in mastery over his mind.

Pleasure born of sensuality is nothing compared with the rapture of the inner peace of mind which can be procured through a process of Buddhist meditation. Sense pleasures are preceded and followed by troubles and pains; it is like scratching a rash—whereas rapture of meditation is free from such troubles and pain either way. It will be difficult for you, looking from a sensuous field, to appreciate what that joy is like. But, I know you can also enjoy and have a taste of it for comparative valuation. There is therefore no reason to suppose that Buddhism teaches something which will make you feel miserable with the nightmare of suffering. Please take it from me that it will give you an escape from the normal conditions of life, a lotus as it were in a pond of crystal water, immune from its fiery surroundings. It will give you that 'peace within' which will satisfy you that you are getting not only beyond the 'day-to-day troubles of life' but slowly and surely beyond the limitation of life, suffering, and death.

What then is the origin of suffering? The origin of it, Buddha said, is craving. Once the seed of desire is sown, it grows into greed and multiplies into craving or lust, either for power or for material gains. The man in whom this seed is sown becomes a slave to these cravings and he is automatically driven to strenuous labors of mind and body to keep pace with them until the end comes. The final result must surely be the accumulation of the evil mental force generated by his own actions, words, and thoughts which are motivated by desire and anger inherent in him.

Thus, it is the mental forces of actions (sankhara) which react in course of time on each individual. These become responsible for continuing the stream of mind and matter, the origin of suffering within.

Only the accomplished saint, only the arahat, can fully understand the truth of suffering. As the truth of suffering is realized, the causes of suffering become automatically destroyed, and so one eventually comes to the end of suffering or ill. What is most important in the understanding of the Buddha Dharma is the realization of the truth of suffering or ill through a process of meditation in accordance with the path set out by the Buddha.

What then is the path leading to the extinction of suffering? The path is none other than the noble eightfold path taught by the Buddha in his first sermon. This eightfold path is divided into three main states; namely, virtue, meditation, and wisdom.

VIRTUE. The three characteristics of virtue are:

1. Right speech.
2. Right action.
3. Right livelihood.

By right speech is meant speech which must be true, beneficial, and neither foul nor malicious.

By right action is meant fundamentals of morality which are opposed to killing, stealing, sexual misconduct, and drunkenness.

By right livelihood is meant way of living by trades other than those which increase the suffering of all beings—such as slave-trading, manufacture of weapons, or traffic in intoxicating drugs.

These represent generally the code of morality as initially pronounced by the Buddha in his very first sermon. Later, however, he amplified it and introduced separate codes for monks and lay disciples.

I need not worry you with what has been prescribed for monks. I will just let you know what the code of morality or precepts for a

Buddhist lay disciple is. This is called the *five precepts*, which are:
1. Abstention from killing any sentient beings. (Life is most precious for all beings, and in prescribing this, Buddha's compassion extends to all beings.)
2. Abstention from taking what is not given. (This serves as a check against improper desires for possessions.)
3. Abstention from sexual misconduct. (Sex desire is dormant in man. This is irresistible to almost all. Unlawful sexual indulgence was therefore prohibited by the Buddha.)
4. Abstention from telling lies. (This precept is included to fulfill by way of speech the essence of truth.)
5. Abstention from intoxication. (Intoxication causes a man to lose his steadfastness of mind and reasoning power so essential for the realization of truth).

The five precepts therefore are intended to control actions and words and to serve as a foundation for concentration and equanimity of mind.

Whoever is desirous of undergoing a course of training in Buddhist meditation must go along with the noble eightfold path. For the first step, the student will have to maintain a minimum standard of morality by way of a promise to keep the five precepts. This promise is not, I believe, detrimental to any religious faith.

MEDITATION. We now come to the mental aspect of Buddhism, right meditation. In the second stage of the eightfold noble path are included:
1. Right exertion.
2. Right attentiveness.
3. Right concentration.

Right exertion is, of course, a prerequisite for right attentiveness. Unless one makes a determined effort to narrow the range of thoughts of his wavering and unsteady mind, he cannot expect to secure that attentiveness which in turn helps bring the mind by right concentration to a state of one-pointedness and equanimity. It is here that the mind becomes freed from hindrances, pure and tranquil, illumined within and without. The mind, in such a state becomes powerful and bright. It experiences a light which is a mental reflex, with the light varying in degrees from that of a star to that of the sun. To be plain, this light which is reflected in the mind's eye in complete darkness is a manifestation of purity, tranquility, and serenity of the mind.

The Hindus work for it. To go from light into the void and to come back to it is truly Brahmanic. In the *New Testament* in

Matthew, he speaks of a "body full of light." We hear also of Roman Catholic priests meditating regularly for this miraculous light. The *Holy Koran* too, gives prominence to the "manifestation of divine light."

This mental reflex of light denotes the purity of mind within, and purity of mind forms the essence of religious life whether Buddhist, Hindu, Christian, or Muslim. Indeed, purity of mind is the greatest common denominator of all religions. Love which alone is a means for the unity of mankind must be supreme, and it cannot be so unless the mind is transcendentally pure. A balanced mind is necessary to balance the unbalanced minds of others. "As a fletcher makes straight his arrow, a wise man makes straight his trembling and unsteady thought, which it is difficult to guard, difficult to hold back." So said the Buddha. Exercise of mind is equally necessary as exercise of the physical body. Why not, then, give exercise to the mind and make it pure and strong so that you may enjoy the peace of concentration, the 'jhanic peace within'.

When inner peace begins to permeate the mind, you will surely progress in the knowledge of truth. It is our experience that under a proper guide this inner peace and purity of mind with light can be secured by one and all irrespective of their religion or creed provided they have sincerity of purpose and are prepared to submit to the guide for the period of trial.

In this respect, the guru is merely a guide.[1] However, the success in the development of the power of concentration to perfection depends entirely on the right exertion and right mindfulness of the candidate concerned. The achievement of absorption-concentration or access-concentration is a reward which goes only to highly developed candidates.

When, by continued practice, one has complete mastery over his mind, he can enter into absorption states and gradually develop himself to acquire attainments which will even give him super-normal powers. However, such a practice, which gives supernormal powers in this mundane field, was not encouraged by the

---

[1] *U Ba Khin viewed the role of teacher as most important in the student's development. He wrote that, "One cannot rise to a level of pure mental attitude without the help of a teacher." He considered himself just a guide. But as one who had traversed the terrain once before, he had the power to dispel certain obstacles and thus speed the student's progress toward insight. This is what he meant by his frequent use of the word* qualified *in describing a teacher.*

Buddha, whose sole object of developing concentration was to have the purity and strength of mind essential for the realization of truth.

We have in Buddhism forty methods of concentration, of which the most outstanding is anapana; that is, concentration on the incoming and outgoing breath, the method followed by all Buddhas. The student at the International Meditation Center is helped to develop the power of concentration to one-pointedness by encouraging him to focus his attention to a spot on the upper lip at the base of the nose, synchronizing the inward and outward motion of respiration with the silent awareness of in-breath and out-breath. Whether the induction of life is from the mental forces (sankhara) of one's own actions, as in Buddhism, or from God, as in Christianity, the symbol of life is the same. It is the rhythm, pulsation, or vibration latent in man. Respiration is, in fact, a reflection of this symbol of life. The anapana meditation technique (mindfulness of respiration) is followed at the center. Its great advantage is that the respiration is not only natural, but also available at all times for the purpose of anchoring one's attention to it, to the exclusion of all other thoughts. By concentrating with a determined effort, one can narrow down the range of thought waves first to the area around the nose, then to a spot on the upper lip, with just the touch of the warmth of the breath, while respiration becomes shorter and shorter. There is no reason why a good student in meditation should not be able to secure firm one-pointedness of mind in a few days of training. There are always pointers to the progress of this meditation when it is steered in the right direction, by way of the appearance of visual symbols taking the form of something 'white' as opposed to anything 'black'. At first, they are seen in the form of clouds or cotton wool, and sometimes in shapes of white as of smoke, cobwebs, flowers, or discs, but when the attention becomes more concentrated, they appear as flashes or points of light or as a tiny star or moon or sun. If these pointers appear in meditation (of course, with eyes closed), then it should be taken for granted that concentration is being established. What is essential, then, is for the student to try after each short spell of relaxation to get back to concentration with the pointer of 'light' as quickly as possible.

"Just as a man who makes a journey on a wild horse without the ability to control the reins does not get very far, so also a disciple with weak concentration will not make good progress in his or her practice. So I remind you not to become prey to your mind but to

245

tame it with a revolutionary spirit and make use of it." When you can do this, you are ready to be switched to Vipassana meditation to gain insight into the ultimate truth and enjoy the great peace of nirvana. If one is able to focus his attention to one point at the base of the nose with a minute point of light remaining stationary for some time, it is all the better, because at that time he reaches the level of mind known as access concentration.

246

"Mind is intrinsically pure," said the Buddha. "It becomes polluted, however, by the absorption of impurities." In the same way as salt water can be distilled into pure water, so also a student meditating on the breath can eventually get his mind distilled of impurities and brought to a perfect state of purity. This is the power of the practice of concentration, built upon a base of virtue.

WISDOM. I will now take up the philosophical aspect of Buddhism in the third state of the noble eightfold path—wisdom or insight.

The two characteristic aspects of wisdom are:

1. Right aspiration.
2. Right understanding.

Right understanding of the truth is the aim and object of Buddhism and right aspiration is the analytical study of mind and matter, both within and without, to come to a realization of truth. Mind is so called because of its tendency to incline toward an object of sense. Form is so called because of its impermanence due to perpetual change. The terms in English are close but the meaning is not exact.

Mind, strictly speaking, is the term applied to the following:

1. Consciousness (vinnana).
2. Feeling (vedana).
3. Perception (sanna).
4. Volitional energies and mental qualities (sankhara).

These, together with form in material states, make what we call the *five aggregates*. It is in these five aggregates that the Buddha has summed up all the mental and physical phenomena of existence which in reality is a continuum of mind and matter coexisting but which to a layman is misperceived as personality or ego.

In right aspiration, the disciple who by then has developed a powerful lens of concentration, focuses his attention into himself. By introspective meditation makes an analytical study first of the nature of matter and then of mind and mental properties. He feels, and at times also sees, the kalapas in their true state. He begins to realize that both matter and mind are in constant change—

impermanent and fleeting. As his power of concentration increases, the nature of forces in him become more and more vivified. He can no longer deny that the five aggregates are suffering. He longs for a state beyond suffering. By continued practice he can eventually get out of the bonds of suffering, and move from the mundane to the supramundane state, entering the stream of nirvana. At this point, he becomes free from (1) ego, (2) doubts, and (3) attachment to rules and rituals. With further practice comes the second stage of liberation, which is a level of wisdom in which sensuous craving and ill will become attenuated. By continued practice the yogi then ceases to have any passion or anger. Eventually he experiences the full freedom of arahatship as the final goal. Each of those who have experienced nirvana can repeat this experience as many times as he may choose by going to the fruition stage which gives him the 'nirvanic peace within'.

This 'peace within' which is identified with nirvana has no parallel because it is supramundane. Compared to this, the state of absorption, or peace within, which I mentioned earlier in dealing with concentration, is negligible. While the 'nirvanic peace within' takes one beyond the limits of all planes of existence, the 'jhanic peace within' will still keep one within these planes.

The development of wisdom and eventual insight into what is the truth of existence and nirvana, is based directly on the practice of meditation. In our center, when the student has reached a certain level of concentration (preferably access samadhi), after following the breathing meditation for several days, the course of training is changed to Vipassana or insight. This requires the use of the powerful lens of concentration already developed and involves an examination of the inherent tendencies of all that exists within one's self. The student is taught to become sensitive to the ongoing processes of his own organism, where he experiences the reactions taking place in all living beings. When the student becomes engrossed with such sensations, which are the products of nature, he comes to the realization, physically and mentally, of the truth that his whole physical being is after all a changing mass. This is the fundamental concept of impermanence in Buddhism— the nature of change that is taking place in everything, whether animate or inanimate, that exists in this universe. He also experiences the corollary, the concept of suffering or ill which becomes identified with life. This is true because of the fact that the whole structure of a being is made up of atoms (kalapas) all in a state of perpetual combustion. The last concept that becomes clear is that of non-self. You call *substance* what appears to you to be a substance. In reality, there is no unchanging substance as such. As the course of meditation progresses, the student comes to the realization that there is no substantiality in his so-called self, and there is no such thing as the core of a being. Eventually he breaks away the ego-centralism in him—in respect to both mind and body. He then emerges out of meditation with a new outlook, alive to the fact that whatever happens in this universe is subject to the fundamental laws of cause and effect. He knows with his inward eye the illusory nature of the separate self.

Now, let me go into more detail regarding the essence of our practice. In the development of insight at our center, we work especially with the truth of anicca or impermanence. If you know impermanence truly you know the truth of suffering and the truth of egolessness as well, for the three appear together.

Impermanence is, then, the essential factor which must be first experienced and understood by the practice. A mere reading of the books on Buddhism or book-knowledge of Buddha Dharma will not be enough for the understanding of true impermanence because the experiential aspect will be missing. It is only through experience and understanding of the nature of impermanence as an ever-changing process within your very self that you can understand it in the way Buddha meant for all to understand.

To understand impermanence, one must follow strictly and diligently the noble eightfold path. In this connection I should like to explain that each action, either by deed, word, or thought, leaves behind a force of action, karma, which goes to the credit or debit account of the individual according to whether the action is good or bad. This invisible something which we call *sankhara* or *forces of action* is the product of the mind with which each action is related. It has no element of extension. The whole universe is permeated with the forces of action of all living beings. The inductive theory of life has the origin, we believe, in these forces, each individual absorbing continually the forces of his own actions, at the same time releasing new forces of actions by deeds, words, and thoughts, creating, so to say, an unending cycle of life with pulsation, rhythm, and vibration as its symbol. Let us take the forces of good actions as positive and the forces of bad actions as negative. Then, we get what we may call the positive and negative reaction, which is always taking place everywhere in the universe. It is taking place in all animate and inanimate objects, in my body, in your body, and in the bodies of all living beings. There is constantly an accumulation of karma which becomes the source of energy to sustain life, which inevitably is followed by suffering and death. One may be a saint today but a rogue thereafter. He may be rich today but may soon become poor. The vicissitudes of life are very conspicuous. There is no man who is stable, no family which is stable, no community which is stable, no nation which is stable. All are subject to the Law of Karma. As this karma comes out of mind which is ever-changing, the effects of karma must necessarily also be changing. It is by the development of the power inherent in the understanding of impermanence, suffering, and non-self that one is able to rid oneself of karma which becomes accumulated in one's own personal account. Daily we are making new karma with our actions, and only through the development of insight into impermanence can we cut into this process. It can be a matter of a lifetime or more to get rid of all of one's own karma. He who has got himself rid of all karma comes to the end of suffering, because by then there is no remainder to give the necessary life energy to sustain him in any form of life. This is the end of suffering reached by the Buddha and arahats on the termination of their lives, when they passed into final nirvana. For us of today who take the Vipassana meditation it should suffice if we can understand impermanence very well and reach the first stage of enlightenment and begin to limit the lifetimes we must continue to suffer.

This impermanence which opens the door to the understanding of suffering and non-self and then leads to the end of suffering eventually, can be encountered only through a Buddha, or after he has passed away, through his teaching relating to the noble eightfold path and the factors of enlightenment.

For progress in Vipassana meditation, a student must keep knowing impermanence as continuously as possible. The Buddha's advice to monks is that they should maintain the awareness of impermanence (or suffering or non-self) in all postures, whether sitting, standing, walking, or lying down. The continuity of awareness of impermanence and so of suffering and non-self is the secret of success. The last word of Buddha just before he breathed his last and passed into parinirvana was: "Decay and impermanence is inherent in all compound things. Work out your own salvation with diligence."

This is in fact the essence of all his teachings during the forty-five years of his lifetime. If you will keep up the awareness of impermanence that is inherent in all component things you are sure to reach the goal of freedom in the course of time.

In the meanwhile, as you develop in the understanding of impermanence, your insight into 'what is true of nature' will become greater and greater. So much so that eventually you will have no doubt whatsoever of the three characteristics of impermanence, suffering, and non-self. It is then only that you will be in a position to go ahead for the goal in view.

Now that you know that understanding impermanence is the first essential factor, you should try to focus with clarity on what impermanence means as continuously as possible. More and more you will see that the real meaning of impermanence is decay. This is the inherent nature of everything that exists in the universe, animate or inanimate.

To know that our very body is composed of tiny kalapas all in a state of change is to know what is true of the nature of change or decay. The nature of change or decay (impermanence) occasioned by the continual breakdown and replacement of kalapas is unsatisfactoriness, the truth of suffering. It is only when you experience this change as suffering that you come to the realization of the four noble truths on which so much emphasis has been laid in the teachings of Buddha. Why? Because when you realize the subtle nature of suffering from which you cannot escape for a moment, you become truly afraid of, disgusted with, and disinclined to your very existence with body-matter and mind, and look for a way of escape to a state beyond—beyond the cycle of moment-to-moment rebirth, beyond to the end of suffering. What that final end of suffering would be like, you will be able to taste even as a living human being, when you reach the level of stream entry, when by enough practice you go into the unconditioned state of peace of nirvana within.

In speaking of the development of the Vipassana meditation so far I have stressed seeing impermanence in the kalapas, in the elements of the body. Viapassana meditation also includes contemplation on the changing nature of thought-elements or attention projected toward a process of change of matter. At times the attention will be on impermanence of matter only. At times the attention may be on impermanence of thought-elements. When one is contemplating impermanence of matter, one realizes also that the thought-elements arising simultaneously with the awareness of impermanence of matter are also in a state of transition or change. In this case one can understand impermanence of both matter and thought-elements (mind).

All I have said so far relates to the understanding of impermanence through body-feeling, the process of change of matter and also of thought elements depending upon such changing processes. You should know also that impermanence can be understood through other types of feeling as well.

Awareness of impermanence can be developed through feeling:[2]

By contact of visible form with the sense organ of eye.

By contact of sound with the sense organ of ear.

By contact of smell with the sense organ of nose.

By contact of taste with the sense organ of tongue.

By contact of thought with the sense of mind.

In fact, one can develop the understanding of impermanence through any of the six organs of sense. In practice, however, we have found that, of all the types of feelings, the feeling by contact of touch with the component parts of the body in a process of change covers the best area for introspective meditation. Not only that, the feeling by contact of touch (by way of friction, radiation, and vibration of the kalapas within) with the component parts of the body is more tangible than other types of feeling and therefore a beginner in Vipassana meditation can come to the understanding of impermanence most easily through body feeling. This is the main reason why we have chosen the body feeling as a medium for quick understanding of impermanence. It is open for anyone to try other means but my suggestion is that one should have oneself well established in the understanding of the impermanence through body feeling before any attempt is made through other types of feeling. However it is done, Vipassana meditation is concerned with mindfulness of the process of moment-to-moment change and as suggested above, we have found that the touch and sensation in the body and six senses is the best station for developing this mindfulness.

At our center, when meditation is changed from the breath to awareness of impermanence, the teacher instructs the meditator with a specific formula for beginning the practice of sweeping the attention through the body, part by part, feeling the impermanence of all touch and sensation. As the awareness of impermanence continues, the meditator will see how the power of his concentration and mindfulness can unblock the flow of energy in the body. Then the sweeping becomes more rapid and more clear. As the body becomes clear for the flow of energy and the impermanence (and suffering and non-self) of all sensation becomes more

251

[2] Feeling *in this usage refers to bodily sensation.*

apparent, the focus of attention of the meditator moves to the center (the heart). Now mindfulness and concentration on changing sensation and feeling are so strong that all senses, even the movement of mind, are experienced as changing, as vibrations. Perception of the whole world, matter and mind, becomes reduced to various levels of vibration in a constant state of change. The meditator refines and penetrates with Vipassana to see the true nature of existence. It is this clear penetration that leads him to the cessation of this constant moment-to-moment change, the peace of nirvana.

The development of awareness of impermanence will lead to the arising of the various levels of insight knowledge. The practice should be reviewed and adjusted by a competent teacher to best help the meditator through the new experiences and insights of each level. One should avoid looking forward to any attainment of insight, as this will distract from the continuity of awareness of impermanence which alone can and will lead to the highest truth.

The meditator who has practiced until final penetration into the Dharma of the Buddha can truly appreciate the six attributes of the Dharma:

1. The Dharma is not the result of conjecture or speculation, but the result of personal attainments, and it is precise in every respect.
2. The Dharma produces beneficial results here and now for those who practice it in accordance with the techniques evolved by the Buddha.
3. The effect of Dharma on the person practicing is immediate in that it has the ability to remove the causes of suffering as the understanding of the truth of suffering grows.
4. The Dharma can stand the test of those who are anxious to do so. They can know for themselves what the benefits are.
5. The Dharma is part of one's own self, and therefore withstands ready investigation.
6. The fruits of Dharma can be fully experienced by any meditators who reach at least the first experience of enlightenment. The nirvanic peace within is available to all of the 'noble disciples'. They may enjoy it as and when they may like to do so. They gain access to the state of peace called *fruition*, the supramundane consciousness in relation to the peace of nirvana where no feeling can be aroused through any of the sense centers. At this time, body posture becomes erect. This state is one of perfect physical and mental calm; the

peace of nirvana is the highest bliss.

Let me now deal with Vipassana meditation from the point of view of a householder in everyday life and explain the benefit one can derive from it, here and now, in this very lifetime.

The initial object of Vipassana meditation is to 'activate impermanence'[3] in oneself or to experience one's inner self in impermanence and to get eventually to a state of inner and outer calmness and balance. This is achieved when one becomes engrossed in the feeling of impermanence within.

253

The world is now facing serious problems threatening mankind. It is just the right time for everyone to take to Vipassana meditation and learn how to find a deep pool of quiet in the midst of all that is happening today. Impermanence is inside everybody. It is with everybody. Just look into oneself and there it is to be experienced. When one can feel impermanence, when one can experience impermanence, and when one can become engrossed in impermanence, one can at will cut away from the world of ideation outside. Impermanence is for the householder the gem of life which he will treasure to create a reservoir of calm and balanced energy for his own. It strikes at the root of one's physical and mental ills and removes gradually whatever is bad in him, the sources of such physical and mental ills. In the lifetime of Buddha the number of householders who took to Vipassana meditation was great. Impermanence is not reserved for men who have renounced the world for homeless life. In spite of drawbacks which make a householder restless in these days, a competent teacher or guide can help a student to get impermanence activated in a comparatively short time. Once it is activated, all that is necessary is to try to maintain it. The meditator must make it a point, as soon as time or opportunity presents itself for further progress, to attain the level of knowledge of the fast changing nature of all material and mental phenomena. If he reaches this level, there will be little or no problem because he should then be able to experience impermanence without much ado and almost automatically. In this case, impermanence will become his base, and he can return there as soon as

[3] *U Ba Khin sometimes used the term* to activate impermanence. *It seemed to imply that moment when the awareness could fully experience the* actual *sensation of anicca, the rapid dissolution within the mind-body continuum described as 'the falling of rainwater on the surface of a lake'. At that moment, the mind generates this force of purification which he called nibbana dhatu.*

the domestic needs of daily life are over. There is likely, however, to be some difficulty with one who has not as yet reached the stage of insight which sees the fast change of mental and material phenomena. It will be just like a tug of war for him between impermanence within and the physical and mental activities outside the body. So, it would be wise for him to follow the motto of "work while you work—play while you play." There is no need to be activating impermanence all the time. It should suffice to confine practice to regular periods set apart in the day or night for the purpose. During this time an attempt must be made to keep the mind/attention inside the body with the awareness exclusively on impermanence. Awareness of impermanence should be moment to moment, so continuous as not to allow for interpolation of any discursive or distracting thoughts which are definitely detrimental to progress. If this is not possible, go back to respiration mindfulness, because concentration is the key to being able to activate impermanence. Remember that to get good concentration, virtue has to be perfect, since concentration is built upon virtue. Then, for mindfulness of impermanence, concentration must be good. If concentration is excellent, awareness of impermanence will also become excellent. There is no special technique for cultivating impermanence other than cultivating attention directed to the object of meditation. This means drawing attention back to body feeling, in order to feel impermanence on or in the body; it should first be in the areas where one can get attention easily engrossed. This can mean changing the area of attention from place to place, from head to feet, and from feet to head, at times probing into the interior. It must be clearly understood that no attention is to be paid to the anatomy of body but rather to the direct experience of the formation of matter (kalapas) as sensation and the nature of their constant change.

If these instructions are observed, there will surely be progress. The rate of this progress depends on ability and the devotion of the individual to the work of meditation. If he attains high levels of concentration and wisdom, his power to understand the three characteristics of impermanence, suffering, and non-self will increase and he will accordingly come nearer and nearer to the goal of enlightenment which every person should keep in view.

This is the age of science. Men of today have no faith in a future utopia. They will not accept anything unless the results are good, concrete, vivid, personal, and here and now.

Nowadays, there is dissatisfaction almost everywhere. Dissatisfaction creates ill feeling. Ill feeling creates hatred. Hatred creates enmity. Enmity creates enemies. Enemies create war. War creates enemies, and so on. It is a vicious circle. Why? Because there is lack of proper control over the mind. Man is, after all, mental forces personified. What is matter? Matter is nothing but mental forces materialized, a result of the reaction of the moral (positive) and immoral (negative) forces. Buddha said, "The world is mind made." Mind, therefore, predominates everything. Let us then study the mind and its peculiar characteristics and solve the problem that is now facing the world.

255

When Buddha was alive, he said to the Kalamas:

> *Listen, Kalamas. Be not misled by report or tradition or hearsay. Be not misled by proficiency in debate, nor by reason of logic, nor reflection on and approval of some theory; nor because it conforms with one's inclination nor out of respect for the prestige of a teacher.*
>
> *But, Kalamas, when you know for yourselves these things are unwholesome, these things are blameworthy, these things are censured by the intelligent, these things are practiced and observed, conduce to loss and sorrow— then indeed do you reject them.*
>
> *But, if at any time you know of yourselves, these things are wholesome, these things are blameless, they are praised by the intelligent, these things are practiced and observed, are conducive to welfare and happiness, then Kalamas do ye, having practiced them, abide therein.*

The time for the revival of the practice of Vipassana has occurred. We have no doubt whatsoever about definite results accruing to those who, with an open mind, sincerely undergo a course of training under a competent teacher. These results will be seen as good, concrete, vivid, personal, here and now—results which will keep us in good stead and in a state of well-being and happiness for the rest of our lives.

May all beings be happy and may peace prevail in the world.

ACHAAN DHAMMADARO

CHAPTER
FOURTEEN

Achaan Dhammadaro was a family man (two wives they say) who ordained later in his life. A man of enormous energy and self-confidence who had studied several meditation techniques and felt them inadequate, he found a temple where they offered him a room to continue his study of meditation on his own. For many months he remained alone in this room until he had discovered for himself a route to the heart of the Buddha's teaching. On coming out of this room he traveled in south Thailand and eventually began teaching insight meditation at Wat Tow Kote in Nakorn Sri Thammaraj.

Wat Tow Kote is a large town monastery on the outskirts of Nakorn Sri Thammaraj. This area must once have been a beach, as the ground is sand and trees are quite sparse. More than half of the temple is given to two large compounds for male and female meditators. The monks' section has more than fifty tiny cottages surrounding a large open square, where several hours of walking and standing meditation are done en masse daily. In addition, the compound contains one of the town's burning grounds, where meditators can periodically observe cremations, undertaking the 'cemetary meditations' to add perspective to their practice. Meals are taken together early and late morning in a large hall. Intensive practice is encouraged and Achaan Dhammadaro is very accessible for questions and problems. Often he will stand or walk outside with his meditators and there are tape-recorded talks on meditation played over the temple loudspeakers daily. More than a dozen Westerners have studied at Wat Tow Kote, and Achaan Dhammadaro is especially pleased to teach them. He cannot speak English, but there are usually several people around who can translate for students. At the time of publishing this book we have received word that Achaan Dhammadaro has moved to a temple several provinces north of Makorn Sri Thammaraj, and is receiving Thai and Western students there.

In his meditation Achaan Dhammadaro emphasizes mindfulness of *sensation* (a word he uses interchangeably with *feeling*). Through constant mindfulness of changing sensation we can see all our experience as moment-to-moment arisings and vanishings. This is clear, he explains, because form, and therefore sensation, is the basis for all five aggregates. The perception of the five aggregates as they arise and vanish is what the Buddha meant when he directed us to be mindful of body in body, feeling in feeling, mind in mind, and Dharma in Dharma. Achaan Dhammadaro uses moment-to-moment awareness of sensation as perceived in the body, feelings, and even in subtle movements of mind as a direct means of experiencing inner truth. In explaining the development of the meditation, he describes how mindfulness of sensation will lead us to experience all the senses directly at the heart base (the heart is traditionally known as the seat of mind). When all experience, even mind, becomes perceived as clear sensations arising and passing away at the heart base, we see the truth of impermanence, suffering, and non-self. This leads us to the deepest truth of all, the end of suffering, the experience of nirvana.

Questions And Answers on the Nature of Insight Practice

14

Question: Would you begin by explaining basic Buddhism?
Answer: The Buddha taught the path to ultimate happiness and peace. This path leading from the understanding of suffering to the cessation of suffering was most simply and directly taught as mindfulness meditation. Mindfulness is the basis of all proper practice.

Q: Can we understand this path through our reading and thinking about the four noble truths and the noble eightfold path?
A: Books as distinct from practice only point to the possibility of ending suffering by the noble path of the Buddha. Intellectual understanding comes from books and teachings. Practice is different. It is like actually performing experiments in the laboratory of your own body and mind. When one meditates under a teacher and develops perfect mindfulness and perfect concentration, one realizes fully the path in oneself. This can be achieved by continual vigilance. In other words, being mindful every moment with respect to the processes of body, feelings, mind, and mind objects. These are the foundations of mindfulness.

Q: What is the result of the path of development of mindfulness, of insight meditation?
A: Mindfulness is practiced in order to realize the Dharma within us. When it is properly practiced it leads to giving up attachment to sense objects, and is able to put a stop to the stream of suffering, the endless rounds of rebirth. Ignorance and the distraction of mind are the basis for this suffering. All of our senses—eye, ear, nose, tongue, touch, and mind—arise in conjunction with the six sense objects. When consciousness arises and mindfulness is absent, the knowing of objects through the senses leads to liking and disliking. This leads to craving for continued pleasure and further

to clinging, action, and rebirth. Our whole being, body and mind, which is made up of the five aggregates, arises and manifests itself at each rebirth of consciousness at the six sense doors. When liking and disliking occur, leading to karma-producing action, we continue on the rounds of rebirth and suffering. Insight meditation is the cure for this ceaseless craving.

260

Q: The Buddha talked about the need to develop mindfulness and concentration. Could you say more about concentration?
A: There are three kinds of concentration developed in meditation. Two of them are developed on the path to absorption (jhana) and these are access and full absorption concentration. Each of these is developed by fixing the mind one-pointedly on a single meditation object. Such meditations include visualizations of fixed forms or colors, or concentrating the mind on one particular feeling like loving-kindness. When access and absorption concentration are developed, bliss and tranquility arise, the meditator is fully absorbed in the object, and no hindrances can disturb him. This provisional eradication of defilements—a state free from desire, aversion, and confusion—lasts only so long as the meditator keeps the mind on the meditation object. As soon as the mind leaves its absorption in the object, bliss disappears and the mind is again beset by the flow of defilements. There is additionally a danger of this fixed concentration. Since it does not generate wisdom it can lead to clinging to bliss or even misuse of the powers of concentration, thereby actually increasing defilements.

The third kind of concentration is what is referred to in the eightfold path as right concentration, or perfect concentration. This is concentration developed on a moment-to-moment basis in insight meditation. Only moment-to-moment concentration following the path of mindfulness leads to the destruction of defilements. This concentration is not developed by fixing the mind motionless to one object, but by being mindful of the changing bodily sensations, feelings, consciousness, and mind objects. When properly established in the inner body and mind, moment-to-moment concentration leads to the destruction of the rounds of rebirth. Through this concentration, we develop the ability to see clearly the five aggregates—form, feeling, perception, volition, and consciousness—which make up what we conventionally call *men* and *women*.

Q: Would you elaborate more on developing moment-to-moment concentration?
A: There are two important points to make. First is that it is through the feelings arising from contact at each of the sense doors that we must develop insight. The aggregate of form is the basis for the development of moment-to-moment concentration and the resulting wisdom. Therefore we must be mindful of the *sensation* or feelings arising from contact at the eye, ear, nose, tongue, body, and mental sense bases.

261

The second important point is that continuity is the secret of success in meditation. The meditator must strive to be mindful night and day, every moment, and thus quickly develop proper concentration and wisdom. The Buddha himself stated that if a meditator is truly mindful moment by moment for seven days and nights he will reach full enlightenment. Therefore, the essence of insight meditation is continuous moment-to-moment mindfulness of the sensation arising from contact at all six bases.

Q: How is the mindfulness you speak of different from our ordinary state of mind?
A: Everyone has some degree of mindfulness. The ordinary business of life, driving a car, baking bread, and so on requires that we are mindful or attentive to the present moment to some extent. But this usually alternates each minute with long lapses of forgetfulness. A person who has no mindfulness at all is mad, completely scattered, and out of contact. But all of this ordinary mindfulness we can refer to as mundane or worldly. Even the mindfulness involved in virtuous acts is worldly. To reach nirvana, mindfulness must become supramundane. Through this precise mindfulness, attending to body, mind, and mind objects we can understand the whole universe inside ourselves. To realize this all we have to do is establish continuous mindfulness in the body in all postures, moving or not.

Q: How does this practice relate to the eightfold path of the Buddha?
A: Whenever there is right mindfulness it is automatically accompanied by right concentration and right understanding, the other two essential elements of the eightfold path. What this means practically is that the eightfold path is developed when we establish right mindfulness on body, feeling, mind, and phenomena to the point of experiencing clearly the contact feeling at these four stations. This means especially paying attention to the momentary

arising and ceasing of our experience. Mindfulness of any of these four aspects of body and mind is equally good as they all have the aggregate of form as their basis.

Rather than answering any more questions, let me explain in greater detail about practice. Mindfulness can only be present on one of the four foundations at a time. With this mindfulness established, and the accompanying concentration and understanding, the meditator will be able to see the four elements that make up form on a moment-to-moment basis. He will also begin to distinguish between the inner and outer body.

These are two important points. Remember that I said that all of the four foundations of mindfulness have the aggregate of form as their basis. Because this is so, we emphasize meditation that begins with mindfulness of the body as its focus. We must develop mindfulness of the six senses by experiencing them as subtle sensations manifest in the body.

The other important point is that the Buddha instructed us in his great *Discourse on Mindfulness* to become aware of the body in body, feelings in feelings, mind in mind, and Dharma in Dharma. It is absolutely essential to our practice that we understand what the Buddha meant by this.

How can we be mindful of body in body? What is inner body, what is outer body? The outer body is composed of the four elements of hardness, fluidity, warmth, and vibration (earth, air, fire, and water) in the ratio of 20:12:5:4. This body is produced and sustained by karma that we make from ignorance. The outer body is born, grows, and decays. Hair turns white, teeth fall out, all against our will. Eventually, it is burnt after death, this body which we dress and scent so carefully.

But the Buddha found the way to overcome death. His technique was to understand the inner body with the help of the outer. In the inner body, he saw only the five aggregates constantly in flux. In our normal state of desire and clinging, however, the inner body cannot be seen. Desire and clinging create an illusion of continuity and therefore the arising and ceasing of the aggregates cannot be realized. Hence, the practice of mindfulness is necessary. If one does not practice mindfulness, one cannot see the inner body, one cannot see the five aggregates, one cannot destroy defilements, and one cannot understand the four noble truths. The practitioner should aim at seeing the aggregates of the body arising and ceasing as continuously as possible. This is very difficult for the ordinary man. Therefore he does not see the truth in himself. Only when the meditator has sufficient concentration and mindfulness will the inner body's true characteristics be revealed. Then the meditator will experience for himself the truth of the Buddha.

To see the inner body, the meditator must observe with the mind the outer or conventional body. One must establish mindfulness wherever there is sensation, for example, stretching and bending. Through continuous precise awareness of this sensation, one will then realize the true characteristic of impermanence in all bodily postures and movements. One will see how the body arises and ceases moment to moment. As soon as one realizes this he sees the true inner body, he sees the five aggregates. Realizing this inner body is right effort. *The four foundations of mindfulness, therefore, are to be traced in our sensations inside the body*, not outside. They are to be experienced by seeing body in body, feeling in feeling, mind in mind, and Dharma in Dharma.

Mindfulness of the body is the first aspect of insight meditation. Next is mindfulness of feeling. There are five kinds of feeling: (1) pleasant bodily feeling, (2) unpleasant bodily feeling, (3) pleasant mental feeling, (4) unpleasant mental feeling, and (5) feeling of indifference. To have an experience of this type of feeling, at an ordinary level is outer feeling. By *ordinary level* is meant the ordinary attachment to pleasure and aversion to pain. This attachment may be there and one may not be aware of it, or if one is aware one may not admit it openly. In such a case, attachment exists in a more dormant state. Yet always the experience seems to be experienced by 'I'. This means that there is attachment. This comes from the identification with the feelings, believing them to be 'I', 'mine', 'myself'. Even in the feeling of indifference there is delusion and identification. Thus, any feeling which has clinging, condemning, or identification, which has greed, hatred, or delusion with it is the outer feeling. Outer feeling generates clinging and leads us around the wheel of birth and death.

Insight meditation leads to knowing the inner feeling. By destroying identification and the passions, the practitioner can experience the inner feeling. Feeling 'I have suffered' shows the existence of identification with outer feeling. In order to bring about understanding, the meditator must see through the outer feeling to the inner feeling or the five aggregates. Whenever there is contact, feeling arises. Whenever there is feeling, craving arises. Whenever there is craving, attachment arises at all the six sense doors. If the practitioner sees feeling inside feeling he can end attachment. The meditator must *see inner feeling by establishing* awareness in all four foundations of *mindfulness of sensations* as experienced in body, feelings, mind, and mind objects. Thus he will realize how feeling arises based on the aggregate of form.

Though the Buddha taught meditation at all sense doors, it is easiest to observe feelings through bodily sensations. This can be done in any posture. For example, while the meditator is in sitting posture, he should concentrate on that portion of the body which touches the ground and should experience the sensation of contact. As his meditation progresses focusing on contact, he will see how the five kinds of feelings arise where contact arises based on the aggregate of form.

When one sees form as the basis of feeling and also when one sees form and the body as impermanent, feeling too will be seen as impermanent. Extending this insight, the meditator will realize that all the aggregates including those of perception, the factors of mind and consciousness itself, are also impermanent. They are impermanent, unsatisfactory, and without an abiding self. The three characteristics are not experienced prior to meditation because of the presence of attachment. As soon as the attachment is destroyed one can realize the experience in one's own body of the four noble truths.

Now we must understand how to be mindful of mind in meditation, both outer mind and inner mind. Outer mind means superficial mind, that which deals with external objects. This is the mind that thinks about one's house, wife, children, past, future, and so on. In other words, it is the mind which thinks about everything and does not experience the five aggregates directly. Outer mind is accompanied by craving, grasping, discriminating, and so forth.

To know inner mind, we must search, using the aggregate of form as its basis, as we did in the case of feeling. This is done best by *contemplating* on the feeling arising from mind contact, the *subtle bodily sensation arising from mind.* When there is contact through any of the six sense doors with whatever object, then one experiences the feeling sensation arising from mind contact. Thus we see by this procedure mind in mind. This is known as the inner mind. By contemplating on the feeling arising from mind contact, one will understand directly the five aggregates, namely the aggregates of form, feeling, perception, factors of mind, and consciousness, and will see how they are always arising and vanishing.

When the meditator's practice has reached the subtlety of perceiving the inner mind, there may arise different kinds of images such as those of the moon, sun, stars, or imaginary bodies. At this, the mind sometimes becomes passive and realizes bliss or experiences delightful sensations or even the impression of freedom from defilements and belief that one is enlightened. One may become attached to this state of meditation. The meditator must use his wisdom to penetrate all those experiences and see the three characteristics. That is to be done by always returning to sensation, by comtemplating on the feeling sensation that arises from contact of mind. It is only by this process that one develops the highest purification of virtue and wisdom. Let not the mindfulness depart from the sensation arising from contact of mind.

The meditator, while noticing the nature of sensation arising from mind contact, should see further how it arises and how mind consciousness perceives things. The meditator will see that the consciousness that arises in conjunction with mind knows things more clearly than consciousness of the eye, ear, nose, tongue, and body. The meditator should further see how the different senses are functioning, For example, he should observe how we perceive different forms through eye, form, and eye consciousness coming together. Experiencing this process as all that is involved in sight, he can understand how our world is void of self or soul. This is the natural result of the development of proper meditation.

Sometimes when mindfulness and concentration are strong and the meditator departs from the four foundations of mindfulness, the mind is elevated and experiences void as if there is no self, both inside and outside. When this takes place, one may feel as if he is free from defilements. But clinging is still present in a dormant state in this voidness. Whenever this happens, the meditator should note that he has gone astray from the true path to nirvana and is going toward absorption. Note that the voidness of nirvana is quite different from absorption. Such a voidness is the outcome of meditation directed toward nirvana as object. To experience this means cultivating continuous mindfulness. When the inner mind is seen, one will see it as a group or cluster of many things. When the insight develops further, one can perceive change each thought moment. Then one's sense of solidity or self is broken and the sense of emptiness of self is established. This destroys the myth of soul. The other characteristics of existence become equally clear. When postures are constantly watched mindfully, the body is seen as the basis of pain. The myth of happiness is broken and the true suffering inherent in the body is experienced. The realization of impermanence seen arising and ceasing in mind and body from moment to moment automatically breaks the myth of continuity. The meditator can see the three characteristics of impermanence, suffering, and non-self in every phenomena he experiences.

Mindfulness of inner and outer Dharma is the last aspect of the meditation. Whether a man is good or bad, whether he is happy or unhappy, whether he is going to realize nirvana or not, all depends on mind. One must exert right effort in the foundation of Dharma and see the true inner Dharma. The inner and the outer Dharma are interrelated. The practitioner must separate them distinctly. That means the meditator should not be attached to outer Dharma which is the words and form of the teachings. It is correct to compare outer Dharma to a map indicating inner Dharma. The outer Dharma, says the Buddha, are eighty-four thousand aspects of teachings described according to the mental conditions of individuals. The nature of the outer Dharma was made clear by the Buddha when he picked up a handful of leaves and asked his disciples whether his handful of leaves was more or less than those in the forest around him. The monks replied, "Less, sir." The Buddha then said, "Dharma which I have taught is comparable to the leaves in the forest. But a man of wisdom knows how to apply Dharma practically so that a handful of Dharma like a handful of leaves is sufficient." This handful refers to the four foundations of mindfulness. All water in the ocean has a taste of salt. So too, whatever extensive discourses the Buddha delivered, all were aimed at liberation and deliverance from defilements. The various discourses serve to show us the path from different angles of vision. Therefore, these discourses or outer Dharma are important and useful, but only for one who has wisdom and intelligence. If one has no intelligence, one may cling to the words, to the concepts of the outer Dharma. It is like a two-edged sword. Even the terms *five aggregates* or *the four noble truths* are outer Dharma. Meditators must destroy the clinging to outer Dharma. Because of the attachment one gets caught up in outer Dharma, quoting the Buddha or simply thinking about his teaching. Meditators must break through the outer Dharma and penetrate into the inner. We can say that the outer Dharma is the symptom and the inner Dharma is the cause. All the Dharmas have a cause of arising. The practitioners must penetrate the inner Dharma by continuously having *mindfulness of the sensation arising from the contact of mind* as their chief object. By practicing in this manner, the meditator will see all of the true Dharmas, the aggregates within him. It is in regard to this technique of practice that Buddha said, "He who sees me, sees the Dharma" and vice versa. So he who sees the body in body, mind in mind, feeling in feeling and mind objects in mind objects, or Dharma in Dharma understands the profound significance of these words.

Now it should be noted that all Dharmas are found in all foundations of mindfulness. That means that when one sees body in body there is also included feeling, mind, and mind objects. The same for seeing feeling in feeling, mind in mind, or Dharma in Dharma. All the four can be found in each because they cannot arise separately. When the five aggregates are seen arising and ceasing in each of the four foundations of mindfulness, the statement "All aggregates are impermanent" will become clear to the meditator. He will see all compounded things are impermanent whether they are internal or external, animate or inanimate, visible or invisible.

All Dharmas are devoid of any self or soul. Outer Dharmas, concepts, and words, even inner Dharmas, the five aggregates which are a part of our true nature, are without any permanent self. When the Dharmas are seen, understood, and penetrated through like this, the meditator will destroy the need for grasping. He will then experience the noble path which further destroys the defilements and the illusion of self.

To develop this practice, the only thing needed is faith and earnestness. Even children, drunkards, madmen, those who are old, or those who are illiterate, can develop mindfulness. If there is faith in the possibility of Buddha's enlightenment and in the four noble truths, one can progress along the path.

Traditionally, one can uphold the Dharma or the teachings in three ways. First, he can provide material things to those who are practicing. Second, he can uphold the Dharma through the study of the scriptures and transmissions of the original teaching. Third, he can uphold the teachings by practice and realization. This is the fulfillment of the perfections. In fact, everyone should uphold the teachings by practice leading to realization because realization and liberation is the essence of Buddhism. This is what the Buddha really taught. Every person is capable of that realization because truth is inherent in every being. The one who practices sincerely is the one who upholds Buddhism. This is the highest merit.

We must have proper determination. We must have the determination to contemplate body in body, feeling in feeling, mind in mind, and Dharma in Dharma in the present moment always. We must practice all four foundations of mindfulness. Desire arises at

267

all six sense doors. *Thus mindful contemplation using sensation to abandon desires at all sense doors is the key to practice.* It will lead to the end of attachment and to liberation.

Let us take practice and liberation seriously. We should not indulge in collecting flowers from outside the path, because there is a long path yet to go. The path is taught for us to become free from the suffering that results from birth, old age, and death. This path is the one that leads to nirvana, to cessation and liberation, to the end of the illusion of self, to peace.

268

DETAILED METHOD OF PRACTICE

The practice of Vipassana according to the fourfold path of mindfulness begins by attending to the body within our body. This is best done by becoming mindful of the sensation in the center of the hand (between the wrist and fingers) and raising the hand and forearm in small, three-to six-inch increments from horizontal to vertical and back down again. Fix the (mental factor of) mindfulness to the subtle sensation that arises and ceases in the hand each time the hand moves. At first it will feel just like raising the hand in the ordinary way. Later when the factor of mindfulness is stronger in attending to the hand movement, there will arise a much clearer sensation than at first, often like a mild electric current. When the hand stops moving, this sensation will disappear. With increased practice and attention, insight will arise so that the meditator will see increasingly clearly how the sensation in the hand arises and ceases each time the hand moves. Further, mindfulness and concentration on this sensation will lead to seeing the sensation arise and cease throughout the body. This will lead to the experiencing of the heart base, which means the meditator will feel sensations arising and passing away in the area of his heart at the same time the sensations arise and vanish in the hand. After some further practice, the power of concentration and mindfulness will be strong enough to notice the arising and passing away of subtle sensation at the heart (base) simultaneously with any other sensation noted in the body. Moment-to-moment awareness of sensation in hand movement or other body movement will come directly to attention at the heart base.

This is to be further developed in all the postures. Practicing continuously throughout the day, the meditator may alternate postures. While in standing posture, he should be mindful of the sensation arising from the contact of the feet on the ground. If practicing walking meditation, he should make an effort to note the moment-to-moment change of sensation at the sole of the moving foot. While meditating in a lying posture, mindfulness should be turned to the sensation of the places where the body touches the mat.

In all of these postures, mindfulness will develop from a coarse, continuous sensation to the clearer perception of the arising and passing away of all sensation each moment. With stronger mindfulness, too, the meditator will note more clearly the simultaneous arising and passing of sensation at the heart. It is then unnecessary for the meditator to move his hand to experience the sensation at the heart base.

269

Practice should be developed as continuously as possible in all postures. Now the sensations at the heart base will be stronger. Sharp symptoms or pain may be experienced. All of the sense doors will become part of the meditation. At first, sounds will be heard as normal. Then they will become perceived as sensations on the ear drum. Finally, with strong concentration and mindfulness, sounds will be noted like bodily sensations—as sensations arising and ceasing at the heart base.

More subtler still, the other senses will be drawn into the meditation. Eventually, taste, smell, and sight will be perceived as changing sensation, first at the organ of perception, and then at the heart base. The use of mindfulness of sensation as it comes and goes is a direct tool to cut attachment to any particular form or pleasure as the senses arise.

Most subtle of all, the mind, which is the sixth sense, will also become clearer as it arises and vanishes. Then the meditator will experience the sensation that arises from mind contact. As a thought arises, there will be perceived a sensation at the heart base. This is the feeling arising from mind contact. Meditators will now have enough power of mind to catch movement of mind from the beginning of thoughts to the end. They will also be able to feel the path of sensation as the mind moves from heart up the back of the neck and over the head.

At this point the meditator may experience the arising of various visions and bright lights, white or colored. These are fascinating and can blind us to the truth of our experience. Therefore the meditator should not pay special attention to such phenomena. Instead, stay focused directly on sensation itself as it is experienced at the heart center. In each moment of clear attention you will see the process of arising and passing away of experience. Thought may arise but will pass quickly. Memories, plans, will pass too. All of this will pass quickly as the force of mindfulness in the present moment penetrates clearly the sensation of being. When practice deepens we are able to see even more clearly the distinction between the inner experience and outer forms until we penetrate to the truth of our deep inner experience.

270

What is essential in practice is that the meditator maintain continuous mindfulness of sensation in all postures. This way he will experience directly the body in the body, feeling in feeling, mind in mind, and mind objects in mind objects. Sensation, contact, and the development of moment to moment awareness through the heart base is the key.

Ultimately, the meditator will perceive how all five aggregates are arising and ceasing moment to moment. This direct experience of the flux of the aggregates is the truth of the Buddha. When the mind is sufficiently purified, concentrated, and balanced, the meditator will perceive the whole world, all six senses, as sensation at the heart base. The entire world, now just sensation or vibration that arises and completely vanishes with each moment, will no longer have a hold on him. He will see clearly the truth of the three characteristics. We are made up solely of the five aggregates. These are all arising and vanishing rapidly moment to moment. The whole world, now perceived as varying vibrations, is impermanent. It is painful, this momentary birth and death. Sensation at any of the six sense bases is pain. Birth and death. Arising and ceasing. Finally, the meditator will experience the peace beyond birth and death, nirvana. This is the true path of the Buddha.

It is very important that we use our opportunity in this life to practice. There is only one way to put an end to suffering. May this teaching be of benefit to all. May all beings be happy.

ACHAAN JUMNIEN

Born in a rural village, apprenticed at an early age to the village folk doctor who was a blind lay priest and astrologer, Achaan Jumnien began meditation practice at the age of six. His first instruction was in concentration practices and loving-kindness meditation. He also trained as a folk healer and was admonished to constantly work on his meditation and remain celibate. By adolescence, many local people were turning to him for help, and at age twenty he ordained as a monk in the Theravada Buddhist tradition. He proceeded to practice various concentration meditations with well-known teachers in Thailand, traveled as a wandering ascetic, and then was trained in intensive insight meditation by Achaan Dhammadaro at Wat Tow Kote.

When Achaan Jumnien was asked to teach eight years ago, he was in his early thirties and just becoming known among local people for his wisdom in expounding the Dharma and for the power of his loving-kindness. He was specifically requested by the people of the Wat Sukontawas to come and teach, as they were having great problems. This area of lush forest and rubber tree groves in southern Thailand was a focus of prolonged and occasionally violent conflict between government forces and the communist-style insurgents in the mountains. When he arrived and began to teach he was told to leave the area or be shot. He continued to teach. Through the power of his Dharma he eventually was able to teach the government soldiers in town and was later invited to teach the insurgents in the mountains as well. Each side thereupon offered to 'protect' his monastery. Keeping in harmony with the true Dharma was all the protection he needed, he replied.

Achaan Jumnien is an extremely open teacher who makes use of many methods of practice. He has studied different techniques and rather than focus on only one approach he will prescribe different meditations for his students depending on their needs and their personality or predominant attachments. Yet no matter what technique is developed, he eventually directs the student back to the insight practice of seeing the true nature of the mind-body process as changing, unsatisfactory, and empty of self. It is a part of his teaching that there is no *one* correct path. He teaches growth in the Dharma as an experiment and investigation into our own desires and suffering, watching our meditation progress as just another aspect of the development of insight. Though he will guide students very closely, especially when they are developing high states of concentration or are breaking through pain in intensive practice (two of his special ways of working). He reminds you often that your path in the Dharma is one of constant observation and investigation. As he says, "It is important to know that people must take responsibility for their own growth in the Dharma." Practice is for him and all of us a lifelong process and though we may use particular meditation techniques for a time, it is the permanent end of all desires, this final peace, that is the true conclusion to our spiritual practice.

Wat Sukontawas extends up a hillside with meditators' cottages fit between rows of rubber trees. During the rainy season there are between one and two hundred monks and nuns studying together under Achaan Jumnien's guidance. Half a dozen Westerners have studied here, and although Achaan Jumnien does not speak English, a translator can usually be found. Achaan Jumnien is young and laughing and easily approachable.

Now, at the time of publishing this book I have heard that Achaan Jumnien has moved his monastery to a series of caves in the mountains of Krabi, a southern Thai province.

275

Recollections of an Interview

15

with Achaan Jumnien at Wat Sukontawas
Surrathani, Thailand

Questions: What type of meditation do you teach here?
Answer: Here you will find people practicing many meditation techniques. The Buddha outlined more than forty kinds to his disciples. Not everyone has the same background, not everyone has the same abilities. I do not teach just one type of meditation but many, selecting the appropriate one for each disciple. Some here practice meditation on the breath. Others do meditation based on watching sensations in the body. Some work on loving-kindness. For some who come I give instruction in beginning insight practices, while for others I teach concentration methods that will eventually lead them into higher insight practices and wisdom.

Q: You say there are many good ways to practice. What about all the teachers who claim that their way or their method is the real way of the Buddha and that other practices do not lead to enlightenment?
A: The whole of Buddhist practice can be summed up in one sentence: Cling to nothing. Often even very wise people will still cling to the one method that worked for them. They have not yet been able to completely let go of their method, their teacher. They are

not in tune with the commonality in all our practice. This does not mean that they may not be good teachers. You must be careful not to judge them or cling to your own idea of how a teacher should be. Wisdom is not something we can hold on to. Simply the absence of clinging allows wisdom to flow.

I was fortunate. I mastered the practices of many teachers before starting to teach. There are many good practices. What is important is that you devote yourself to your own practice with faith and energy. Then you will know the results for yourself.

Q: Do you usually start your students directly with insight meditation or with a concentration practice?
A: Most often they start with an insight practice. Sometimes, though, I will teach a concentration (jhana) practice first, especially if they have had past meditation experience or if their mind tends toward concentration easily. Eventually it is most important that everyone return to insight practice.

There is a discourse in the Pali scriptures in which the Buddha, while receiving some lay visitors, speaks to this point. He indicates the various natures of the monks sitting in groups in the grove before him:

> See how those monks with tendency toward great wisdom are gathered there with Sariputtra, my wisest disciple. And there, how those who tend most toward powers are clustered with my great disciple MahaMoggallana. And those with a tendency toward monastic discipline are with Upali, the master of the Vinaya, while those in whom jhanic tendencies predominate . . .

So we see that from the time of the Buddha, teachers have allowed predisposition to help in selecting the proper practice for meditators.

Q: What are some other factors involved in selecting a proper meditation?
A: In guiding a student I look at his past practices and propensities. I also consider how much time and energy a student has to devote to meditation. Is he a lay person who will practice one hour a day, or a monk wishing intensive round-the-clock practice? Temperament. Does this person's temperament lend itself to a practice? Loving-kindness for some angry people is a good way to

start. Meditation on equanimity is good for those who are overly concerned about people around them, instead of their own practice. There are many factors that can be considered in choosing a meditation. Meditation is in fact a way of life. We are talking here of meditation as techniques to use to further a way of being, but we must remember that everything in life can be meditation. In terms of techniques, if you choose any of the basic Buddhist practices leading to insight, and practice sincerely, you cannot go wrong.   277

Q: Can you give any more pointers as to how to direct our practice?
A: Practice should be directed opposite your predominant hindrances or attachments. If you are honest with yourself you can identify these easily. For example, if your temperament is one that leads you to indifference you should make an extra effort to cultivate compassion. If lust is a problem, use the contemplation on the repulsiveness of the body until you can see its true nature more clearly, unhindered by your desires. If you are deluded and confused, cultivate investigation and sensibility in relation to your experience, study and watch clearly to overcome this tendency. But you must practice with devotion and sincerity, you must have devotion to your own path directed with an unceasing desire to know the truth. Otherwise your practice will stagnate and become like a ritual. Only the end of greed, hatred, and delusion in the heart will do. Bit by bit, moment to moment, you must continue your way with constancy. Practice fearlessly right into the direction of your attachments and do it until liberation. That is all.

Q: Is it better then to practice meditation alone or in a group situation?
A: It varies. In the case of new meditators, if they are serious and ardent, it is good to place them alone and to supervise carefully their initial practice. For those who are not so serious or self-disciplined, or who are especially unbalanced and need to be close to a teacher, they should practice in a structured, supportive group. This way they can be helped and inspired and can use the energy of the group to strengthen their practice. As for more experienced students, if they are strict and sincere, solitude and silence is best. These students can help themselves and their path will deepen without being pushed by a teacher or group. With those less disciplined, even if experienced, it is better for them to stay in a group setting. The discipline and hard practice will help them break through their inner resistance until they see for them-

selves the true Dharma. Then their practice will flower alone or in a group, unhindered.

Q: Do you often recommend really intensive meditation practice done in isolation?

A: Certainly. For those who are prepared, strict intensive meditation is extremely useful. If it is combined with isolation, the meditator can quickly develop strong concentration and clear insight. Even now, I myself go off for one month a year with only my robes and bowl to live alone in the forest and practice intensively. Most students here are encouraged to do the same. As they gain experience they can then find their own balance between going off for periodic intensive retreats and otherwise living a meditative daily life.

As for practice in intensive retreat, on longer retreats my students usually practice simple Vipassana, observing the changes in body and mind. For shorter periods they will often work on a particular concentration exercise or try breaking through a posture. Eventually though, practice must return to insight and letting go. This is the aim of all Buddhist teaching.

Q: Would you describe the process of breaking through a posture?

A: Our fear of pain and our attachment to the body interfere with clarity and wisdom. For those disciples who have the energy and inclination, I recommend an insight practice, concentrating on the movement of sensation in the body. This is done while holding to only one posture—sitting, standing, lying, or walking for a long period of time. As the meditator holds any posture, attentive to the body, pain increases. As he continues to hold still, the pain continues to increase and he must concentrate directly on these feelings. Bodily pain is a precise object on which to concentrate. Eventually the mind perceives the pain not as pain but as a clear sensation neither desirable nor undesirable arising and ceasing in the body. Often meditators will sit or stand for a whole twenty-four hours in one position. As soon as we stop moving, the suffering inherent in our bodies shows itself. Sometimes four or five, sometimes eight hours or more will pass before a meditator breaks through his attachment to bodily pain. Then there is no need to move. The mind becomes extremely clear, concentrated, and malleable. A great deal of joy and rapture accompany this breakthrough. The meditator is able to see clearly with equanimity, bodily and mental phenomena arising and ceasing. With bodily desires stilled and strong concentration developed, wisdom arises.

Breaking through a posture is one of many practices we use here. It is only used with serious students under close supervision.

Q: Many teachers of Vipassana will stress starting with one particular aspect of awareness such as sensation, feeling, or consciousness. Won't mindfulness developed on any of these lead to the same place, a deep, overall mindfulness?

A: Of course. In each instant and in each experience is reflected the whole of the Dharma. This means that whatever aspect of body or mind we observe can lead to deepening of concentration and understanding of who we are. In seeing the totality of who we are, we will also see how the whole universe has the same characteristics. We will see impermanence, the flux of all experience, we will see the insecurity in holding to any state, and most importantly we will recognize the emptiness of all things. One may meditate on any part of our direct experience, sight, sound, taste, smell, sensations, feelings, or elements of mind. To focus on any one of these areas is a fine way to deepen concentration and insight together. But at some point the mind becomes so clear and balanced that whatever arises is seen and left untouched with no interference. One ceases to focus on any particular content and all is seen as simply mind and matter, an empty process arising and passing away of its own, or seen as just vibrations or energy, empty experience. It is out of a perfect balance of mind with no reactions that we find true liberation, beyond suffering, beyond self. There is no longer any doing and no longer even a sense of one knowing, simply the empty universe as it stands.

Q: Is there any use for contemplation on thinking, using thought in meditation?

A: When we first start to practice we begin to see the nature of our normal thought process. An endless stream of ideas, fantasies, regrets, plans, judgments, fears, desires, commentary, worry, and on and on. It can be helpful, especially in initial stages of meditation, to work with thinking, to direct the thinking mind into our practice. What this means is to cultivate thoughts related to the Dharma, such as reflecting on the four elements. Contemplate how all we know constantly changes form, that our world is simply a play of changing elements. We can also direct thinking to contemplate the three characteristics in all situations of our daily life. We can think about life and impending death as a way to understand our experience in terms of the Dharma. All of this is the cultivation of right understanding. From books and teachings we move to our own directed thought and consideration, and finally to meditation for a deep, silent understanding in our own mind.

Q: Does discussion of the Dharma have any value for practice?
A: If the mind is concentrated and silent then wisdom can indeed grow when we hear the Dharma from those who speak wisely. Certainly, if you must talk, speaking about the Dharma is the most suitable conversation. Yet talking often exaggerates our lack of clarity. Only when the heart is silent can we hear the Dharma in a fresh real way, within ourselves and in the words of others who have understanding. For most people the mind is already too full of words and thoughts and the best practice is to cultivate concentration and silence.

Q: In relation to the various practices here, how do you recommend disciples eat?
A: The content of the diet is not particularly important. It should be sufficient to maintain body health only. What is important is how food is eaten. Normally we have many strong desires associated with eating. Our meditation is a way to get beyond our desires. Food should be received, prepared, and eaten with careful attention to the process involved. Some kinds of eating meditations include viewing all food and substances around you in terms of the four elements (earth, air, fire, and water). You can then perceive the flow of elements in and out of your body. Or else you can be aware of contact while you eat. The sensation of the touch of the food on your hand and your mouth, the touch of the smell at your nose, the touch of your hand on the bowl. Focus clearly on contact, the sense of touch in the whole eating process, and you will go beyond your desires. If your desires are especially strong you might meditate on the repulsive aspects of food during its preparation, digestion, and elimination, or meditate on the constant change in the food from the farmer's field to the stomach. Most simple would be to be clearly aware of the whole process of getting and eating food. Watch the mind as consciousness changes, desires come and go, intention to eat, chewing, tasting . . . whatever becomes conscious, watch that process. Any of the food meditations will help us break through desires to the clarity and freedom beyond desire.

Q: What about Hatha Yoga and other body-oriented practices?
A: These may be useful to keep the body healthy, but such practices are not essential to our work. As meditation progresses, the body automatically begins to become balanced. Increased concentration and mindfulness automatically lead to better posture and freer energy flow in the body. As your meditation practice deepens, you will feel your body as lighter, more balanced, energetic. You need not worry about this or add it to your list of desires. It will come of itself.

281

I myself have never practiced Hatha Yoga nor anything like it, yet I now find less than three hours sleep sufficient. I feel always light and energetic and have walked through the mountains without food for days without stop, feeling no ill effects—all by keeping my mind disciplined using meditation. Certainly do take care of the body, but do not perceive bodily attainments as a necessary foundation in our practice.

Q: How essential is the practice of virtue and morality in our practice?
A: Absolutely inevitable. There are three important levels of virtue. First is refraining from doing unskillful actions, keeping the basic precepts. Second is the virtue of sense restraint, keeping all six senses including the mind directed toward practice and away from desires. Third is the true inner virtue beyond any rules or precepts that comes from a silent, purified mind. In this, wisdom arises in conjunction with all six senses and every moment of being in the world is mindful, beyond selfishness. We must all begin practicing the first two kinds of virtue, and as our minds become clear and silent then inner virtue will come. It will grow out of the harmony of body and mind, out of letting go of desires and from the deep understanding of the emptiness of the world.

Q: How much time do you recommend for a householder or lay person to practice?
A: For one still doubtful or weak in practice they should take it an hour at a time, whenever they like, not forcing, yet continuing enough to see the benefit for themselves. Those who have seen more clearly the fruit of practice should meditate as much as they can in their work day, perhaps an hour in a quiet setting each morning and evening. For those who know the true nature of practice, working in the world is no hindrance. Mindfulness and clarity can be cultivated all the time. They understand how all situations

are teachings and that true meditation is not apart from life but cultivating inner stillness and wisdom in all circumstances. Then one's practice of Dharma goes beyond the realm of time or situation.

Q: I have heard many conflicting stories about absorption states.[1] *Some say almost no one can attain them these days. Some say they are necessary to attain for access to nirvana. Others now claim they hinder wisdom. Which is correct?*
A: There are still people who achieve jhanic absorption these days. Though it is not necessary for access to nirvana, absorption is the best route for some people. People also attain nirvana doing Vipassana without absorption. My own disciples practice both ways.

Those who do concentration practices use breathing or visualization (kasina)[2] meditations until they achieve absorption. Then they switch to insight practice after coming out of absorption. At times I will meditate along with them, staying on the same levels, to monitor their practice. If one can attain absorption as well as insight, there are additional benefits. In the scriptures there are many references of various enlightened disciples of the Buddha entering absorption. They clearly benefited from this practice, even after they became fully enlightened. So, for us too, the strength of mind that results in absorptive attainment is useful in adding to equanimity, bodily well-being, and penetrating the Dharma.

Q: On fully penetrating the Dharma does one experience the nirvanic peace only once for each stage before full enlightenment, at the stages of stream enterer, once-returner, non-returner, and final liberation? (Note: These four are the stages of enlightenment as traditionally described in the Buddhist scriptures. They are further described as progressive cutting of the fetters listed below.)
A: One may repeat the experience of fully penetrating the Dharma (nirvana) without necessarily cutting more fetters. The ten fetters that bind us to the wheel of becoming are:
1. False view of self.
2. Doubt and uncertainty.
3. Adherence to rites and rituals.
4. Sense desires.

[1] *See Glossary and "Maha Boowa."*
[2] *See Glossary and first pages of "Sunlun Sayadaw."*

5. Anger and resentment.
6. Desire for fine material states.
7. Desire for fine immaterial states.
8. Pride and conceit.
9. Agitation and curiosity.
10. Ignorance.

The stream enterer has fully cut the first three fetters with his first penetration into the Dharma. The once-returner weakens the re- 283 maining, while the non-returner has cut all but the last five. An arahat, one completely free of defilements, free from new becoming, has cut all the fetters.

Q: The provinces around your temple have been deeply involved in the government/communist political struggle common to Southeast Asia. Do you see a role for monks or teachers like yourself in this struggle?
A: One way that the Buddha's teaching has survived for more than twenty-five hundred years is by monks not taking sides in politics. The Dharma is above politics. Our temple is a refuge from the battleground, just as the Dharma is a refuge from the battleground of desires. I share my teaching equally with all who come, and when I go out I teach to all people who ask. In the mountains I have preached the Dharma to the revolutionaries and in the towns to the government soldiers—only after each side laid down their arms. True peace, true happiness, will not come from a change in the social order. Both sides in these fights may have legitimate complaints, but the true peace is an inner one that can only come through the Dharma. For monks and lay people alike, security comes from the Dharma, from wisdom which sees the impermanence of all things in the world.

Q: Do we need to have a teacher to guide our practice or can we do it ourselves?
A: If one has read much and heard good, correct Dharma then it is perhaps possible to practice without further guidance. However, even with very thorough knowledge one can easily get stuck or deceived by the subtleties of the mind. I always recommend strongly that practice be done under the direction of a teacher who has a clear understanding of the path and its pitfalls. It is also helpful to become part of a Dharma community where spiritual friends can aid each other. Our desires and unclarity have held us and ruled our lives for so long it is most skillful to get all the support and guidance we can to uncover our true nature and become free.

Q: Is it important to have very pure intentions when coming to a temple to meditate?

A: Many causes bring people to the Dharma. Sometimes we can see them, sometimes not. It is possible to have an unwholesome desire bring you to hear the Dharma or meditate and then for you to get wholesome results! There are nuns here who have told me that a part of their original reason for coming was that they found me or one of my assistant teachers particularly handsome or attractive. Yet after being here they let go of the original reason for coming and are now fine meditators and serious students of the Dharma. For you as a practitioner what is important is now. You must try to be aware not of what brought you to the Dharma, but of your mind, your desires, your intentions in the present moment. Mindfulness and insight practice has the power to cut through past karma. The moment we are truly mindful and aware we let go of our desires and we stop making new karma. Some of our old karma will bear fruit, but mindfulness makes it possible for us to break the chain of following past karma or past patterns.

Q: You have often linked three words: Dharma, nature, and the ordinary or commonplace. Can you explain this?

A: These all have the same basis. Nature unfolds of itself in a natural, spontaneous way. The common or ordinary is that which happens without interference. And the Dharma is the truth of the way things are, while the Dharma as teachings is a reflection in words of this truth. The Dharma directs the mind back to what is natural, to our true nature. Then we see that all is just as it is— nothing special, ordinary, and common in the deepest sense. So the Dharma brings us back to nature and to the truth in the ordinary. And seeing nature and our ordinary existence more clearly, we are brought to a deeper understanding of the Dharma. This circle continues until the heart and mind are one with nature, until all aspects of nature and our existence become clear as simply the Dharma unfolding.

Q: What kinds of things do you still find a problem for yourself in your practice?

A: When I first began teaching I was overly concerned with how well my students were doing. I wanted them to understand the Dharma and to benefit from their meditation quickly. Similarly, I was concerned about the general discipline around my temple. It was important that it look good to the lay supporters, that everyone was meditating seriously. I felt that I must keep close supervision of all that went on. Now I have almost completely let go of that. The temple runs fine by itself. My disciples learn and progress at a rate that is natural and best for them. I provide teaching and a suitable environment, and the rest is up to them. I still do have some carry over of this problem. From a very young age I have practiced loving-kindness meditation. This is still a strong force in my life, and with it is some attachment to helping people. I want them to benefit from the Dharma, from their meditation quickly. I want them to see the end of suffering. Now, in my own practice, I am trying to transform this loving-kindness and attachment to a more refined compassion and equanimity. It is important to know that people must take responsibility for their own growth in the Dharma. It is a natural process. The Buddha's teachings are a kind of catalyst for the natural growth of wisdom. It is now up to you.

May all beings be happy. May all beings see the end of suffering.

FURTHER QUESTIONS

CHAPTER
SIXTEEN

In this chapter an editor interviews the author. Questions were posed in order to clarify and expand upon the teachings already presented.

Jack Kornfield has studied with many of the masters represented here and currently teaches meditation retreats in the U.S. and Canada.

Question: Let me ask you some questions specifically about the material in this book. First, what do you feel is the most important point made by publishing this collection of teachings?
Answer: This collection shows the richness and variety of the living Theravada tradition. It allows us to see many styles and techniques of practice reflected in different attitudes and personalities of teachers. Yet it also shows how all these teachings come from the same basic underlying realization, the same Dharma. I hope this book assists the reader to pick a suitable style of meditation and inspires him to practice it fully, tasting the Dharma for himself.

Q: What is the role of the teacher in Theravada Buddhism?
A: Theravada Buddhism includes a wide variety of teaching styles. In some temples the teacher becomes an object of devotion. You wash his feet, you imitate his behavior, you follow him extremely reverently—in that respect, he becomes very much the guru. In other temples, such as Buddhadasa's, the teacher considers himself to be merely a kaliyana mita, a good friend. If you want advice on meditation, he'll tell you what he knows from experience. He's very simple and direct, and speaks with you like a brother.

Student-teacher relationships vary greatly. Some teachers use a great deal of love and kind words to express the Dharma. Their mind-states and actions are a model of acceptance and allowance of that non-judgmental clarity that is the enlightenment you're trying to develop. On the other hand, some teachers instruct students in a very harsh, seemingly angry way. They use this fierceness to help you break out of your normal behavior patterns and clinging. Teachers may use 'tricks' to help you develop balance. They may put you in a situation which they know will force you to see clearly your hidden desires. Or they may insist you do a particular practice which is especially hard for you. They may inspire you with stories or magic, or hit you, cajole you, fool you, laugh at you, or even ignore you. They will do whatever is necessary to destroy the particular views or clingings you may have and to bring you back to a balanced center from the particular place where you're stuck. Teachers also use various means to help regulate various mental factors such as love or concentration or energy. For example, if there is too much energy and too little concentration in your practice, they may urge you to sit motionless for a long period, or if there is much anger they may prescribe loving-kindness meditation as a balance. They use all kinds of styles and techniques that come out of their own practice. Whether they have a temperament that allows them to be fierce, or a very loving, soft temperament, they use whatever is available to help you let go—how they do it has no hard and fast rules. In any case, skillful teachers will not allow you to get dependent on them or their instruction. They will direct you to find your own inner truth independent of any outside authority, independent of any opinions, fresh, clear, and totally liberating.

Q: Doesn't the notion that the teacher will give you a specific tool to fit your personality conflict with the idea that all paths are the same?
A: Often one of the greatest tricks that a teacher will use is to say, "My way is the best way, the most direct, the fastest way." That gives the student enough faith to put in the energy and effort to continue the practice through inevitable difficult spots, and thereby get results from it. This does not conflict with the fact that there are indeed many practices that lead to eventual freedom. Often when you first come to teachers they will teach very open Dharma to get your interest. Once you start meditation they will then guide you into a more specific practice and work with the difficulties that come up within that method. Part of the skill of the

teacher involves playing with this paradox, being able both to reveal the whole truth to you and at the same time to direct your effort and concentration in a specific way that will be fruitful to your development.

In seeking a teacher, as I mentioned earlier, the choice can come from your own intuitive sense of what feels right, of which teacher or what style appeals to you. It can come out of a desire for balance: If you're not very disciplined it is good to find someone who will encourage you with discipline. On the other hand, if you're someone who is compulsively disciplined, it would be skillful to find a teacher to help you let go, relax, and just flow. There are a multitude of factors involved.

The Buddha said that it was good for people to spend at least five years with their first teacher. It's to be remembered that no matter which path one chooses there is rarely quick and instantaneous development of enlightenment. The image used by the Buddha was of the ocean floor gradually sloping to deeper and deeper depths, a gradual development, of equanimity in the face of change, of wisdom and understanding.

So, you may shop around for a while and may even try a couple of methods for different periods of time, but then it's necessary to be disciplined and to stay with whichever system you pick for a fairly long period of time.

Q: Say more about this notion of shopping around, which is so very American, so very Western. Does it imply that if the first experience of a teaching isn't all you expected, you should get up and leave and go to someone else?

A: Not at all. Although I had difficulty in immediately accepting one or two of my teachers. I stayed with them because I clearly saw in them much to learn. Later I realized that much of my problem was attachment to my own image of a teacher. Even though I felt disturbed by their monastery or their personality or some particular aspect of the teaching, that did not at all overshadow my genuine interest and belief in the ultimate value of what they were teaching. To become open and to get beyond fantasies and prejudices it is often more helpful to look for Dharma as *teachings* rather than as *teachers*. In this way we become open to using all situations as places to practice, to learn and grow. In this way too we can use good teachings without being overly caught up in the form of the teacher who shares them. In selecting a teacher, the more open you become, the more likely you will be to find that

289

person and situation which is appropriate for you at this time. Openness and trust is important.

Q: It seems important to understand that shopping for a teacher or a method is not the same as shopping for a car. Is it true that the teacher and the method that become right for you aren't necessarily the ones that make you feel best, or most comfortable, or affirm your preconceptions?
A: That's correct. The nature of Buddhist practice is to look clearly into oneself, the totality of one's own processes of body and mind. One of the first things you see is the suffering that comes from your attachments. No matter what path you pick, eventually there will be pain and difficulty as a part of the whole unfolding of insight in your practice. The teaching will change from how it first appeared and your meditation will evolve to understandings not at all apparent in the first steps. Pick a teacher you can trust, not one that makes you feel comfortable.

Q: Can meditation progress without periodic intensive retreats from the world?
A: One can progress in the Dharma without intensive practice, simply by developing natural mindfulness such as the way taught by Achaan Chaa or Achaan Buddhadasa. At the same time, intensive practice is also extremely valuable. At best, I would recommend a balance, spending some time in intensive practice and some time in the world. Through intensive practice one develops strong concentration, deep insights into the truths of which the Buddha spoke, very strong faith and firm resolve. By integrating intensive practice with daily mindfulness, no aspect of one's life will be apart from the practice. There will be the opportunity to integrate the deep insights of the retreat into one's daily actions and relations to other beings. Conversely, in deep practice one can take the problems that arise from daily social interaction and see through to the underlying problem: attachments and liberation from them. Wisdom will grow in both intensive and daily practice. As to how often to go on retreat, one has to observe one's own needs and find one's own flow. This whole process is one of observation, investigation, and experimentation. You must be aware, watching and observing your own development. That's all. That's really the key.

Q: Where does all this lead?

A: It leads to freedom. It leads to living more in the moment, fully experiencing what's there, not holding on to it, not greeting things with preconceptions but seeing them clearly as they are. It leads to the letting go of attachments and therefore to less suffering, to less selfishness which means more love and joy, more compassion for other beings and a more gentle flow with what is. It leads to a recognition that one's own being is this mind-body process. There's no one behind it all, nothing to do, nothing to get.

291

Q: What of enlightenment and the ability to experience nirvana in this lifetime?
A: There are several meanings for nirvana. There is final nirvana, which is described as occurring when there is no more attachment whatsoever at the end of this particular life. This final non-attachment ends the force of desire that keeps carrying one through the rounds of samsara; there is no more rebirth. Then there is the nirvana, the enlightenment of an arahat, full enlightenment within this world, liberation during this lifetime. An arahat is one who has no more selfishness, no more greed, hatred, or any kind of delusion arising in the mind. To put it another way, an arahat is always mindful, from moment to moment; a moment never passes without full awareness. The arahat's life is one of total balance and total compassion. We can experience something like this nirvana of an arahat each moment we are fully mindful. In each moment that we are free of clinging and attachment, the peaceful awake state of mind is a kind of nirvana within samsara. And as the mind becomes more deeply silent we can come to understand that which is timeless and unmoving in the midst of the world of form and changes.

Nirvana also refers to a state that can be experienced by meditators. The first taste of this state is called *stream entry* and is a momentary experience of a state of complete cessation, beyond this mind-body process altogether. This is absolute stillness and peace, beyond any movement, any knowing, cessation beyond this world. In some meditation practices, and even in some places in the texts, this particular state is seen as the final goal—even wisdom itself and insight are seen as only stepping stones to this state. However, over and over again, the Buddha spoke of the practice being that of the recognition of suffering and the end of suffering. Experiencing this state beyond the mind-body, beyond samsara, is only the temporary end of suffering. It is extremely profound. It allows one to see the illusory nature of what we call 'self'; it profoundly affects attachments, it can uproot fetters and defilements. Yet you cannot cling to it once it passes. Until one has attained the full liberated state of an arahat, in which there are no more attachments or desires, one must simply continue to practice. The experience of this realm beyond movement, of total peace, will deepen your practice and is a sign that practice is going properly, but in itself it is not the end of practice and cannot be clung to. The end of practice is beyond any attachment, beyond any selfishness; total freedom and compassion for all beings.

292

Q: Can you say more about approaching practice from the absolute level of 'non-doing' versus the relative one of striving for enlightenment?
A: As one gets deeper into practice and more and more observing things as they are, without judgment and without intervening concepts, one becomes more and more comfortable with paradox. In this case, we are talking about the paradox of the description of practice as 'non-doing' from the absolute level, and also the truth of the relative level of 'doing' particular paths and methods. There's a difficulty in clinging to the absolute. People may feel that if, in fact, this is all an illusion, they don't need to do anything. But they do need to do something because they're still caught in the illusion. Somehow, somewhere, they're still taking it to be real. Even teachers like Achaan Chaa and Achaan Buddhadasa still encourage you to practice by continuous mindful noticing of what's happening. Not that you have to attain anything, be anything special, but that you have to see more and more clearly the true nature of what's already there. It's not the effort to gain, to attain, or to do anything special. It's simply the effort to be aware. So, though there is nothing to gain or become, still we must make the effort to practice in order to overcome our delusion and ignorance. All the methods in this book are simply skillful means. The Buddha described his teachings (the relative level of concepts and various practices) as a raft. This raft is to be used to cross the ocean of illusion. When you're on the other side, you no longer need these relative truths; you can discard the raft, or use it to help others across. The Buddha also spoke of the absolute level in the scriptures. He said the teachings and methods are not at all the Dharma. The Dharma is the truth and is beyond all words, beyond all teachings and beyond all methods.

Q: What degree of effort is necessary in practice?

A: It may require enormous effort. The Buddha often directed yogis to put out a great deal of effort in certain ways, to concentrate, to direct attention, or even to direct the thought process into practice, as in the Abhidharma meditation of Mohnyin Sayadaw. Effort must be balanced by equivalent inner stillness and concentration. At times some yogis may practice mindfulness, sitting there fully in the moment, and get up from a session of 'doing nothing' soaked with sweat from the effort that went into simply being attentive moment to moment. That is not always the case, however. Other times it is possible to be very balanced, very laid back, just observing the process as it goes by. The effort is not primarily physical and should simply be one of staying fully aware, fully present, without trying to get or change anything. That is right effort.

Q: Isn't effort necessary to break the conditioned way one usually does things?
A: At times effort is necessary to break out of our patterns of preconception, out of patterns of reaction to the world. Sometimes this effort involves the body as well as the mind. One of the most strenuous practices in Theravada teaching involves doing very long sittings without moving, and allowing an enormous amount of pain to build up in the body. This approach of Sunlun Sayadaw requires simply sitting with it, bearing with it, and penetrating it. The practice eventually breaks your normal identification and reaction against pain and allows you to see that it is not you. The effort alone though is not the cause of liberation. Freedom comes from the clear-seeing insight into the nature of experience.

Sustained effort of another sort is required at times in practice. There will be periods of days, weeks, or even months when one's whole perception of the world is only that of unsatisfactoriness, terror, suffering, and misery. To stick with the practice, to look more and more closely into the true nature of what is around you, to go beyond even the suffering, to the true nature of the emptiness of all phenomena, requires the effort of perseverance and courage. Long enduring effort is the key to awakening of wisdom.

It's also good to remember that many teachers skillfully use non-effort in practice. One can simply watch and let go. It is possible, though unusual, never to experience pain in sitting, or never need to put out a great deal of effort, but simply to sit back and observe clearly the impersonal, changing nature of all phenomena of body and mind and, in this way, to let go of one's attachments in

293

the world, becoming lighter, more spontaneous, and wiser. There is no one way in which practice unfolds.

Q: Can't the emphasis on suffering in Theravada Buddhism be seen as a depressing, negative philosophy?
A: To see it that way is to misunderstand the teachings. We are all seeking happiness for ourselves and others. In order to come to true happiness it is necessary to understand directly the nature of our minds, of our conditioning, of our world. When we look in an honest way it becomes clear that most of the means we have used to find happiness and security are unsatisfactory—in fact, they lead us to suffer. Grasping, clinging, desire—trying to sustain happiness and security in the constantly changing world of sight, sounds, tastes, smells, touch, and mind objects doesn't work. It only frustrates and stirs up the mind, brings inevitable dissatisfaction.

Buddhism is not a philosphy, not just a description of the world. It is a practical means for dealing with our lives, with the problem of our suffering and happiness; it outlines a way to become joyful and content in all situations. This practical process insists we become open to the totality of our experience. We must first see how we create suffering before we can become liberated from it. However, the emphasis must not be only on seeing the suffering in the world; it must lead to experiencing the true emptiness of it all. Then we can let go and come to completion, to inner stillness, to the highest happiness which is peace. For those who understand and practice the Dharma, it means giving up suffering. Their lives become filled with joy, free from worry and desire. They experience the happiness of the Buddha. Meditation is not to learn about the Buddha, it is a way to become like the Buddha.

Q: There is much discussion in this book of pure concentration versus insight practices. Some teachers warn students about developing high states of concentration. If one is developing concentration correctly, won't they also develop the wisdom that would guard against these dangers?
A: In the proper development of concentration wisdom is essential. However, there's good reason for the warnings and cautions of the masters in this book. Meditators often get trapped by the bliss and pleasure of concentration or feeling they have attained something that they should hold on to. This subtle attachment to concentration or bliss then becomes another burden to carry around which

prevents one from being in the moment where true wisdom is found.

It's somewhat artificial to make too great a distinction between concentration and insight practice. Always in the proper development of insight, concentration must be developed. It's impossible to have real insight without some degree of calm, tranquility and one-pointedness of mind. If concentration is developed along with attention to the change of experience as its basis, then it will become very simple for insight to develop.

295

All we have to remember is that attachment to anything, whether it be particular benefits of concentration such as bliss or powers, or the attainment of insights that come from Vipassana, any attachment whatsoever is a block to the natural unfolding of wisdom.

Q: Considering the distinction between knowledge and wisdom, certain teachers such as Achaan Naeb, Mogok Sayadaw, and others who use the Abhidharma approach stress understanding a theoretical framework of Dharma first so you know how to distinguish the different processes within your experience. Is this knowledge helpful or important in developing wisdom?

A: Some people find it is useful to have a theoretical understanding of Dharma. It directs their thinking process and their intellect into deeper self-understanding. Sometimes too, a knowledge of the teachings is used as a cure, a balance for one who has a great deal of doubt or misunderstanding. In the beginning of practice, theoretical knowledge of Dharma aids to direct the mind where to look. After some practice, study can be beneficial in order to communicate, to share the experience of insight and wisdom with other beings. In teaching it helps to have some intellectual framework, some theoretical knowledge. Theoretical knowledge is not, however, necessary. In fact, one could know nothing of the scriptures, the Buddha, or the commentaries, and simply sit down, observe the mind, and come to the identical understanding. One would still experience the three characteristics of existence: the truth of change, the insecure and therefore unsatisfactory nature of this impermanence, and the impersonal nature of all phenomena, including all that which we take to be a 'self' or 'I'.

There's a danger in having too much theoretical knowledge before practice, especially that which is descriptive of particular states that one may experience in meditation. Expectations develop which block clear perception of things as they are. One must be wary of knowing too much of what is supposed to happen in practice. The ideal, perhaps, is to have some framework of understanding on broad aspects of the Dharma. Then simply sit and do your work and see the nature of truth for yourself.

Q: Perhaps the most difficult aspect of the teachings to translate to Western culture with its heavy tradition of free personal expression is that of morality. What is the function of restraint in spiritual practice?

A:Morality as taught by way of rules is extremely powerful and valuable in the development of practice. It must be remembered first that it, like all the techniques in meditation, is merely a tool to enable one to eventually get to that place of unselfishness where morality and wisdom flow naturally. In the West, there's a myth that freedom means free expression—that to follow all desires wherever they take one is true freedom. In fact, as one observes the mind, one sees that following desires, attractions, repulsions is not at all freedom, but is a kind of bondage. A mind filled with desires and grasping inevitably entails great suffering. Freedom is not to be gained through the ability to perform certain external actions. True freedom is an inward state of being. Once it is attained, no situation in the world can bind one or limit one's freedom. It is in this context that we must understand moral precepts and moral rules.

Normally, we spend our time simply reacting to stimuli in ways in which we have been conditioned. Often this conditioning is quite strong and brings about situations in which we act out our selfishness in ways that hurt or infringe upon those around us. By observing moral precepts we begin to set limits on how much we will follow our conditioned reactions and our desires. We stop identifying so strongly with them and say: "Wait, I'm going to stop a minute and simply watch the nature of this process," rather than blindly follow all the desires and impulses that come. It is this stopping, observing, and not being caught in the web of reaction that will lead us to freedom.

The traditional Buddhist precepts are five: 1) *not killing*, not taking of life of any sentient being whatsoever, since almost always there has to be some degree of hatred or aversion or selfishness in the mind to take life; 2) *not stealing*, as stealing comes from selfishness, from following one's desires, wanting to make oneself happy at the expense of other beings (also it is looking for happiness in material goods and comfort, where true happiness doesn't even lie); 3) *not lying,* again a precept that is obvious (lying usually comes out of feeling that there is something to protect or hide, out of selfishness) 4); *no sexual misconduct,* which is primarily interpreted as not performing those sexual acts which can cause pain and suffering to other beings (adultery is the traditional example given); and finally 5) *no taking of intoxicants to the point of dullness and delusion of mind* which leads to the breaking of the other precepts or the losing of awareness, which is our key to understanding and compassion.

297

When one undertakes these precepts, in the traditional Buddhist sense, the phrase used is "I undertake the training rule to abstain from killing." It is explained that this is not absolute morality, for absolute morality comes out of unselfishness in one's own being. A precept is a rule one undertakes to follow, to help develop stillness of mind that will lead to seeing the true nature of things, to help bring one into harmony with the world around oneself. Eventually, the naturalness and compassion take over by themselves.

The precepts are enormously powerful. For instance, not to tell an untruth in any circumstance, alone could be one's whole and total practice. With regard to other beings, it means not misrepresenting anything, being totally mindful and aware of just what is being said and making it as direct and clear a reflection of the truth as one can perceive. Any person you meet who is totally honest and truthful becomes the focus of admiration, of respect, of incredible power, in whatever society he finds himself. This person has the power of the truth, of really representing what is, without being pulled and swayed by various desires, by all the impulses of mind that are, in fact, the opposite of freedom. To carry this precept even further, if one practices the precept of truthfulness within oneself as well, not fooling oneself, not trying to look at things other than as they really are, seeing things mindfully, with full consciousness and awareness, this one precept becomes the whole and entire practice of Buddhism. Not only of Buddhism, but in fact of all religions. As soon as one becomes totally honest, automatically the wisdom of unselfishness arises. One becomes loving in a natural way because one is no longer trying to get or be something other than what is already true.

You can begin to see the great benefit that can be acquired by allowing oneself to undertake these as training precepts. What is true for the precept of honesty is also true for that of not stealing. If you interpret it as not taking that which is not given, it becomes an enormously powerful tool for seeing all of the occasions where one would act in a selfish way in the world. In a greater sense this precept awakens us to our responsibility to the fair distribution of resources in the world, as well as recognition of economic and social stealing. Most basically, it refers to the cultivation of the ability to remain unaffected by the everchanging flow of pleasant and painful experience. Stealing results from the illusion that there is a self to protect, or a self to please, or as though getting momentary pleasure were really where freedom and happiness lie. Instead of acting on greed, one learns to observe its process and to come to the peace of mind which is beyond trying to get and hold on to momentary pleasures. Although these moral precepts are very simple and may sound contrary to "unlimited" action as a conception of freedom, they become incredibly powerful tools in developing a liberated mind when properly used. I cannot help but add here a Zen-style reminder—don't cling to the precepts blindly nor use them to judge others. Know when to keep them and when to break them.

298

Q: Concentration develops wisdom, and now morality develops wisdom; yet at the same time doesn't wisdom develop morality?
A: The Dharma is developing in the West in a fashion quite different from the traditional progression. In the East, it is taught that one successively develops morality, concentration, and finally wisdom. Living a moral life calms the mind and then one can sit and develop strong concentration and one-pointedness of mind. One then uses this to examine the process of who one is, developing insight into the three characteristics, which leads to wisdom and eventual liberation.

In the West in some ways it has been the reverse. Many people here have experienced disatisfaction with their lives or the society around them. Some have had glimpses of other deeper understandings through psychedelics. Some wisdom has arisen first. They've often gone from that taste of wisdom to learn concentration, to explore various ways of stilling and directing the mind. Finally people are realizing, both in relation to themselves and society, that it is essential to also develop a way of being that is not harmful or injurious to those around them. So in the West we find this reverse development—first of wisdom, then of concentration, then of morality; which is of course cyclical and will develop, in turn, greater concentration and more wisdom.

Q: Can one look at one's spiritual development as a linear progression?
A: Here we come back to the question of seeing things from the level of absolute or relative reality. In teaching or in practice, it is often useful to think of the deepening of meditation and insight as the development of more frequent moments of wisdom, over a period of time. Thus, on this relative level, practice is a progression, an improvement over time. In fact, from the absolute level, time does not exist. Time is a concept, the only thing that exists to our perception is here and now. There is only the present moment. The use of time and the use of the word *path* is only a relative way of speaking. With this absolute understanding, we come fully into the moment, and the path is complete. There is no improvement, only being here now. Yet all of the greatest teachers including the Buddha, Ramana Maharshi, and Lao Tzu use concepts such as these in trying to communicate this absolute reality to people in a way they can understand. The Buddha is said to have reminded his disciples that: "When I speak of time, or when I speak of myself, I do not mean a 'self', I do not mean 'time'. I use these terms in a relative sense to communicate in a useful way that which will be helpful to you to perceive the direct nature of reality."

Q: Does insight always occur in a certain order?
A: As practice develops, there is often a common order to the deeper and deeper penetration of the nature of existence. It is a striking experience to witness oneself or another yogi going through the classical stages of insight on the path. However, a precise progression does not always occur, especially with the natural development of wisdom as described by Achaan Chaa or Achaan Buddhadasa. Instead of experiencing stages, one may simply feel a dropping away of desires and a more and more clear awareness of the present, just being with what is, without any clinging. This can occur without the very deeply concentrated perception of the moment-to-moment stages of insight that Achaan Naeb has described. Even when one does go through the classical stages, one may not perceive each of the levels of insight in a distinct manner, but may seem, in experience, to skip from one level of perception to another. At times it may seem like practice is a spiral or even multi-dimensional, holographic process—and at times it goes beyond the concept of development altogether.

Q: How should one approach the concept of time and the spiritual path in practical terms?
A: There are several answers. One is to beware not to adopt intellectually the absolute perspective on the world. To say, well there's nothing to do, it's all empty (and it is all empty!) is fine, but if you're not perceiving it directly and deeply as all empty, you are just clinging to the concept of emptiness. This becomes another barrier to the direct perception of what is, to the unfolding of wisdom on a moment-to-moment basis.

To answer your question in another way, it is quite useful to think of our practice as part of a great journey and to develop the long enduring mind or, as Achaan Chaa would emphasize, just to continue your practice without regard to how long you have practiced. One well-known Buddhist teacher has said that practice simply means turning oneself in the right direction, following the path, and walking—not considering how many days or hours or events have passed. The very walking itself is the goal because each moment that you are mindful, fully in the present, freed from greed, hatred, and delusion, is a moment of liberation as well as a step toward final liberation. Spiritual practice becomes, at minimum, a lifelong task; unless one is totally liberated and fully enlightened, there's always more to be done. This relative viewpoint is very useful. As long as there's still attachment and suffering and delusion, an effort to be aware and mindful and in the present moment is still necessary, no matter which particular teaching or technique one adopts.

The practice of spiritual development will have ups and downs. Some on a moment-to-moment basis: moment-to-moment emptiness, moment-to-moment depression, moment-to-moment elation, moment-to-moment insight, moment-to-moment delusion. Some will be on an hourly basis: On one day, one's meditation or one's daily activities may be very clear, may be very precise, there may be a lot of equanimity; while on the next day it may be dull, sluggish, and unclear. On a month-to-month and year-to-year basis, too, one's practice may deepen or one may spend several months in a great deal of depression seeing suffering, seeing despair, seeing only that aspect of the world. One must have faith and trust in the process, to allow the waves of impermanence both on a moment-to-moment and even on a year-to-year basis pass with a certain kind of long abiding equanimity. It is this quality of mind which allows things to flow as they will, allows the Dharma to unfold without our preconceptions. It is also this long abiding quality which, with the force of compassion, brings the Dharma to the aid of all beings.

It should also be mentioned that the development of wisdom which is the end of suffering is not only for oneself but, in fact, the end of suffering for all beings. When selfishness completely disappears there is no more greed, hatred, or delusion in the mind. Then there is no more separateness, there is no more 'I', no more 'me' or 'they'. Without this separateness, the automatic manifestation of wisdom is loving-kindness, compassion, and sympathetic joy in the world; one's actions become selfless, totally in harmony with the good of all beings. In the world one becomes, in this state of wisdom, like the Buddha. And there's no need to worry about not entering enlightenment in order to save other beings first, because the development of wisdom breaks down the separation between oneself and all other beings. The bodhisattva vow of wishing to save all beings does not mean that a particular person will save all other beings, but rather that through the development of the practice, the illusion of oneself separate from all beings will fall away and the universal love and compassion that exists as part of wisdom will become apparent.

301

Q: And one last question: Is it really 'all One'?
A: The Buddha did not teach Buddhism, he taught the Dharma, the Truth. What techniques he taught were means to see this truth. If one looks into the mind with silent awareness, then the mind becomes quiet as all clinging, thoughts, ideas, and concepts drop away, then what is left is exactly what there is in the present moment, nothing but that. That experience must be the same for whatever person in whatever country, in whatever tradition they're practicing. This silence of mind may be referred to as *sunyata* or *nirvana* or *mahamudra* or by many other terms, but that's all there is and it cannot be different.

OTHER MEDITATIONS IN THE THERAVADA TRADITION

CHAPTER
SEVENTEEN
In order to represent more fully the living Theravada tradition as found in Southeast Asia, this chapter will briefly review some additional systems and approaches to meditation used by modern Theravada teachers. Theravada Buddhism encompasses an extraordinarily large range of spiritual practices. Many of these practices are those which are thought to be found solely in other traditions, such as Mahayana or Vajrayana Buddhism, Hinduism, and the many yoga, Sufi, and Western spiritual schools. Each major religious tradition around the world has developed a variety of similar techniques and methods within its own framework for assisting those on the spiritual path. Theravada Buddhism incorporates many of these ways of practice. Some of these approaches to practice are variations on standard concentration or insight meditation techniques. Others involve the skillful cultivation of certain attitudes and lifestyles as a basis for spiritual growth. To present clearly these approaches we will start with more specific meditations and follow by commenting on various broader ways to approach practice found in modern Theravada teachings.

Concentration and Absorption. Practices which lead to high levels of concentration and absorption are central to Theravada Buddhist training. Often they are combined with insight meditation as described by such teachers as Achaan Maha Boowa previously in this book. Sometimes they are cultivated for their own benefits of purity and power, quite separately from insight practice.

Teachers use many meditation objects to lead meditators to the various levels of absorption, but in each case the principle of the meditation is to focus the mind so totally on one object that it becomes absorbed into it, completely stilled and unmoving. The power of making the mind completely concentrated on one object (such as an inner light, visualization, sound, feeling, etc.) is enormous. When the mind is so trained by repeated return to an object that it remains steady without fluctuation, the meditator obtains access to a whole range of higher absorptions or states of consciousness. These include absorption into light, into the four basic elements, into infinite loving-kindness, compassion or equanimity. This absorption is the cause for the arising of great rapture, bliss and many extraordinary states on the level of 'concentrations of form'. On an even higher level, the meditator can use the power of concentration to be trained to enter absorption into (or become one with) infinite space, infinite consciousness and the subtleties of neither perception nor non-perception. These trainings are a traditional part of the purification of mind, still practiced and taught by Theravada masters, including many of those represented in this book. Although attainment in absorption is difficult, requiring a well-controlled and unmoving mind, it is a source of great peace and inspriation on the Buddha's path of purification and can be used as a basis for development of deep insight and equanimity.

Visualizations Visualizations are meditation exercises which involve the use of a color or form, either internal or external, as a meditation object. The use of visualizations is common among Theravada teachers. The most popular visualizations are concentration meditations on colors (kasinas) or colored discs. This exercise is traditionally used to produce an after-image of the color in the mind, which is followed by further concentration leading to absorption. Some teachers and centers use visualizations of colored lights, of Buddha images, of the body, or of parts of the body or corpses. In some cases, more complex visualizations are used, some of which resemble the creation of an internal visual mandala. For example, one large meditation center in Bangkok uses a meditation system which starts by developing a white light from concentration; into the light are projected visualizations of various heavenly beings. Other forms and mandalas are created from the four elements or the various realms of existence.

In some cases, visualization in meditation is simply used as a device to develop concentration. In other ways, visualizations such as those on the parts of the body not only deepen concentration but also help develop detachment and equanimity, and lead to the arising of wisdom, understanding the true nature of the mind and body.

Mantra and Chanting The use of mantra or the repetition of certain phrases in Pali is an extremely common form of meditation in the Theravada tradition. Simple mantras use repetitions of the Buddha's name, 'Budho', or use the 'Dharma', or the 'Sangha', the community, as mantra words. Other mantras that are used are directed toward developing loving-kindness. Some mantras direct attention to the process of change by repeating the Pali phrase that means 'everything changes', while other mantras are used to develop equanimity with phrases that would be translated, 'let go'. Very often mantra practice is combined with breathing meditation, so that one recites a mantra simultaneously with in-breath and out-breath to help develop tranquility and concentration. Mantra meditation is especially popular among the lay people. Like other basic concentration exercises, it can be used simply to still the mind or it can be the basis for an insight practice where the mantra becomes the focus of observation of how life unfolds, or an aid in surrendering and letting go.

Chanting is used extensively to develop faith and concentration and is part of a daily meditation regimen in Theravada Buddhism. Chanting is usually recitations from the Pali scriptures. There are chants that honor the Buddha or his teachings, chants of loving-kindness, chants of the most important concepts in the Buddha's discourses, and chants of the Buddhist psychology. Hours of chanting are often practiced in meditation temples to help develop concentrated mind-states and open hearts. Among lay people, too, chanting in temples provides a popular form of meditation which is both a reminder of the contents of the Buddha's teaching and a basis for stillness of mind from which clarity and wisdom can grow.

Meditation on the Breath Theravada teachers use many breath-related practices in addition to the basic breathing meditations already described in this book. Some teach breath control similar to yogic pranayama exercises, while others use breathing meditation as a basis for the cultivation of a whole range of high states of concentration and absorption. Often the use of breath is combined with other practices, such as the recitation of a mantra coupled with noticing in- and out-breath, or meditations which synchronize breathing with awareness of bodily movements. Some form of concentration on breath in meditation is the most common formal practice found in the Theravada tradition.

Postures and Movement As touched upon earlier in this book, Theravada teachers use particular postures, change of postures and bodily movements, space, and such ritual movements as prostrations for meditation. In some systems, the holding of particular postures—such as standing without moving, or lying without moving, or sitting in a certain position—is considered important in the development of concentration that will lead to wisdom. In other systems, a great deal of attention is paid to movement, first to the mental cause of movement and then to the actual physical movement as it takes place. This changing of postures and flow of movement becomes the focus of some Theravada meditation teachers' systems. Particular ways of walking are adopted as meditation exercises in almost every meditation system, as well as awareness of the body in relation to robes and environment. Teachers make conscious use of confined and/or open space for different kinds of meditation in some Theravada temples. In other places the use of frequent prostrations, both as a body-movement meditation and as a way to reduce pride, is employed as part of daily practice. In all cases, the use of particular postures, movements, and prostrations must be accompanied by careful cultivation of mindfulness to properly derive the benefits that come from this meditation.

Meditation with the Intellect The intellectual aspect of the mind is made use of in many ways in preparation for, or in conjunction with, meditation. As a part of practice, one is often encouraged to study before sitting. This study may be of sutras and discourses of the Buddha, the description of meditation practices, or the Abhidharma, Buddhist psychology. The knowledge that is gained by study is then applied to certain kinds of meditation. For example, use of the Abhidharma is very common in Burma and in Thailand. Here the meditator first learns in detail all of the categories of mind-states and the process or conditions for their arising and passing away. He learns all the parts of the material universe, the various elements and their relations. When he has mastered them, he then applies this knowledge to his meditation. This is done by observing all mind-states that arise and all interactions between the mind, body, and environment. This ongoing process is observed and analyzed into its component parts. When the causes, the conditions, and the transiency of all these mind-states are learned first through the intellect and then observed through direct experience, wisdom develops. One sees clearly how the world is simply a series of empty mental and physical processes, void of any permanent self.

Another way of study involves contemplation of basic Dharma questions which ultimately bring one to logical paradoxes. The direct experience of meditation beyond the intellect is then necessary to resolve and understand these questions. Other teachers prescribe meditations that are contemplations on specific aspects of the Dharma. For example, one is directed to contemplate the extent of change in the universe, or the nature of the four great elements, or the meaning of emptiness. In cultivating the meditation using the elements, one might examine all experiences throughout the day to see that they are just the four great elements arising and passing away in different combinations.

By far the most common study is of the basic Buddhist doctrine and is used to develop right understanding of the nature of the world through the intellect. This understanding, especially in relation to the nature of happiness and suffering and who we really are, is the ground for strong faith and energy. The student is then encouraged to persevere in meditation and to develop the fruits of practice for oneself.

Meditations on Feeling States In the realm of feeling states, the highest, the realms of divine abodes, are most popular for meditation. Almost every teacher in the Theravada tradition incorporates meditation on loving-kindness and compassion as a part of practice. Often one begins practice by cultivating this love and compassion toward oneself and then develops it toward all living beings. At times, it is developed by repeating a mantra such as 'May all beings be happy', while other teachers employ visualizations to assist in cultivating a mind filled with love. In addition to compassion there are specific meditations taught to develop feelings of sympathetic joy for others' happiness and meditations to strengthen equanimity. As meditation deepens, the mind becomes still and unselfish, and wisdom grows. Wisdom sees the underlying unity of all things and is naturally the source for great love and compassion. Thus love and compassion can be cultivated as specific meditations on feeling states, or allowed to develop naturally as the basic fruit of Buddhist practice.

Devotional Practices Devotional exercises form the backbone of the most common Buddhist religious practice. These practices range from daily prayer and surrender to devotional ceremonies and initiations, and on the highest level to devotion to the truth, the Dharma. Many Buddhist lay people go to temples and pray to the Buddha or surrender to his will. It is a common misunderstanding among Buddhists that the Buddha is a god rather than an enlightened man. Devotional attitude is reinforced by various rituals performed by the monks. These range from simple blessings and holy water at weddings and special rites at funerals, to more complex exorcisms and shamanic-type practices at certain temples. In each country, Buddhist practice has incorporated elements of rites from other religions and early animist roots. In the best cases, these devotional practices and rituals serve an important function for lay people as symbols for deeper meaning in their lives, and as reminders of the importance of the teachings of the Buddha. Devotion and surrender become a source of comfort and peace of mind for these Buddhists in times of change or life crisis.

Initiations and ceremonies, too, celebrate the connection to the Dharma and the twenty-five-hundred-year-old tradition. Ancient ritual helps create an atmosphere of trust and surrender in which the deepest meditation practices can be followed most fruitfully. In the sophisticated teachings, it is clearly understood that the disciple is not surrendering to a god or deity, but simply opening himself up to the Dharma, to the unfolding of his own spiritual development. The use of ritual and devotional practices is encouraged to assist meditators in developing the states of mind that lead to openness of heart and wisdom. So, although Buddhism is not a theistic religion, we find that the use of ritual and devotional practices is extremely widespread. Even in some of the strictest and 'purest' of the meditation centers, devotional practices are integrated into the daily schedule. Prostrations, chants to the Buddha, and devotional chants about the Buddha and his teaching and the community of monks form a part of daily life for most monks. The use of various rituals, lighting of candles, offering of flowers and incense, and devotional chanting are all part of meditation in these temples and centers. In the end, the path of devotion, to the Buddha, the Dharma or to the teacher must lead back to oneself. Devotion becomes a vehicle for surrender of selfishness and from this surrender one can grow in love, compassion and wisdom, until the Buddha and Dharma are not apart from oneself.

Rules and Discipline In some of the ascetic and strict meditation monasteries, and other strict meditation monasteries, the use of very intricate and precise rules of discipline is part of the meditation. One is encouraged to be as mindful as possible in following the many hundreds, even thousands, of rules and to use them to help break down the need for one's own individuality which comes   309 from the illusion of self. The refined use of discipline as part of meditation practice is an extremely important part of many well-known meditation centers. It is difficult to understand its full value unless it has been personally practiced. Through the use of precise discipline, one becomes very mindful of body and speech, and one's actions become harmonious with the rest of the community. This in turn creates a very strong basis for further meditation practice and helps one cut to the root of personal desire systems. One follows the rules of the community rather than basing behavior simply on one's desires in the moment. Strict and precise discipline can be an enormous and valuable aid to the development of wisdom when used in conjunction with day-to-day mindfulness and loving-kindness.

Service and Charity The use of forms of social meditation which are service oriented, such as teaching, helping the sick, and drug rehabilitation, are also an important part of the Theravada Buddhist tradition. A large number of monasteries are set up for cultivating purity through surrender and service as the main form of meditation. This service may include teaching meditation in formal ways; teaching other skills and knowledge, such as reading and writing, to lay people; assisting those who are very poor or sick; and other, more specialized functions. Some temples are set up particularly to take care of young children and to teach and train them. Other temples serve as drug rehabilitation centers for those who have been addicted to opium or heroin and need a place to go where there is love and assistance. The value of giving, both of service and of material goods, was stressed often by the Buddha and is an integral part of the Theravada meditation systems and the Buddhist way of life. Charity, the sharing of one's work and possessions with others, is fundamental to the cultivation of inner renunciation and peace. It is the manifestation in action of nongreed and compassion in the mind. Giving, letting go on all levels, is the root practice leading to unselfishness and purification of mind and, as such, is a particularly important and widespread form of meditation.

Higher Teachings and Other Practices For the sake of completeness it seems important to note that though the teachings elaborated in this book contain the essence of Buddhist meditation, there also exist practices and understandings that go beyond what is written here. The 'higher practices' fall into two classes, the first being the deeper levels of insight and purity that come with the vipassana practice. The second class includes various concentration and yogic practices taught to complement the wisdom of insight and to cultivate the power to express this wisdom in compassionate ways for oneself and all beings. Many of these teachings include practices and descriptions of experiences beyond the first taste of nirvana. Mahasi Sayadaw writes elsewhere at length about the higher attainments including absorption, nirvanic fruition, states of cessation, and especially the path of purification after the first experience of nirvana. Similarly, Achaans Dhammadaro and Jumnien and the U Ba Khin tradition teach practices that involve not only absorption and cessation but also work with opening chakras or energy centers in the body and with the use of energy and light, luminous cords, 'nibbana dhatu', transmission of power and more. Other teachers cultivate other bodily and psychic powers in advanced students. Most of the teachers represented are not only acknowledged masters of insight who stress the essence of Buddhist wisdom in their teachings, but are also known as masters of absorption and are reputed to have cultivated many varieties of powers. Powers are not wisdom, though, and they, and this book, prefer to teach in a way that leads most directly to insight and liberation.

In understanding the higher levels of insight, one is usually guided directly by a teacher. Theravada's tradition stresses the development of practice up to the profound experience of the first taste of nirvana, after which a meditator needs few guidelines, though often much more practice, to continue to final liberation. As the mind becomes purified, the luminous and self-existing nature of all experience is revealed. The Dharma unfolds naturally, following the basic principles outlined in the very first talk of the Buddha on the four noble truths. When the basic teachings are understood, all that remains is perseverence in putting them into practice.

There are certainly many other techniques and forms of meditation used in Theravada countries not represented here, although this chapter gives a fair sampling. One other aspect of practice worth mentioning is that of healing. Either as a part of the standard meditation teaching or developed specially, there are a number of systems of healing in the Theravada tradition. These include, to name but a few, the use of meditations which concentrate on particular parts of the body, the use of colored lights in relation to the body or diseases, the use of special concentration visualization exercises, the use of herbs and water that have been collected and treated in special ways by monks, and the sprinkling of holy water. The laying on of hands and various kinds of exorcisms, rites, and rituals are involved in healing ceremonies performed by monks. Astrology and palmistry is also a part of certain healing traditions. The Buddha stressed the importance of monks taking care of others who are sick, expressing it very strongly in this way: "Those who take care of one who is sick, my friends, take care of the Buddha himself." In fact, all of the teachings and meditation systems in this book deal with healing. Some of them deal with the healing of particular bodily ills, but for the most part they deal with the healing of our mental suffering. Suffering that comes from our ignorance, our attachment and desires can be healed: This is the greatest and most important message of the Buddha.

Hinayana, Mahayana, and Other Yanas In exploring the variety of Buddhist practices, students often have questions about the different schools and traditions of various countries. Buddhism is often described in terms of vehicles: Hinayana, or the lesser vehicle; Mahayana, or the greater vehicle; or Vajrayana, the Diamond vehicle. Where does Theravada teaching fit into this scheme?

The division into yanas can be understood in several ways. One is that the yanas refer to the historical-cultural evolution of Buddhism. In this scheme, Hinayana refers to the early schools in India that evolved into the Theravada Buddhism found in Ceylon and Southeast Asia. Mahayana refers to the Buddhism which developed in the cultures of China, Korea, and Japan while the Vajrayana approach is found particularly in the evolution of Buddhism in Tibet and Mongolia.

Another popular way to understand the division of Buddhist yanas is based on some misunderstanding of each tradition. In this approach, Hinayana, or the lesser vehicle, is considered the early teachings of the Buddha that deal with the lesser practices leading

311

to the attainment of limited enlightenment. Hinayana is seen as practice in which one separates oneself from others and attains a limited freedom without helping anyone else. Mahayana, on the other hand, is the greater vehicle based on later teachings of the Buddha, which leads to liberation for oneself and all other beings—teaching based on great compassion. The Vajrayana schools are seen as having the highest teachings of the Buddha, through which one transcends even the duality of saving all beings or of liberation and non-liberation. This misunderstanding of the yanas is compounded by the identification of Hinayana with Theravada, Mahayana with Zen and other east Asian schools, and Vajrayana with Tibetan Buddhism.

When one truly understands Buddhism, it becomes clear that all three vehicles are present in each tradition, and that the essence of all Buddhist practice is the same everywhere. The real meaning of the yanas is seen as a description of the natural evolution of practice for each individual, regardless of school or culture. Hinayana refers to the initial stage in practice where one is primarily motivated by self-centered desire. We wish to end suffering, or we want to understand or to find bliss or truth or want to become enlightened. Practice begins because we want something for ourselves. This limited approach is the natural starting place. Later, as understanding deepens through practice, the truth of emptiness of self becomes clear. No longer bound by the illusion of a separate self, practice becomes Mahayana. There arises automatically great compassion and practice becomes based on the unselfish intent to save all beings because one no longer makes the distinction between self and other. This is the great vehicle. Practice for all beings come when we transcend selfish practice, seeing clearly that there is no self to gain anything. Continuing, practice naturally evolves into the supreme, non-dualistic vehicle, when even the distinctions between practice and no practice break down. As understanding of emptiness deepens, there is the increasing ability to transmute all situations and energy into forces for liberation. Finally, any desire to be liberated or any illusion of other beings to liberate dissappears. All the world becomes simply a place of the manifestation of Dharma where no event is apart from practice. The true nature of all things is manifest beyond any conceptual interference and there is nothing left to be done. What life is left is beyond desires and beyond distinctions, where appropriate action is taken simply as the natural course of events.

When one understands the vehicles as a natural unfolding of practice, it is clear that each school (such as Theravada or Zen) contains all of the yanas within it. One goes from self-centered to selfless practice as wisdom grows. Since all Buddhism aims toward the eradication of greed, hatred, and delusion, there can be no real distinction between the purposes of the different schools. This is not to deny the richness of each of the historical-cultural traditions in Buddhism, or their valuable differences in emphasis and techniques of practice. It is simply important to make clear that Buddhist practice leads to putting oneself in harmony with the four noble truths by coming to the end of all grasping and illusion, and that any path that leads to this is full and complete.

313

Finally, we must transcend the yanas completely. They are but another artificial distinction on the path. As it is said traditionally, Buddhism is like a raft used to cross the stream to the shore beyond selfishness, beyond desires. After crossing, there is no need to carry the raft any further. Or, as was written by a modern Buddhist poet, Tom Savage, "Greater vehicle, lesser vehicle; all vehicles will be towed away at owner's expense."

Return to Wisdom When we consider all of the different approaches to meditation in light of the seven factors of enlightenment (concentration, investigation, energy, rapture, tranquility, mindfulness, and equanimity), it becomes simple to see how each of the approaches can be helpful in developing at least some of these qualities of mind that lead to liberation. However, it must be remembered that meditation in the form of a particular practice, method, or technique is simply a tool to use. When one has developed meditation leading to wisdom and liberation, eventually all systems, all techniques, and all practices must be let go of. Then meditation is no longer viewed in isolation, but becomes integrated as a way of life, and life itself becomes meditation. Simple. Direct. Unselfish. Moment-to-moment being.

It is stated in the final discourse of the Buddha to his monks (the *Maha-parinibbana Sutta*), "So long as the brethren shall exercise themselves in the sevenfold higher wisdom, that is to say in the development of the seven factors of enlightenment, so long then may the brethren be expected not to decline, but to prosper." The Buddha addressed the brethren with his last words and said, "Behold now, Brethren, I exhort you, decay is inherent in all compound things. Work out your salvation with diligence."

May the words of the Dharma as transmitted through this book be of benefit, of merit, and of use for beings to be relieved of the burden of suffering. May all beings be happy. May all beings be free from illusion. May all work out their salvation with diligence.

BASIC GLOSSARY

ANAPANA: a concentration technique based on noting the coming and going of the breath.

CONCENTRATION (SAMADHI): the mental factor of one-pointedness of mind, steadyness of mind on an object.

CONCENTRATION (SAMATHA): those meditation practices which develop strong concentration and tranquility by focusing on a steady object.

CONSCIOUSNESS (VINNANA): the knowing faculty of mind, that aspect of mind which knows the sense objects arising, and passing away with them at the six sense doors.

DEFILEMENTS (KILESA): the mental factors of greed, hatred, and delusion.

DELUSION (MOHA): the mental factor of cloudiness of mind which does not allow objects to be seen clearly in the light of impermanence, suffering, and emptiness.

EIGHTFOLD PATH (ARIYA-MAGGA): the Buddhist path to purification and liberation—right understanding, right thought, right speech, right action, right livelihood, right effort, right mindfulness, and right concentration.

ELEMENTS (DHATU): usually refers to the four great elements of solidity (earth), cohesion (water), temperature (fire), and movement or vibration (air). Also used to refer to secondary physical elements and at times to elements of mind.

EMPTINESS (ANATTA): emptiness of self or soul; refers to the basic understanding that there is no one, no self to whom all experience is happening and that what we are is simply a changing process.

FEELING (VEDANA): the mental factor of pleasant, unpleasant, or neutral feeling that arises in relation to an object.

FOUR FOUNDATIONS OF MINDFULNESS (SATIPATTHANA): the four fields for awareness that are our whole experience and where we must pay attention to develop insight. They are: (1) the body and material elements, (2) feelings—pleasant, unpleasant, and neutral, (3) consciousness, and (4) all mental factors, all objects of mind, such as thoughts, emotions, greed, and love.

FOUR NOBLE TRUTHS (ARIYA SACCA): the most basic teaching of the Buddha: (1) the truth of suffering, (2) the truth of the cause of suffering—clinging and desire, (3) the truth of the end of suffering, and (4) the path to the end of suffering—the eightfold path.

GREED (LOBHA): the mental factor which causes the mind to grasp or stick to an object or experience.

HATRED (LOBHA): the mental factor of aversion which causes the mind to dislike or strike against an object or experience.

IGNORANCE (AVIJJA): that basic force which does not see clearly the nature of the world and is the root cause of grasping and of our desire systems.

IMPERMANENCE (ANICCA): the basic truth that all phenomena which have the nature to arise must pass away.

INSIGHT MEDITATION (VIPASSANA): seeing clearly; meditation that focuses on the basic nature of the mind-body process to understand its true characteristics.

KALAPA: the smallest subatomic unit of physical matter which is in constant vibration.

KARMA: the law of cause and effect which describes the relationship between events in the realm of mind and of matter.

MATTER (RUPA): the physical world made of the four basic elements.

MENTAL FACTORS (SANKHARA): in the five aggregates, this refers to volition and the various other mental factors which arise in relation to consciousness and an object.

MIND (NAMA): includes consciousness plus the various mental factors which color consciousness.

MINDFULNESS (SATI): that quality of mind which notices what is happening in the present moment with no clinging, aversion, or delusion.

NIRVANA: that state of total coolness beyond the movement of the mind-body process. Also refers to liberation from all greed, hatred, and delusion in the mind of an enlightened being.

PERCEPTION (SANNA): the mental factor which perceives or recognizes objects.

SAMSARA: the world of conditioned phenomena, of the elements of mind and matter, all of which are subject to constant change.

SENSE BASES (AYATANA): the six subjective-objective sense bases are: (1) the eye and visible objects, (2) the ear and sounds, (3) the nose and odors, (4) the tongue and tastes, (5) the body and bodily impressions, and (6) the mind and mind-objects.

SIGN (NIMITTA): an internal mental image that arises when the mind becomes concentrated.

SUFFERING (DUKKHA): the basic unsatisfactory, insecure nature of all transient phenomena.

VIRTUE (SILA): initially refers to following certain moral precepts; more deeply refers to acting in the world without greed, hatred, or delusion.

317